D. H. LAWRENCE

AND THE DIAL

By

Nicholas Joost *and* Alvin Sullivan

Southern Illinois University Press CARBONDALE AND EDWARDSVILLE

Feffer & Simons, Inc. LONDON AND AMSTERDAM

FOR
THE MEN AND WOMEN
WHO MADE THE *DIAL* POSSIBLE
Scofield Thayer
James Sibley Watson, Jr.
Marianne Moore
AND
Kenneth Burke, Gilbert Seldes, *and* Ellen Thayer

CONTENTS

LIST OF ILLUSTRATIONS

between pages 114–115

FOREWORD

THE AMBIENCE OF THE 1920's is, in some ways, as extinct as the dodo, as exotic as Timbuctoo. No other statement can explain the fairly recent revival of the Charleston, the boyish bob, and musical comedies and movies spoofing our naïve grandparents who suffered and splurged through the years of drinking fake Scotch and spending February at the Roney Plaza. Hardly a man is now alive . . . .

What *were* the 1920's like? Were they altogether Main Street and the booboisie, gangsters and flappers, movie stars and butter-and-egg men? Indeed they were not, that is, if there is any validity to the account that follows, the story of David Herbert Lawrence, the *Dial*, and their relationship in those days when Scofield Thayer, James Sibley Watson, Jr., and Marianne Moore edited and published their magazine. To be sure, the *Dial* caricatured the flapper and editorialized about tycoons. It was aware of the lonely anguish of the Marooned Individual on Main Street—and it spoke to the Carol Kennicutts of America.

But the 1920's one views through the magic lantern of the *Dial* are also akin to the enchanted landscape Keats saw. (Keats was always a favorite of Scofield Thayer.) In the lingo of its decade, the *Dial* is a magic movie projector, a frame and setting similar to Keats's charm'd magic casements opening on the foam of perilous seas in faery lands forlorn, and how forlorn they are to the generation of 1970. As two very minor apprentices to some very major magicians, Alvin Sullivan and I have tackled the dusty apparatus of the dismantled projector and have tried as best we could to fit it together again to rerun some of the old pictures. The story they tell is partial and incomplete, and our reels may occasionally flicker in the rerunning; yet, we like to think, something of the pristine magic remains. There are no gangsters, one or two flappers, two or three millionaires—not enough perhaps for Cecil B. de Mille or Lowell Sherman. But we do show the desert with Lobo Mountain rising in the distance; we show the busy editorial office in New York, bringing out month after month the most fascinating magazine of arts and letters of its decade; London and Capri and the Riviera serve as backgrounds to the action; and then, of course, there is the star, D. H. Lawrence himself, with (as they say) a brilliant supporting cast. An *homme* as *fatal* as Byron and with as wicked a sense of humor and with as black a sense of despair, loved by a German baroness no less, petted by English aristocrats and American millionairesses, despised by Mrs. Grundy, and hounded by the police of two continents. Surely all this recreates for a few moments a milieu magically fresh to the audiences of *The Boy Friend* and *Thoroughly Modern Millie*?

Still another enchantment wafts over us, the subtler and more delicate, the profounder nuances of this story. The 1920's were the last really cosmopolitan age in modern history, and placed in that kaleidoscopic context, Lawrence's travels and agonizings and lovings as he wrote his way around the world constitute a nostalgic and, for all his relative poverty and his recalcitrance to glamor, a rather glamorous spectacle. Would he be able to pass today so easily through the customs at Ceylon? Could he today afford a villa in Sicily? And how would he force himself today to accept the bounty of one of the great charitable foundations that have replaced Ottoline Morrell and Mabel Dodge Luhan? Moreover, Lawrence's and Scofield Thayer's strong, shared affinity for Germanic culture —it was still the culture common to all of Central Europe—would no doubt render them even more suspect than it did in 1923.

Most vitally and importantly, today no *Dial* exists for a relatively "unacceptable" writer like Lawrence, although there are havens for mousy people (or superlatively clever people) at the universities, and Valhallas for the hacks of television and the movies. Yes, that magic is gone, only to be evoked when the rackety, taped-together movie projector shines its enchantment: and then one visits the publishing and Bohemian milieux of the 1920's, the magazine office down in Greenwich Village, the ranch house out in Taos, one shares in the passions and hangovers and Jungian gropings after primitive reality.

The deepest and most troubling enchantment is that wrought

by D. H. Lawrence himself—a wounded spirit in a sick body, relentlessly pouring out of himself that flood of stories and novels and travel sketches and poems and book reviews and opinions which the world has been rediscovering ever since March 2, 1930, the day he died. For here is the heroic sorcerer, who in his life and art prophetically adumbrated today's rebellion against mass communications, mass technology, and mass man.

Magic is illusion and so veils the truth; yet if in these moments the viewer understands Lawrence as a white magician like Merlin, the true seer, his particular magic paradoxically creates a vision (as it were) of the truth that the appearances of this world veil from ordinary sight. Our reassembled projector thus will serve, we trust, to shed added light on D. H. Lawrence in his own age and to interpret his magic for ours.

FOR PERMISSION to publish previously unpublished letters by D. H. Lawrence and to reprint two previously published letters by Lawrence to Marianne Moore we gratefully acknowledge the kindness of Laurence Pollinger, the literary representative of Montague Weekley.

For permission to use and to publish material from the *Dial* papers we gratefully acknowledge the kindness of Scofield Thayer's representative, Charles P. Williamson.

We also acknowledge the encouragement of the Worcester Art Museum, specifically of its director, Daniel Catton Rich, its curator, Louisa Dresser, and her assistant, Elizabeth Henry. For aid in the procedures of publication and for released time for research we thank Southern Illinois University.

We gratefully acknowledge the aid of Donald C. Gallup, director of the American Literature Collection of the Beinecke Library, Yale University, without whose advice and permission this work could not have proceeded to its conclusion. Further, we are grateful to James Sibley Watson, Jr., for permission to quote a portion of a holograph letter. Finally we acknowledge the permission to publish their correspondence of the following: Gilbert Seldes; for Llewelyn Powys, Malcolm Elwin, his literary executor; for Alyse Gregory, Rosemary Manning, her literary executor; and Marianne Moore, also for her gracious kindness and, in years past, her advice. Quotations from Harry T. Moore's edition of Lawrence's *Collected Letters* are used with the kind permission of Laurence Pollinger Limited, the Estate of the Late Mrs. Frieda Lawrence, William Heinemann, Ltd., and Viking Press. In her letter to Nicholas Joost of March 14, 1969, Ellen Thayer disavowed the authorship of two letters, dated April 13 and May 16, 1927, and printed in Chapter 4. We thank Mrs. Ernest Thayer Clary and Monsignor James Suddes for their kind help with special aspects of this study, and Professors John Ades and Leslie Thompson for their helpful comments on an earlier version of some of these pages.

For permissions to reproduce pictures and sculptures illustrated in this study we thank the following: Charles P. Williamson, representative of Mr. Scofield Thayer; the Worcester Art Museum; Dr. James Sibley Watson, Jr.; Professor Warren Roberts, Director, Humanities Research Center, University of Texas; the National Portrait Gallery, London; Gilbert Seldes; the Kraushaar Galleries; and Professor John Richardson, who graciously accepted our request for a portrait of D. H. Lawrence and permitted its use on the jacket. And for her aid, we thank Professor Betty Hoyenga.

Nicholas Joost

Southern Illinois University
Edwardsville
SEPTEMBER 30, 1969

D. H. LAWRENCE AND *THE DIAL*

ABBREVIATIONS

QUOTATIONS from the works and letters and manuscripts of Lawrence are identified in the text by the following abbreviations:

AA   *Assorted Articles* (New York, 1930).

AR   *Aaron's Rod.* Compass Books (New York, 1961).

CL   *Collected Letters*, ed. Harry T. Moore. Two vols. (New York, 1962).

CP   *Collected Poems.* Vol. II (London, 1928).

CSS   *The Complete Short Stories.* Three vols. Compass Books (New York, 1962).

FU   *Fantasia of the Unconscious.* Compass Books (New York, 1960); in the same volume with *PU*.

G   Ivan Bunin, *The Gentleman from San Francisco and Other Stories*, transl. D. H. Lawrence, S. S. Koteliansky, and Leonard Woolf (New York, 1922).

H   *Letters*, ed. Aldous Huxley (London, 1932).

P   *Pansies* (New York, 1929).

Ph   *Phoenix: The Posthumous Papers of D. H. Lawrence*, ed. Edward D. McDonald (New York, 1936).

PU   *Psychoanalysis and the Unconscious.* Compass Books (New York, 1960); in the same volume with *FU*.

RDP   *Reflections on the Death of a Porcupine.* Midland Books (Bloomington, Ind., 1963).

SeSa   *Sea and Sardinia.* Compass Books (New York, 1963).

SLC   *Selected Literary Criticism*, ed. Anthony Beal. Compass Books (New York, 1966).

Ted   *The Frieda Lawrence Collection of D. H. Lawrence Manuscripts*, ed. E. W. Tedlock, Jr. (Albuquerque, 1948).

1

IN THE BEGINNING, 1913–1920

MY DEAR SCOFIELD, wrote Llewelyn Powys from the White Nose near Dorchester, "A rumour came to us that you might be coming abroad this year. If you have a chance, I beg you to direct your wayfaring towards us. . . . Sylvia Warner was staying with my brother T. F. last week end, but Lord she needed you to subdue her—She is too clever for me." The 1920's had ended: the date of Llewelyn Powys's invitation was April 24, 1930. And his letter is instinct with a nostalgic realization that with the closing of the great decade, all its achievement was transmuted into the raw material—the rubble, mortar, sand, and piled-up bricks—of the edifice of history. That spring was a period of hushed waiting, a transition from the glamorous prosperity of the 1920's to the depression and forebodings, the bloody minor wars and noisy marchings of the 1930's. At the White Nose the swallows had already arrived, but Llewelyn Powys had not yet heard the cuckoo: "Every where in his world there is trouble and yet if anywhere there is a blessed peace to be found in these trills. It is sad that D. H. Lawrence should be dead. He had his inanities and yet he was a writer of great spirit and passion. The lobster and crab season has begun and I trust I shall live through the summer so that I shall be able to enjoy a diet of these delectable fish."

With spring the swallows would return, and another season for lobster and crab would begin; but man's world, his edifice of history and culture, had undergone an irrevocable change. Scofield Thayer, now ill and retired to the privacy of hushed rooms and tortured loneliness, could not come to England to stop by for a visit with his old friends Llewelyn and Alyse Powys, to reminisce about the years they wrote for and edited that courageous and beautiful magazine the *Dial*. Thayer's generous solicitude for the artists and writers of the avant-garde, struggling for recognition during the 1920's, was already sorely missed. In London, when the news came, during the height of the 1929 season, that the *Dial* had closed shop, Osbert Sitwell wandered about Bloomsbury in pain and disbelief, exclaiming to all his friends, "The *Dial* is dead, the *Dial* is dead!"

And gone, sadly even for those who recognized his inanities, was D. H. Lawrence, that writer of great spirit and passion. Of all the group who distinguished the issues of the *Dial* throughout the 1920's, from the beginning in January 1920 until the final number for July 1929, of all that cosmopolitan and forward-leading throng—T. S. Eliot and Picasso, Pound and Matisse, Cummings and Chagall, Lawrence and Georgia O'Keeffe, Thomas Mann and Edvard Munch, and the others, their brothers in spirit—of them all, Lawrence was the earliest to die. Yet of them all, none was more closely linked with the *Dial* in his rise to fame than was Lawrence.

Indeed, the story of Lawrence's American publication and renown that the 1920's witnessed is to an appreciable and even an essential extent an account of his publication by Scofield Thayer and James Sibley Watson, Jr., in their *Dial*.

From 1909 until 1958, works and letters by Lawrence appeared in seventy-six periodicals, by the record of his bibliographer Warren Roberts. Except for the novels, virtually all his writing appeared first in magazines in England and America. Yet critics and scholars largely ignore this vital fact of Lawrence's publication, even though an understanding of it is necessary if the general reader is to get to know what Lawrence created in the context within which it shocked and delighted the English-speaking world. True, there has been a general recognition of the role played by Ford Madox Ford as editor of the brilliant *English Review*, from late 1908 until early 1910, in first publishing D. H. Lawrence's writing and thus presenting him to a readership both sympathetic and sophisticated. By publishing such work as Lawrence's early stories and reviews, Ford secured the reputation of his journal for discovering new writing of high quality. Further, there has been recognition of the importance to Lawrence of the various magazines his disciple and rival John Middleton Murry edited or established sometimes as outlets for the master—for example, *Signature* (1915), *Adelphi* (1923–30), and the *Athenaeum* (1919–21)—but these have importance primarily insofar as they enter into an account of the relationship of Lawrence and Murry.[1]

Thus in England the *English Review* was uniquely important because it not only first published Lawrence's work but printed so much of it. He had to struggle on for another decade before a second magazine accorded him a similarly generous welcome, and this second time that welcome came not from an English but an American source. Next to Ford's *English Review*, Thayer's and Watson's *Dial* first published the greatest number of Lawrence's works. And like the *English Review*, which had so signally helped to establish Lawrence's reputation in his own land, the *Dial* helped more than any other magazine to establish his audience in America. Like the *English Review*, which published Lawrence pretty consistently from the beginning of his career until 1923, the *Dial* consistently published his work throughout the entire decade of his mature achievement, 1920–29. Thirty of Lawrence's works in four literary genres appeared in twenty-five issues of the magazine, and in eighteen issues during the 1920's, the *Dial*'s reviewers discussed his novels, plays, essays, and stories.

Well over half of Lawrence's publication in American magazines appeared in such outlets as the *Smart Set*, the *Forum*, and *Poetry*, but the frequency with which Lawrence's work appeared in the *Dial* as well as the quality of that work justifies this emphasis on the part the magazine played in the development of his career. In the context of the 1920's, a view of Lawrence's *Weltanschauung* and the editorial policies of the *Dial* has a wider and perhaps deeper significance than might appear on the surface. It helps one understand the rather narrow "why" of the matter (*why* did his writing appear in so many issues of the *Dial*, a quarter of the total?); it also helps the general reader to understand the "how" (*how* did Lawrence succeed in reaching an American readership as sympathetic and as sophisticated as the group he first reached through the *English Review?*); and finally, such a view helps one to observe a great writer in his time, not as a tailor's dummy engulfed by statistics and value judgments but as a human being—the writer of great spirit and passion despite his inanities, whom Llewelyn Powys knew—striving always to realize himself before his peers and his growing number of readers. When one compares Lawrence's contributions to the *Dial* with other writing in the magazine, certain relationships emerge to view that suggest why the *Dial* published some of his works to the exclusion of others. Then, too, Lawrence's correspondence with the staff of the *Dial*, which has never been published, contains fascinating accounts of his relations with his own circle of friends and with the *Dial* staff and casts new light on the literary and artistic achievement of the 1920's.

When the editors of the *Dial* published a story by D. H. Lawrence in its issue for September 1920, they thus signalized the start of a hospitality that would last as long as the magazine survived, indeed almost until Lawrence's death on March 2, 1930.

Five other American magazines had already published Lawrence—the *Forum*, *Smart Set*, *Playboy*, *Poetry*, and the *Seven Arts*—but none of them had published his work in all the genres in which he wrote, and none of them would publish him as frequently and for as long a span of years as the *Dial*.[2] Nevertheless these American magazines are important to the story of D. H. Lawrence and the *Dial*: they reveal Lawrence's

consistent efforts to secure an audience outside his own country, and after the British suppression of *The Rainbow*, when he
was a pariah at home, these magazines provided his major
income.[3]

The *Forum* was the first magazine in America to publish
any writing by Lawrence; his short story, "The Soiled Rose"
(later called "The Shades of Spring") appeared in the issue
for March 1913. For a while the *Forum* appeared to be the sole
American outlet for his work. Its editor, Mitchell Kennerly,
was also a venturesome though erratic book publisher and was
shrewd enough to secure the manuscripts of *The Trespasser*,
Sons and Lovers, and *The Rainbow;* at the same time he was
foolish enough to try to pay Lawrence and other contributors
with worthless checks.[4] As a result of Kennerly's chicanery,
over thirteen years lapsed between Lawrence's second publication in the *Forum* for September 1913—the last chapter of *Sons
and Lovers*, entitled by Kennerly "Derelict"—and his essay
"Fireworks" that the magazine next published, in its issue for
May 1927. Toward the end of Lawrence's career, however,
and under new editors, the *Forum* became his spokesman, as it
had originally shown promise of becoming. In September 1927
the magazine published an essay, "The Nightingale," and in its
number for February 1928 appeared the first portion of Lawrence's controversial interpretation of the Christ story, "The
Escaped Cock," which he later expanded into the short novel
The Man Who Died. In spite of the uproar the story caused,
the possibility that the *Forum* would be censored, and the
certainty that it would lose subscribers, the magazine went on
in its issue for January 1929 to publish Lawrence's "Cocksure
Women and Hensure Men," which English newspapers had
refused.[5] Certainly the *Dial*, its eye ever to the lurking censor,
would not have published either of those works.

The second American magazine to publish Lawrence's
work was also influential in attracting an audience to his writing. The circulation of the *Smart Set* at one time reached as
high as 165,000; the equivalent of that number in proportion to
today's magazine audience would be perhaps five times

greater.[6] At the time Lawrence contributed to the magazine, its circulation had dropped to sixty thousand, still a large number in comparison to the circulation of the *Dial*, a figure that never exceeded eighteen thousand and averaged ten thousand.[7] In its issue for September 1913, the *Smart Set* published two poems by Lawrence, "Kisses in the Train" and "Violets," followed in November 1913 by a poem, "The Mowers," in March 1914 by a story, "The Shadow in the Rose Garden," and in October 1914 by another story, "The White Stocking"; then ensued a hiatus of almost ten years until the *Smart Set* published Lawrence's story, "The Border Line," in its issue for September 1924.[8]

Although his contributions to the *Smart Set* were few, Lawrence valued the magazine for its generosity. All of his work for it except the last story was purchased for the magazine by the saturnine Willard Huntington Wright, editor from February 1913 until February 1914 and one of the most important editors for the artistic vanguard. To contributors whose work he liked, Wright often paid as much as ten times the customary rates of a cent a word for prose and twenty-five or thirty-five cents a line for poetry. It is understandable that a letter in 1916 from Lawrence to his agent sounded a tone of regret in announcing that the *Smart Set* was "under other management" (*CL* 469); and it is revealing that H. L. Mencken as editor (1914–23) of the *Smart Set* published at most a single work by Lawrence ("The White Stocking"), for the story entitled "The Border Line" was accepted after the Hearst interests had taken over the *Smart Set* in 1924. In 1922, when the *Dial* was publicizing Lawrence as one of its most distinguished contributors, in his own *Smart Set* Mencken scathingly reviewed *Aaron's Rod*—a chapter of which had recently graced the pages of the *Dial*—as "A great nose-blowing, grunting and eye-rolling about nothing. . . . A few months ago, so the papers say, Lawrence's *A Lost Girl* was awarded a prize in England as the best novel of the year. Well, we can match that in America. On the Tuesday following the first Monday in November, 1920, Warren Gamaliel Harding was elected President of the United States."[9]

Two other magazines which published Lawrence before 1920 played less important roles in his early career. *Playboy* and the *Seven Arts* lasted only for a short time, the first from 1919 until 1924, the other from November 1916 until October 1917. *Playboy* serialized in two issues in 1919 an essay on contemporary poetry which Lawrence later appended as the introduction to *New Poems* and which the *Dial* in turn later reviewed.[10] During its brief and controversial year of existence, the *Seven Arts* published two stories by Lawrence, "The Thimble" in March 1917 and "The Mortal Coil" in July 1917. Both present a mordant view of war and thus were welcomed by a little magazine resolutely opposed to America's participation in World War I. The importance of the *Seven Arts* for Lawrence is not so much that the magazine attracted new readers to his work but that it served as a link with the *Dial*, which effectively absorbed the subscription list of the *Seven Arts* when it closed in 1917.[11]

The *Forum*, *Seven Arts*, *Playboy*, and *Smart Set* had either ceased publication altogether or else had stopped publishing Lawrence by 1920. For over ten years, from March 1914 until September 1924, the *Smart Set* published nothing by Lawrence. From 1913 until 1927 none of Lawrence's works appeared in the *Forum*. The *Seven Arts* was defunct, and *Playboy*, which lasted irregularly until 1924, published nothing else by Lawrence after the essay, "Poetry of the Present," in 1919. Only one magazine, Harriet Monroe's *Poetry*, was publishing Lawrence's poems at the time the *Dial* became his most important outlet; from January 1914 until April 1923, twenty-seven of his poems appeared in *Poetry*, but after the latter issue even Miss Monroe proved inhospitable. During the entire decade of the 1920's, the *Dial* was the only magazine in America to publish a sizeable group of his poems, as *Poetry* last did in 1918. Either Harriet Monroe refused his poems, or Lawrence did not continue to submit them to her after he gained entry to the *Dial*. The latter course seems the more probable, for Lawrence's final contribution to *Poetry* in April 1923 was "Saint Matthew," the only poem of the group of four entitled "Apostolic Beasts" that the *Dial* had not previously published in April 1921 along with "St. Mark," "St. Luke," and "St. John." Moreover, when Lawrence's *Collected Poems* appeared in 1929, Miss Monroe reviewed the volume in her journal with less enthusiasm than was shown by any of the reviewers in other periodicals; and in her strong-minded way she contended that Lawrence's revision of the poems that had appeared first in *Poetry* had damaged them.[12]

Lawrence found American outlets for his early writing through the regular trade publishers as well as through periodicals. In 1911 the New York firm of Duffield published *The White Peacock*, his first novel, one day before Heinemann's brought it out in London. Lawrence's second novel, *The Trespasser*, both Mitchell Kennerly in New York and Gerald Duckworth in London issued in May 1912. Kennerly thus initiated an important if short-lived relationship with Lawrence. In 1913 he brought out *Love Poems and Others* and *Sons and Lovers*, the latter the novel that determined Lawrence's success as a writer. The last of Lawrence's works that Kennerly published was *The Widowing of Mrs. Holroyd* in 1914. It was to be expected that Kennerly should use Lawrence's shorter fiction for the *Forum*. And Lawrence was willing; he had recently pleaded with Edward Garnett to "entreat some Review or other to print me" (*CL* 104). Garnett himself was a well-known author and an esteemed editor for the young firm of Gerald Duckworth, Lawrence's English publisher in these years, and thus was precisely the right person to act informally as Lawrence's first American agent and to send Lawrence's story "The Soiled Rose" to Mitchell Kennerly in New York.

The *Smart Set* first secured Lawrence's work through Ezra Pound, its English agent, who later worked in Paris as European representative for the *Dial*.[13] Pound was impressed with his first reading of the poems by Lawrence that appeared in the *English Review* and wrote Harriet Monroe that Lawrence "learned the proper treatment of modern subjects before I did."[14] The *Seven Arts* and Lawrence became acquainted probably through Esther Andrews, a friend of the magazine's agent in Europe. For Egmont Arens's ambitious but underfinanced *Playboy* there is no recorded link to Lawrence; on the strength of Arens's early editorial pronouncements, Lawrence's agent may have sent along the essay *Playboy* serialized. For *Poetry* the link was at first Ezra Pound and later the editor herself, who corresponded directly with Lawrence, selected poems that he submitted, and arranged them in the order he requested (*CL* 288).[15]

Lawrence's publication in the *Dial* was also apparently accomplished by Ezra Pound, with the immediate aid of Richard Aldington. For Lawrence as for so many others, Pound's characteristically generous advocacy was qualified by his fault-finding. In a letter to T. E. Lawrence in August 1920, Pound remarked that "two stories (or somethings) by D. H. Lawrence have been accepted [by the *Dial?*] through no particular fault of my own save that I asked Aldington to ask D. H. Lawrence to send 'em in." An earlier letter to Harriet Monroe explains Pound's admiration for Lawrence's work, tempered though it was by a personal dislike: "Lawrence, as you know, gives me no particular pleasure. Nevertheless we are lucky to get him. . . . If I were an editor I should probably accept his work without reading it. As a prose writer I grant him first place among the younger men." [16] Pound's qualified opinion of Lawrence's talent was familiar to the editor of the *Dial*, Scofield Thayer, who confided to Alyse Gregory in a letter dated July 30, 1921, that at close quarters Pound was much more fair in his judgments than his correspondence and his books would warrant one to believe: "For example he acknowledges that D. H. Lawrence is one of the two or three most important young men writing English today, and he confesses very sweetly to being so opposite in temperament and interest as to be unable to read the Veil." [17] Years later, in 1931, Pound acknowledged querulously that he felt differently toward Lawrence—"Life wd. have been (in my case) much less interesting if I had waited till Joyce, Lewis, Eliot, D. H. Lawrence, etc. complied with what my taste was in 1908." [18] In 1920, however, Pound preferred not to approach Lawrence, even grudgingly, and for an intermediary turned instead to Aldington, a minor figure with whom he would not have to contend as an equal.

Lawrence had known Aldington and his wife, the poet Hilda Doolittle, since 1914, when they met at a dinner party in London.[19] Actually, the key to the Lawrence-Pound acquaintance was Hilda Doolittle, "H. D.," as she preferred to be published. The daughter of a professor at the University of Pennsylvania, H. D. had been one of Pound's college friends, and they had shared their undergraduate artistic yearnings. The occasion of the dinner party at which Lawrence met the Aldingtons, the hostess, Amy Lowell, had arranged in order to persuade Lawrence to give his poems for an Imagist anthology she was preparing; the evening resulted not only in Lawrence's appearances in Imagist anthologies—appearances that made him out to be what he was not (he was not an Imagist)—but also in his friendship with the Aldingtons. And the association with Amy Lowell may in part account for Pound's ambivalence toward Lawrence; for Pound deserted Imagism as a cause when Amy Lowell appeared on the literary scene to appropriate as *her* cause what Ezra contemptuously labeled "Amygism."

Lawrence's friendship with the Aldingtons proved enduring. His fiction was shocking; his disengagement from British wartime patriotism seemed damagingly irresponsible. But the climactic objection was his alliance with one of the enemy, Frieda, née the Baronin von Richthofen, cousin to the most famous German war ace, and until recently wife of Professor Ernest Weekley; she had deserted husband, children, and hearth for the uncertainties of life with this collier's son gone literary. The Lawrences nevertheless had their protectors. There was Lady Ottoline Morrell, sister to the Duke of Portland, mistress to Bertrand Russell, and a great hostess and aristocrat who presumably was above any middle-class obsession with the war; and also there were the Meynell family, who took in the Lawrences out of the kindness of their hearts and who, like Lady Ottoline, received the reward of Lawrence's most savage irony. She was distorted as the Hermione

Roddice of *Women in Love;* Winifred Meynell's husband, Percy Lucas, was caricatured as the Egbert of *England, My England*. Hilda Aldington nevertheless was deterred neither by Lawrence's politics nor by any speculation about Lawrence's way with his friends and benefactors; after his more patriotic countrymen expelled Frieda and himself from Cornwall in 1917, H. D. offered them rooms in London. Just after the war, in 1919, Richard Aldington took over Lawrence's cottage in Berkshire when he left England for the Continent, Australia, and America. After the American experience, in 1926 Lawrence met Aldington again in England, and in 1928 Lawrence and Frieda stayed at Aldington's house at Port-Cros.[20]

A leading Imagist poet, a novelist, translator, essayist, and biographer, Aldington was a frequent contributor to the *Dial* from 1917 on and therefore was an obvious go-between for Pound to approach in attracting Lawrence to the *Dial* of Thayer and Watson. It is likely, too, that in 1920 Lawrence was not altogether aware of the difference between the *Dial* of Thayer and Watson and the *Dial* of the war years, controlled by Martyn Johnson. In that earlier version of the magazine had appeared Aldington's series of poems, "Letters to Unknown Women," as well as his essays, such as "Poet and Painter: A Renaissance Fancy" in the issue for January 11, 1917, and his reviews, such as the one of *New Paths*, an anthology that included work by Lawrence.[21] Under the circumstances, it seems strange that in his memoirs, *Life for Life's Sake*, Aldington makes no reference to the *Dial;* concerning Lawrence, he merely comments that from 1919 until 1926 he "had not seen [the Lawrences]" and that their correspondence "had been extremely irregular." [22]

Lawrence's diary provides a little more information about his first transaction with the *Dial*. The entry for June 20, 1920 reveals that he "sent Richard Rex to go with Adolf for the Dial" (Ted 90). The only other reference to these early sketches, "Rex" and "Adolf," the first two contributions by Lawrence printed in the *Dial*, is a note in the diary for July 26,

1920 that he received nine pounds, seventeen shillings, and sixpence "via Richard" for "Adolf" (Ted 91). The opinion of Tedlock is that "Richard" in the diary refers to Aldington, and this tentative suggestion is fortunately borne out not only by Pound's *Letters* but also by the *Dial* papers. The magazine's records reveal that payment for the two sketches was sent to Aldington for Lawrence; a letter from Lawrence to Aldington that accompanied "Rex" is in the *Dial* papers.

Perhaps more important than the details of Lawrence's first publication in the *Dial* is the reason that his work did not appear earlier in the magazine. Seven years passed after the publication of *Sons and Lovers*—and seven years after the first periodical publication of Lawrence's work in America—before the *Dial* published Lawrence's writing. By 1920 Lawrence was the author of two plays, *The Widowing of Mrs. Holroyd* in 1914, and *Touch and Go* in 1920; a book of travel sketches, *Twilight in Italy* in 1916; most of *Studies in Classic American Literature*, in 1919; five volumes of poetry, *Love Poems* in 1913, *Amores* in 1916, *Look! We Have Come Through* in 1917, *New Poems* in 1918, and *Bay* in 1919; a collection of short stories, *The Prussian Officer* in 1914; and six novels, *The White Peacock* in 1911, *The Trespasser* in 1912, *Sons and Lovers* in 1913, *The Rainbow* in 1915, and *Women in Love* and *The Lost Girl* in 1920.[23] In some respects, the years 1913–20 were Lawrence's most brilliantly productive period of creative work.

Yet during those years no work by him appeared in the *Dial*, and the magazine printed only five reviews of his work. The first of these, in the issue for January 16, 1915, was Homer E. Woodbridge's compendious notice of Lawrence's *The Widowing of Mrs. Holroyd* and sixteen other plays by such dramatists as J. M. Barrie, Atherton Brownell, and E. A. Robinson.[24] Woodbridge's critical strategy consisted of an attempt to compare the various plays; he may have included *The Widowing of Mrs. Holroyd* only because its subject was the same as that of another play under review, J. O. Francis's *Change*, both being concerned with the tragic clash of the old and new in a Welsh mining village. Francis's *Change*, "as is often the case with prize plays and stories," said Woodbridge, was "rather dull"; he praised Lawrence's play for its attention to characterization rather than social propaganda and perceptively commented that Lawrence would be "well worth watching."

The next notice of Lawrence's work, a general survey of his output at that time, occupied half the cover page of the fortnightly *Dial* for November 16, 1916. Edward Garnett, Lawrence's friend who had helped him into print, was the critic and entitled his piece "Art and the Moralists: Mr. D. H. Lawrence's Work." [25] In the first part of the essay Garnett defended Lawrence as a "pure artist," true to his artistic vision, who refused to separate "sensuous perceptions" from spiritual life. Of Lawrence's poetry Garnett observed that "his range of mood is very limited, his technique is hasty, his vision turns inward, self-centered; but in concentration of feeling, in keenness, one might almost say in fierceness of sensation, he seems to issue from those tides of emotional energy which surge in the swaying ocean of life." In the second part of his essay Garnett traced Lawrence's progress as a novelist, story writer, and playwright, with specific reference to *The White Peacock*, *The Trespasser*, *Sons and Lovers*, *The Widowing of Mrs. Holroyd*, and stories from *The Prussian Officer*. All of Lawrence's works, according to Garnett, would naturally be misunderstood by moralists; " 'the good' as conceived by the moralists confines to too narrow a circle our tides of emotional energies." Garnett—not surprisingly for a progenitor of the "Bloomsberries"—concluded that taste, not morals, should be the criterion for judging works of art.

Then in the issue for March 22, 1917, Henry Blake Fuller reviewed *Twilight in Italy* and *The Prussian Officer* and thereby became the first of several *Dial* reviewers to complain of Lawrence's meticulous and relentless analysis of people and places. [26] In *Twilight in Italy*, said Fuller, Lawrence pursues so deeply and thoroughly the thesis that Italians are oversexed that the reviewer admitted he was forced to ask, "Man, man! is the Italian the only one under the curse?" This may seem the caviling of a genteel moralist, but actually Fuller's opinions are, rather, those of a severely professional writer, a distinguished novelist; both books under review are weakened, he concluded, by excessive description and overly stylized phrases, while *The Prussian Officer* contains stories that are merely descriptive sketches.

Two further reviews of Lawrence's work in Martyn Johnson's *Dial* were, like Woodbridge's earlier review, catchall pieces that considered books of poems by various hands. In the issue for April 19, 1917 Lawrence's *Amores* was included along with *Green Branches* by James Stephens, *Wild Earth and Other Poems* by Padraic Colum, and *Swords for Life* by Irene Rutherford McLeod.[27] The reviewer, William Aspenwall Bradley, was on the staff of the *Dail* and thus should have been sympathetic to the poetry under review, all of it by "new" voices; while Bradley did praise the Georgian lyrics of Stephens, he identified Lawrence as an Imagist and criticized the poetry of *Amores* because it was concerned with painting images and neglected the basically lyrical nature of verse. Not only was Bradley inaccurate in grouping Lawrence with the Imagists, he also erroneously saw Lawrence as a Puritan who rejected beauty in his poems because he denied sensuousness.

Two years later, reviewing *Look! We Have Come Through* in the issue for August 9, 1919, Conrad Aiken also criticized Lawrence's poetry for its neglect of what Aiken called "the melodic line": "That sort of brief movement when, for whatever psychological reason, there is suddenly a fusion of all the many qualities, which may by themselves constitute charm, into one indivisible magic."[28] In Lawrence's love poems, according to Aiken, he came closest to writing melodic lines, but in none of his poetry did he achieve the necessary fusion. Aiken's diagnosis was that Lawrence tried too hard to be both patient and psychiatrist: "the soliloquy of the patient —the lyricism of the subconscious—is forever being broken in upon by the too eager inquisitions of the analyst. If Mr. Lawrence could make up his mind to yield the floor unreservedly to either, he would be on the one hand a clearer and more magical poet, on the other hand a more dependable realist." The generally adverse view of Lawrence's work—not only his poetry but his fiction and travel writing as well—by the American reviewers for Martyn Johnson's *Dial* is properly understood only when one sees it as having relatively little connection with the editorial policy of the magazine after 1919. Of these five *Dial* reviewers, only Conrad Aiken continued to discuss Lawrence's work after 1920, in two issues of the *Dial* of Thayer and Watson.

That none of Lawrence's work appeared in the *Dial* between 1915 and 1920—even though the magazine was reviewing his books—is best explained by a brief account of the *Dial* during that period.[29] When the first review of Lawrence's work appeared in its pages, the *Dial* was a Chicago fortnightly of reviews and literary criticism in the genteel tradition. The Browne family, who then controlled the magazine, did not concern themselves in any positive way with the works of the literary vanguard to which Lawrence belonged. Soon after Homer E. Woodbridge's review appeared, the Brownes decided to sell the magazine because of financial difficulties and the growing dissatisfaction of Waldo Browne, the editor, about his job.

In June 1916 the *Dial* was purchased by Martyn Johnson, who had been associated with the *Trimmed Lamp*, one of several avant-garde reviews then being published in Chicago. Johnson transformed the traditional *Dial* into a liberal review; writers of the New Movement—among them Amy Lowell, Edward Garnett, Van Wyck Brooks, and John Gould Fletcher— and left-wing political writers, such as Harold Laski, were the most important contributors Johnson attracted to the *Dial*. To these Johnson added Gilbert Seldes, J. S. Watson, Jr., Paul Rosenfeld, Randolph Bourne, and Scofield Thayer as essayists and reviewers, and all this group except Bourne, who died in December 1918, were on the staff of the *Dial* in 1920 when Lawrence began to contribute to the magazine.

While Johnson was transforming the *Dial* into an avant-garde spokesman for the New Movement and the political left, Lawrence was contributing to *Poetry, Playboy,* and *Seven Arts.* The last of these is important to Lawrence's relationship with the *Dial.* In March and July 1917 his two war stories, "The Thimble" and "The Mortal Coil," appeared in the *Seven Arts.* Actually, at least one of these stories, "The Mortal Coil," was written long before the war itself; Lawrence had spoken of it as "that other Soldier Story" and had suggested it for the *Forum* in 1913 (*CL* 222). Although he regarded "The Mortal Coil" as one of his "purest creations," he was aware that it was "not destined . . . like the holy in the hymn, to land—On the golden strand" of the *Forum*'s pages (*CL* 480). Thus its appearance in the *Seven Arts,* four years later. The inclusion of Lawrence's two stories was one of many coups for the little magazine with cosmopolitan and antiwar aims that lasted only the twelve monthly issues from November 1916 to October 1917.

Lawrence's association with the *Seven Arts* began about the time the editors brought out their first number. In November 1916 Lawrence received at his house in Cornwall two American guests, Robert Mountsier and Esther Andrews (*CL* 484). They were visiting in England and returned to spend the week after Christmas with the Lawrences (H 389). As a result of his visit, Mountsier became Lawrence's agent in America. More pertinently for the *Seven Arts,* Esther Andrews was a friend of the European agent for the new journal.[30] When Mountsier returned to America, Miss Andrews remained for a while with the Lawrences before she traveled to visit S. S. Koteliansky and Catherine Carswell, literary associates and friends as well of Lawrence (H 393, 408–10). Apparently Miss Andrews thoroughly entrenched herself with her hosts. In a letter to Catherine Carswell on January 15, 1917 Lawrence revealed that Frieda and he wanted Esther Andrews to accompany them to America and to "the ultimate place we call Typee or Rananim" (*CL* 499, H 391).

Through Esther Andrews' influence, Lawrence's work appeared in *Seven Arts.* At this time, he gave her manuscripts of his poetry (*CL* 505, H 401), and she read the draft of *Women in Love* (H 382); clearly to some extent Lawrence must have respected her judgment. Lawrence mentioned in a postscript of a letter to Catherine Carswell dated December 11, 1916, that "The Thimble" was to be published in the *Seven Arts* (*CL* 491). And after the publication of both "The Thimble" and "The Mortal Coil," Miss Andrews wrote Lawrence from Paris and asked for more stories (*CL* 518).

Waldo Frank—an editor of the *Seven Arts* along with James Oppenheim—also wrote to Lawrence in July 1917, telling him that both stories had been published and inquiring about *The Rainbow*. Frank had approvingly mentioned Lawrence in an article in the *Seven Arts* for January 1917 and generally admired his work but was apparently put off by the brutality of the characters and, in that connection, asked in his letter whether the war had influenced Lawrence's writing.[31]

Waldo Frank's interest in Lawrence's response to the war and the publication in *Seven Arts* of Lawrence's two war stories reflect the acute concern of the magazine with the conflict. Like Lawrence, the editors of the *Seven Arts* were firmly opposed to the war; and they opposed, also, war in general. Their rallying force was Randolph Bourne, who published an article decrying the war and American intellectuals for not preparing public opinion for the events leading to the declaration of war. Bourne's famous essay, "War and the Intellectuals," appeared in the issue for June 1917, and by the following September the pacifists writing for Oppenheim and Frank had alienated their financial supporter, Mrs. A. K. Rankine, and thus were bringing about the end of the magazine.[32] The significance of Lawrence's appearances in *Seven Arts* is all the more intense when one observes their context of publication in a leading journal of the intellectual-pacifist vanguard. Indeed, it may well have been in *Seven Arts* that Lawrence came to the attention of Scofield Thayer, Bourne's staunchest friend and later the editor of the *Dial*. Both Lawrence and Thayer agreed about the war, as they did about other issues: art, sexual freedom, and censorship.

In reply to Waldo Frank's letter, Lawrence commented on July 27, 1917 that he was aware only of the publication of "The Thimble" and went on to answer Frank's questions about *The Rainbow*. The book, Lawrence explained, had been conceived before the war and its theme was not altered "from its pre-war statement." "What I did through individuals," Lawrence continued, "the world has done through the war. But alas, in the world of Europe I see no Rainbow. I believe the deluge of iron rain will destroy the world here, utterly: no Ararat will rise above the subsiding iron waters." The war had achieved not consummation, as did death by sensual ecstasy in *The Rainbow*, but extinction (*CL* 518–19). Lawrence then turned to matters at hand, mentioning that he had heard from Miss Andrews in Paris and that he had instructed his English literary agent, James B. Pinker, to send manuscripts either to her in Paris or to Frank in New York. An earlier letter from Lawrence to Pinker reveals that the latter had, in October 1916, the manuscripts for "The Mortal Coil" and that Lawrence at that time despairingly suggested its publication in a "cent-a-worder" magazine in America (*CL* 480), that is, an outlet like *Smart Set;* at any rate, the date of the letter is earlier than Lawrence's acquaintance with *Seven Arts*.

Pinker may have followed Lawrence's instructions to send some stories to Waldo Frank. Whatever the case, they were not to appear in the *Seven Arts;* two months after Lawrence replied to Frank, the magazine folded. As Lawrence's funds dwindled, his letters to Pinker after this time grew correspondingly less frequent and more demanding, and they often contained requests for advances against work to be sold. Lawrence had to endure this situation pretty well throughout the war years, and he was lucky to live off the charity of a more prudent and more popular confrere. As early as November 1915 Arnold Bennett, who admired Lawrence's work, gave Pinker forty pounds for his client (*CL* 390), and later Lawrence suggested that Pinker might ask Bennett for a loan (*CL* 538). Eventually bowing to what must long have seemed the inevitable, in December 1919 or January 1920 Pinker suggested that he and

Lawrence should end their unprofitable business relationship, and the accounts the agent returned to Lawrence in January 1920 show a refund of twenty-five pounds to E. A. Bennett (*CL* 611, 621). In his acknowledgment Lawrence asked, "And who is E. A. Bennett" (*CL* 621). Had the letters of these years not been almost solely about money, perhaps we should know what happened to the manuscripts intended for the *Seven Arts*.

The *Dial* and *Seven Arts* have important connections historically. The *Seven Arts* failed in 1917 for the reasons the *Dial* failed in 1919: both became politically oriented toward unpopular causes. When the *Seven Arts* lost Mrs. A. K. Rankine as its principal financial support, Scofield Thayer tried to salvage it. He wished to establish an editorial board, but James Oppenheim wanted to retain his one-man leadership. The two men could not agree, and so Thayer's project collapsed. The *Dial* attempted then to absorb the other periodical by filling unexpired subscriptions and publishing the *Seven Arts*'s contributors. Many of the writers from the defunct *Seven Arts* did appear in the *Dial* of Martyn Johnson, and Lawrence was one of the relatively few who did not.[33]

One can only guess why he did not. First of all, there was the confused state of Johnson's magazine itself, victim of changes only less shattering than those that wrecked *Seven Arts*. In the summer of 1918, Martyn Johnson moved his journal to New York and dubbed it the "Reconstruction" *Dial* to signalize his interest in reconstructing the postwar world through the propaganda of editorials and articles and *Dial*-sponsored rallies. Johnson managed by hook or by crook to attract as editors and contributors Thorstein Veblen, John Dewey, and Helen Marot, all of them prominent in the liberal groups of the time.

But these activities marked the beginning of the end of Johnson's regime, and that end was accomplished largely by Scofield Thayer. Thayer had been attracted to the *Dial* by Johnson's policies and cohorts: its political leanings were Socialist, and it seemed to provide a crucially needed publishing

outlet for his new-found and deeply admired friend, Randolph
Bourne—as well as a means for Thayer's expression of his own
attitudes and ideas about letters and the arts. That the *Dial*
might escape from Martyn Johnson's control was of course not
at all to the publisher's taste. To him, Thayer was important
solely as a financial backer, as the somewhat eccentric innocent
who in 1918 and 1919 contributed thirty thousand dollars to
the cause of the *Dial* without, or so it seemed, attaching any
strings to the gift. When it came to placing Bourne on the
editorial board, Johnson nevertheless would not temper editorial policy to suit his backer, and in the course of 1918, as the
publisher began openly to agree with John Dewey's support of
President Wilson's war policy and to oppose Randolph
Bourne's pacifism, Thayer had some extremely unpleasant second thoughts anent the *Dial* and its drift. When in December
1918 the magazine printed the "Original Decrees of the Soviet
Government" in its "Foreign Comment," the chief backer of
the *Dial* resigned, wallet and all.

Without Thayer's money, the magazine floundered. Johnson tried yet again to borrow funds and to issue new stock
before he finally put up for sale his own stock in the *Dial*. At
this juncture, Thayer and his friend Sibley Watson went into
action; represented by their lawyers, the two young men
bought Johnson out, thus not only ending his regime and
policies but thereby instituting their own. With the new owner-
ship the Johnson editors and contributors scattered. In the final
issue of Johnson's *Dial*, November 29, 1919, Thayer and Watson announced that the new magazine would "diverge in more
important aspects from the *Dial* of the last year and a half"—
that is to say, since the move in July 1918 from Chicago to
New York and the resultant disasters—"particularly in its
greater emphasis on art and literature" and its avoidance of the
"fumy scene of politics." Under the new editors the magazine
became both physically attractive and formally ordered. From
the beginning its outlook was cosmopolitan and eclectic, and it
welcomed works of art with a passionate regard solely for the
aesthetic value intrinsic to the works themselves. It was to this

new *Dial* that Lawrence contributed for the rest of his life. The point is that in 1918 and 1919, the *Dial* was not financially attractive to Lawrence as a potential contributor. Nor could it have printed much of his writing except for an occasional poem or book review.

These conclusions are supported by an examination of the fate of Lawrence's manuscripts his agent Pinker tried to sell in 1917–19. They were, simply, not salable in those years when their author offended popular opinion to the point that editors and publishers retaliated by refusing to buy his stories.

Yet Lawrence kept going and bode his time. With the beginning of the 1920's a revulsion against the fever of the war years 1914–18 was perceptible. That it *was* perceptible to Lawrence is shown in his request in February 1920 that Pinker return, by manuscript post, all the manuscripts the agent had on hand. A diary notation indicates Pinker returned on February 16 "The Mortal Coil" and "The Thimble" that Waldo Frank had published in America in 1917; "Samson and Delilah," which appeared in the *English Review* in March 1917; and nine other pieces (prose and poetry) listed as "Miracle," "At the Gates," "John Thomas," *The Fox*, "Wintry Peacock," "Fanny and Annie," "Monkey Nuts," and "You Touched Me." In the same note Lawrence indicated Pinker still was keeping "Witch à la Mode," "Once," "The Primrose Path," and "Love Among the Haystacks." Out of this very mixed bag of masterpieces and inconsequentialities, one of the manuscripts not yet published, *The Fox*, was later serialized in four issues of the *Dial*, May–August 1922.[34] The recognition of Lawrence's talent in America would come very soon.

In the same February of 1920, Lawrence wrote his American publisher Benjamin Huebsch, with whom he had done business since 1916 when Huebsch had published *The Prussian Officer*, that he had several stories he wanted to place in America, averred in one paragraph that he needed "a good New York agent," and promised in the next paragraph to have "no more agents: and no more vagueness." He concluded that "I feel it is my business now to secure an American public. I have been fooled long enough" (*CL* 621–22). His quest would soon end successfully. Four months after the complaint to Ben Huebsch, Richard Aldington sent off Lawrence's two animal stories to the *Dial*, and in its issue for September 1920 the American public—that particular public Lawrence had been seeking—would confront his talent in the refurbished *Dial* of Scofield Thayer and James Sibley Watson, Jr.

2

LORENZO COMES TO *THE DIAL*, 1920–1922

Personally, Lawrence remarked in his essay of 1915 entitled "Note to 'The Crown,'" "little magazines mean nothing to me: nor groups nor parties of people. I have no hankering after quick response, nor the effusive, semi-intimate backchat of literary communion" (*RDP*, p. ii). Were that remark anything less than absolute balderdash, its author would never have written for most of the magazines his work appeared in; nor would he himself ever have become a cult object, during his lifetime and after, venerated as quasi-divine by men and women of otherwise rather divergent tastes. And that Lawrence did have a compulsive hankering after the effusive, semi-intimate backchat of literary communion is borne out by the evidence of two bulky volumes of letters bulging with gossip, blackguarding, and the most intimate personal advice bestowed, as often as not, quite gratuitously upon his correspondents.

By the closing weeks of 1919, Lawrence had decided that little and big magazines alike were not so stifling after all. Writing to his American publisher Ben Huebsch from the temporary roosting place of Chapel Hill Cottage, the Hermitage, near Newbury, Lawrence on May 9, 1919 expressed the "hope the *Seven Arts* will be revived" (*CL* 586). Returning again to his theme, Lawrence, now in Italy, told Huebsch on

December 3, 1919 that he intended to "do various small things —on Italy and on Psychoanalysis—for the periodicals." And, he added plaintively, "I wish I knew the American magazines— weeklies and monthlies. Would you hate to advise me about the placing of these things? It is time we made a sort of systematic attack on the American public. I'll do the writing if you'll help with the placing" (*CL* 599). As things turned out, it was Robert Mountsier who mostly helped place Lawrence's writing in the American periodicals during 1920, and then not in the mass-circulation weeklies such as the *Saturday Evening Post* but in magazines of restricted appeal such as the *Dial* and the *New Republic*.

The very soul of Lawrence lies in the coterie atmosphere of the little magazines with their cults and colonies. For all his dithering about money, for all his search for an ideal place to work in, he responded to the ambience of the small vanguard literary journal about as wholeheartedly as he responded to any other prospect of compensation for his writing. One must not be put off to find that the published correspondence, the biographies, the critical studies have not very much specific information about the mundane business of Lawrence's getting into print in the magazines. In contrast, there is relatively a good deal of comment, usually quite irritated comment, on his dealings with agents, the publishers of his books, and other helpers, about equally luckless in their dealings with Lorenzo. What remains to resolve any biographer's indecision is the indubitable fact of publication, the repeated publication of Lawrence's stories, poems, travel essays, publishers' advertisements of his books, reviewers' adulatory or scandalized considerations of his talent. These evidences express as nothing else can—and in the face of all disclaimers—Lawrence's hankering after quick reference and the literary backchat of the little magazines.

If Lawrence did not hanker after such réclame, his allegiance to little magazines is inexplicable. Two of his peers, Ernest Hemingway and William Faulkner, acted far differently when fame came to them. As soon as they could flee the unpaying clutches of the *Double-Dealer* and the *Little Review*, which had generously accepted their earliest work, both writers rushed into print in the *Saturday Evening Post*, the *Atlantic Monthly*, and other prestigious, remunerative outlets. With their marvelously acute sensing of the possibilities of popular response, Faulkner and Hemingway conformed their writing for sale in the broad marketplace. Generally speaking, Lawrence never conformed to the popular taste of the period from the death of Edward VII to the onset of the Great Depression. He was caviar to the general, and by his own intention. He resisted the allurements of well-meaning friends and agents to publish more lucratively. Only toward the end of his life and the close of the 1920's did he attempt a large-scale popular success; and when he succeeded, it was a *succès de scandale* with the publication of *Lady Chatterley's Lover* by Pino Orioli's small private press in Florence and its immediate proscription by official censors. A few verbal deletions, and the expurgated novel was soon published by Martin Secker in London and Alfred Knopf in New York. It sold well in 1929 mostly because it was misunderstood by the prurient. The doubt remains that it ever would have been a best seller except under such circumstances; and since publication in 1959–60 of a trade edition of the original version, Lawrence's single best-selling work has enriched his estate only because, years after his death, a changing taste has allowed that eventual publication. Unexpurgated: the operative word for the widest possible sale in a soft-paper binding in drug stores and supermarkets, to housewives in curlers and elephant pants, to high-school students in pimples and yearning furtiveness. How disappointed they must be that *Lady Chatterley's Lover* is not another *Peyton Place*. Such—except for the spiritual progeny of the readers of the *English Review* and the *Dial*, the *Double-Dealer* and the *Little Review*—is the result of Lawrence's refusal to conform as did Faulkner and Hemingway: he remains essentially an artist for a coterie widely dispersed but small in number by contrast to those millions who admire the novelists of *Sanctuary* and *The Old Man and the Sea*.

Birds of a feather flock together, and in the 1920's the

warmest nest when like called to like was the *Dial*. Not caring that Lawrence was having difficulty in finding acceptance in any other American magazine, the *Dial* of Scofield Thayer and Sibley Watson remained hospitable to his work throughout the decade of the 1920's, those years in which he was to publish so much of his major work. Six full-scale novels—*Women in Love* in 1920, *The Lost Girl* in the same year, *Aaron's Rod* in 1922, *Kangaroo* in 1923, *The Plumed Serpent* in 1926, and *Lady Chatterley's Lover* in 1928—were to appear during the 1920's. Stories and short novels, such as the collection in *The Woman Who Rode Away* in 1928 and *England My England* in 1922 and *Saint Mawr* in 1925, would all appear while Lawrence was contributing to the *Dial*. Five volumes of poems and ten books and pamphlets of essays and travel sketches, including *Studies in Classic American Literature*, *Sea and Sardinia*, and *Mornings in Mexico*, appeared during the 1920's. For many of these works the *Dial* was the first publisher, and other works, including the early major novels, were reviewed in the magazine when it did not publish them.[1]

The years during which Lawrence contributed to the *Dial* are those which Harry T. Moore calls the wander years.[2] By the end of World War I Lawrence was sick of England. He had been spied upon, forced to leave Cornwall, and regarded with suspicion in every part of his native land, for in addition to his marriage to Frieda, he was also a vocal pacifist. The contempt of his countrymen ostracized Lawrence so completely that in November 1919 he left England, never again to live there permanently. After a trip through Italy, Lawrence and Frieda took a villa at Taormina, using it as their Sicilian *pied-à-terre* from March 1920 until late February 1922. Lawrence had become too restless to remain satisfied wandering about Europe and the Mediterranean and embarked with Frieda on his most fateful search for the great good place. By way of India and Australia, they went on to Tahiti and then, drawn ineluctably by the attraction of a new benefactress, to San Francisco and at last to Taos, the Indian town and pueblo that was to be their New Mexican base for three more years.

Meanwhile, Lawrence was writing steadily for the *Dial*, and long before he landed in San Francisco, it was the *Dial* that was leading him on to Taos, for the crucial period of his career as artist and prophet.

Scofield Thayer and Sibley Watson published the first issue of their new *Dial* in January 1920. Lawrence's first contribution appeared nine issues later in September, and "Notes on Contributors" rather sparely announced that "D. H. Lawrence is the author of Sons and Lovers and of The Rainbow." From his story "Adolf" in that September number until the issue for June 1925, there were to be only nine issues of the *Dial* that did not contain at least one of his works, a review of one or more of his books, or an advertisement from one of his publishers.[3] Only once did the *Dial* go for as long as three months without a reference to Lawrence, and this occurred in the issues November–December 1924 and January 1925, when Alyse Gregory was managing editor. The advertisement in the *Dial* for September 1923 for Thomas Seltzer, Lawrence's chief American publisher, correctly asserted that "probably no modern writer is better known to Dial readers than D. H. Lawrence."

From September 1920 until June 1925–when Marianne Moore effectively became an editor–advertising of Lawrence's work appeared in nearly all the issues of the *Dial;* from July 1925, such advertisements appear in about one-fourth of the issues, and all but one of the last seven of these are house advertisements forecasting Lawrence's next publication in the magazine. Lawrence's work appeared less consistently than did the advertisements; twenty-five issues, or 22 percent of the total number of issues of the *Dial* published after 1919, featured his work. Before June 1925, when Scofield Thayer resigned and Marianne Moore became editor, Lawrence's work appeared in 25 percent of the issues. After June 1925 his work appeared in 19 percent of the issues. Reviews of his work appeared regularly in 15 percent of the issues of Thayer's and Watson's *Dial* before June 1925 and in 17 percent after that.

Such a superficial analysis fails to indicate the range and

quality of Lawrence's writing in the *Dial*, nor does it indicate that the years before 1925 are certainly the most significant for an understanding of the relationship of Lawrence and that magazine. At the time the *Dial* began to publish Lawrence's work, *Poetry* was the only other magazine providing an outlet in America for it and did so in just one of the genres in which he wrote. The *Dial* printed representative examples of Lawrence's work in all its genres except the plays, publishing before 1925 two stories, a novella, three essays, a chapter of a novel, a critical review, a translation of a Russian story, and five poems. After 1924 Lawrence's publication in the *Dial* consisted of only five stories and eleven poems. The reviews of Lawrence's writing that appeared there before June 1925 consisted of five long signed articles devoted solely to his work and, further, three signed articles discussing his work along with that of other writers; there were also short unsigned reviews in the department of "Briefer Mention." After June 1925 only one long signed review appeared as opposed to five short, unsigned discussions of his work and a reference in the departmental "London Letter" to *Lady Chatterley's Lover*.

The first half of the career of the new *Dial* is the more exciting.[4] The beginning of the decade witnessed a complete change in the format of the magazine, a turning away from its brief fling as a left-wing political organ to a very different career as the major critical review in America, which also published the best of the avant-garde art and literature of the 1920's. The early years of the refurbished *Dial* were marked by its publication of such important works as Ezra Pound's *Cantos*, T. S. Eliot's *The Waste Land*, various reviews by Bertrand Russell, and *Death in Venice* by Thomas Mann. The *Dial* published experimental columns, such as Henry McBride's "Modern Forms," which discussed not only Gauguin and van Gogh, but also Gaston Lachaise and Georges Braque. Neither the editor, Scofield Thayer, nor the publisher, James Sibley Watson, Jr., held fast to any ideology. Profound though their sympathies were, neither publisher nor editor completely shared aesthetic interests; rather, each complemented the other, and together they brought to the magazine the eclecticism that allowed the publication of literary and artistic works expressing various points of view. What did matter was that what was published be aesthetically pleasing. The variety and diversity of the art and writing in the *Dial* endowed it with a harmonious effect through the careful ordering and arrangement of art work, essays, fiction, poems, and reviews. The editorial "Comment" and the other monthly departments chronicling and criticizing developments in music, art, and the theatre were composed with sophistication equal to that of the poetry, the fiction, and the pages reproducing sculpture and painting; and the contents of the issues were contributed by artists and writers new and already arrived, European, and even Asian, as well as American.

The aim of the *Dial* was not to make money—although the owners hoped eventually to operate solvently. Instead Thayer and Watson used their wealth to provide talented artists with an outlet that paid substantially to publish their work. In addition to the rates of two cents a word for prose and twenty dollars a page for poetry, the editors established an annual award of two thousand dollars in recognition of a writer's achievement and promise. Aside from its financial importance to its contributors, the *Dial* also offered the most discriminating audience in America; such authors as Marianne Moore, Hart Crane, Kenneth Burke, and E. E. Cummings became famous primarily through their publication in the *Dial*. In its effort to publish only the best—in the accepted forms as well as in the new, despite its contention that it wanted to discover fresh genius—unsolicited manuscripts were not indiscriminately encouraged and often the staff made contact with writers whose work they valued.

Operating the *Dial* was more than an expensive hobby for Scofield Thayer; it was his major creative expression. He spent the months from July 1921 to September 1923 in Europe, meeting artists and buying their work, and he conducted the editorial business of the magazine from his commodious apartment in Vienna. Sibley Watson remained in New York as publisher, while he attended medical school, and in the summers traveled with his family to Europe, where he could meet with Thayer as well as visit artists and authors in whom the *Dial* was interested. In the meantime the managing editor—successively Stewart Mitchell, Gilbert Seldes, and Alyse Gregory—worked daily at the *Dial* office in Greenwich Village. When the last managing editor, Alyse Gregory, resigned in the spring of 1925, Marianne Moore, a frequent contributor and the recipient of the Dial Award for 1924, became acting editor. The job essentially combined the duties of editor and managing editor and was created so that Thayer could be released from his editorial duties in order to devote time to his own creative writing. A year later, in 1926, Thayer formally resigned as editor and relinquished the title to Miss Moore. Although both Thayer and Watson continued to subsidize the review, they became less active in its affairs. At first Thayer helped select the art work, but even this task he gradually gave over to the staff; and Watson's visits to the office, from his family home in Rochester, were now few indeed. Marianne Moore was assisted by Kenneth Burke and Ellen Thayer, Scofield Thayer's cousin and friend who had been appointed assistant editor, but it was Miss Moore chiefly—and, more often than not, solely—who decided the content of the magazine.

Marianne Moore followed the detailed editorial set of house rules that under Thayer's guidance, Alyse Gregory had written for the magazine, and the new editor strove for the same excellence and diversity of work by the same contributors whose work had appeared before 1925. The editorial "Comment" and the unsigned reviews, many written by the editor, continued to be soigné and original. The consistent maintenance of quality is admirable, and certainly the *Dial* remained the major critical review in the country. Nevertheless the format of the magazine seemed to become rigid, the house advertisements appeared always on the same page with the same format, and other advertisements lacked the spark of early ones. Furthermore, as the aestheticism of the twenties gave way to the political ideologies of the approaching thirties, the *Dial* increasingly seemed a *fait accompli;* and, perhaps in consequence, its readership dwindled drastically.

For all the years of the 1920's Lawrence was a featured contributor. In the beginning he needed the *Dial;* while the *Dial* was published, he became famous—a status considerably affected by his many appearances in its pages. Nevertheless in the end the magazine needed Lawrence. In December 1927, in the second issue of *Hound and Horn*, a critical review published by undergraduates attending Harvard University, the youthful editors noted that the *Dial* was "not exactly dull or dreary—but quiet, careful; its ardor was very thin." Yet "fragments" such as Lawrence's short story, "In Love?," did "considerably more than keep the pages turning." [5]

For Thayer's *Dial*, with its cosmopolitan and eclectic outlook and aesthetic standards, Lawrence's work was necessary to exemplify and to round out the magazine's international scope. Representing Germany, there appeared the fiction and the "German Letters" by Thomas Mann, the leading German literary figure of the 1920's and the Nobel laureate for 1929; representing France, there were the poems and essays of Paul Valéry and the belletristic essays of Anatole France; representing Ireland, there were the poems and plays and autobiographies of Yeats; representing England, there were countless contributions by the "Bloomsberries," then at the height of their renown; and, finally, representing America, there was the work of Cummings, William Carlos Williams, Marianne Moore—and, for all their expatriate avowals, Eliot and Pound. By 1920 Lawrence had been hailed by several discerning critics as England's most important young novelist; as such, his writing appropriately graced the pages of the *Dial*.

Lawrence and Thayer shared in significant ways a *Weltanschauung*. The fact that the author and his editor were amenable probably did to an appreciable extent affect Lawrence's frequency of appearance in the *Dial;* yet it is true that an occasional writer such as John Dewey, who had been the leader of the opposition during the war to the views of Thayer's friend Randolph Bourne, appeared in Thayer's magazine. Thayer did not tend to regard contributors dispassionately, but he sometimes swallowed a personal antipathy in order to attract some especially glittering fly into his editorial web. And Lawrence expressed his own awareness of these editorial wiles by once confessing "a hatred of magazines' ways and means" (*CL* 660). In 1921 he doubted that he would ever sell to periodicals "more than an odd thing now and then" (H 520–21). Lawrence's appearance in one-fourth of all the issues of the *Dial* constituted more than a "now and then" proposition, and the reason for the frequency of Lawrence's publication there as well as for the constant attention he received from the magazine lies in the compatibility of Lawrence and Thayer.

One sees several ways in which Lawrence and Thayer were congenial. First, both men were pacifists – and fortunately both were rejected for military service. Lawrence suffered during the First World War from the constant spying of British soldiers. He was expelled from his house in Cornwall on charges that he was a spy, and even after he moved to London, he was kept under surveillance by the police. During this time he dreamed of an ideal colony where his ever-changing circle of friends and Frieda and he could live away from "civilization." As a result of the war, Lawrence exploited new themes in his writing; and for some critics, he wrote less effectively than before the war. During the war Scofield Thayer belonged to the intellectual-pacifist group led by his friend Randolph Bourne. When the *Seven Arts* failed in October 1917 because of its pacifist orientation and its vocal opposition to American participation in the war, Thayer expressed a willingness to keep the magazine going by providing the needed financial support.

Both Lawrence and Thayer were notoriously contemptuous of censors. In 1915 *The Rainbow* was banned both in England and America, and for the same reason, Lawrence's next novel, *Women in Love*, was unable to appear until three years after Lawrence had finished it. In England and America it was printed only for subscription but still did not escape the

censors. In addition to the stringencies of the war, which kept
Lawrence in England at a time when he needed most urgently
to be away, the confiscation of his two books reduced him to
poverty and engendered the despair that permeated his novels
after the war. Similarly, at the *Dial*, the staff was always alert
to possible censorship and was careful to avoid the trouble that
the *Little Review* suffered in 1919–21 for its serialization of
Ulysses. When Margaret Anderson, the editor of the *Little
Review*, came to trial in New York for publishing Joyce's
work, Thayer accompanied the witnesses for the defense and
was ready to testify but was never called.[6]

Other interests that the two men shared were intellectual.
Besides their active resistance to the war and censors, both
Thayer and Lawrence were concerned with the aesthetic
avant-garde, with new art forms. Lawrence, for example, wrote
to several of his friends that *The Rainbow* was unlike any
other novel in English (*CL* 205, 223, 230). Thayer admired
the paintings of Picasso, the sculptures of Maillol and Lachaise, and the poems of Eliot and those of Cummings and
bought as much of the new art as pleased him, reproducing it
in his review and in his great folio of pictures and photographs
of sculpture, *Living Art*.[7]

Both Lawrence and Thayer discovered in the new psychology an understanding and explanation not only for their
own feelings but for the art and literature that they read and
produced. Lawrence wrote at least two long essays, *Psychoanalysis and the Unconscious* and the *Fantasia of the Unconscious* and thus expressed his views of the new theoretical
psychology. Freudianism he rejected because it was rational
and intellectual and made a science of love. For Lawrence love
was the irrational, emotional, and religious defense against
science. Freud was the scientist who merely analyzed the unconscious, Lawrence was the prophet who passionately advocated its powers. Yet both men—Lawrence in his fiction and
Freud in his psychotherapy—showed a ruthless driving inward
to discover the hidden elements in men's personalities. Lawrence regarded Jung's theories with contempt. He once told

Mabel Luhan that Jung was very interesting, in his own sort of fat muddled mystical way: "Although he may be an initiate and a thrice-sealed adept, he's soft somewhere, and I've no doubt you'd find it fairly easy to bring his heavy posterior with a bump down off his apple-cart. I think Gourdjieff would be a tougher nut" (*CL* 938). But Lawrence's annoyance, not to be taken at face value, was directed as much at Mabel Luhan as against Jung. The truth is that the new theoretical psychology fascinated Lawrence. From the beginning his novels were primarily efforts to explain dramatically the inner states of his characters. His analyses of other writers in *Studies in Classic American Literature* are attempts to describe the psychological states of some American writers themselves and the characters they created. Similarly attracted to the new psychology, Thayer went to Vienna and lived there expressly to be psychoanalyzed by Sigmund Freud.[8]

Finally, both Lawrence and Thayer actively sought a new code of intellectual and sexual freedom. All of Lawrence's novels and most of his short stories are concerned with the relations of people in love, with sexual domination, fulfillment, and balance. The sexual behavior of his characters corresponds to their mental and emotional states and serves as the objectification of their inner beings. Thayer, with his interest in the new psychology and new art forms, found in Lawrence's work an enlargement of the new consciousness he tried to bring to art and letters. The intensity of the editor's admiration for his contributor is seen in an *aperçu* jotted in one of Thayer's private notebooks in 1923: "Lawrence: Not since Byron have we had such passion, not since Byron such vulgarity. A collier may be as emotional as a lord, and as vulgar also." [9] And he added in a Lawrentian afterthought, "Because of [the] inhumanity of industrialism Americans take flight into soft Romance, baby-talk, and the nursery where they deify childhood."

For Marianne Moore and D. H. Lawrence there are no such discernible points of agreement or difference. Both writers were interested in the craft of writing, but beyond this shared interest, the fact that Miss Moore, as editor, was sole arbiter of the work that appeared in the magazine indicates that she sufficiently admired Lawrence's work to publish it. While she was editor there appeared in the *Dial* three stories by Lawrence that constitute an important portion of his total contribution to the magazine, as well as two other lesser stories and eleven short poems from *Pansies*. One of these three major stories was purchased before Miss Moore became editor, but apart from that legacy and apart from established editorial policy, at least two pieces of evidence suggest that she was enthusiastic about Lawrence's work in the *Dial*. First, at the back of each issue was printed an announcement of major articles, fiction, and poems to be featured in the next issue of the magazine. Under Miss Moore's editorship, Lawrence's forthcoming work in the *Dial* was always so previously announced.[10] A second and stronger suggestion that Miss Moore admired Lawrence's work occurs in a letter she wrote to him when she was editor. She observed sensitively that some lines of his poetry revealed "certain hurts" but that on the whole they had "an infection of beauty." More overtly, she noted that Lawrence's contributions to the *Dial* were "an eager delight."

The early years of Lawrence's publication in the *Dial* are nevertheless the most important to consider, and to appreciate the variety of Lawrence's contributions, the reader must go to the issues from September 1920 through June 1925, the issues in which Lawrence's work appeared while Scofield Thayer was actively engaged in editing the magazine. It is suggestive that Lawrence's diary for June 20, 1920 noted that he had sent "Adolf" and "Rex" to Richard Aldington for the *Dial;* this entry links up with what one learns from the letters, that Thayer's European agent, Ezra Pound, asked Aldington for Lawrence's first work in the *Dial*. This approach to an author was usual in the years of Thayer's editorship, especially when he was bent on attracting to his magazine a particular writer or artist. Occasionally he approached his prey without the intermediary, and in Lawrence's case, Pound was soon bypassed. With Thayer's tacit cooperation, Lawrence mailed in his contributions through his agents—first Mountsier, then the firm of

Curtis Brown—even when corresponding directly with Thayer and the staff of the *Dial*.

"Adolf," which appeared in the issue for September 1920, had been written originally in 1919 for the *Athenaeum*, which John Middleton Murry had just been appointed to edit. In a letter to S. S. Koteliansky on March 14, 1919 Lawrence commented, "I have been trying to write for the *Athenaeum*. Why is it such a cold effort to do these things?" (*CL* 581). On April 3, 1919, in another letter to Koteliansky, Lawrence noted that he had "heard from Murry, very editorial—he sort of 'declines with thanks' the things I did for him. He will publish an essay next week—too late to ask for it back—and that is the first and last word of mine that will ever appear in the *Athenaeum*. Good-bye, Jacky, I knew thee beforehand" (*CL* 584).

Murry's account of the incident reveals that, as the new editor, he wanted Lawrence to write for the *Athenaeum* but at the same time was "rather nervous." Murry explained, "I knew he was in a condition of rebellion against England and all its works; if he gave full vent to his resentment, it would shock the remnants of respectable readers of that ancient organ out of their skins." Lawrence promised to be "a bit old-fashioned" and offered to write under a pseudonym. The first article he submitted, "Whistling of Birds," Murry thought was "a beautiful one." The second article, "Adolf," was—said Murry—"embittered and angry," and he and Katherine Mansfield returned the piece. In Murry's words, "Lawrence was angered and sent us nothing more." [11]

The terms "angry and embittered" hardly describe that sketch about a rabbit the Lawrence children owned. Murry's objections to the sketch were doubtlessly focused on the playful, tongue-in-cheek incident at the conclusion of the story. Four paragraphs from the end of the sketch, Lawrence observes that when the rabbit turned away from him, showing its "insolent white tail," it reminded him of "a certain rude gesture, and a certain unprintable phrase, which may not even be suggested." Lawrence goes on to correct those naturalists who "say that the rabbit shows his white tail in order to guide his

young safely after him"; *his* rabbit flipped his tail and said
"*Merde!*" "Bob! bob! bob! goes the white tail, *merde! merde!
merde!* it says to the pursuer." Only the ending of the sketch is
perhaps bitter. In death, according to Lawrence, the rabbit
seemed to say, "I am the meek, I am the righteous, I am the
rabbit. All you rest, you are evil doers, and you shall be *bien
emmerdés!*" (*Ph* 13). Was Adolf a persona for Lawrence? In
the story, was Lawrence's father symbolic of the hostile British
public who drove Lawrence out of his native land to wander
the earth?

The *Dial*, then, at the beginning of the 1920's published
work by Lawrence that other periodicals turned away; perhaps
the magazine doubted whether any censors would be cultivated
enough to read French. Moreover, the editors were apparently
pleased with Lawrence's first contribution and perhaps requested "Rex," a second sketch about a childhood pet, which
appeared in the issue for February 1921. The holograph sketch
was mailed to Aldington on May 30, 1920, along with a
letter: [12]

> Here is the other sketch for The Dial if it'll suit them.
> The money is very attractive.
> At last we're back from Malta—a dry chip of a place—
> didn't like it—frightfully hot. Hot also here—the corn cut,
> the earth autumn-pale. Alas! I can't bear to think of cowslips.
> There are no flowers like Englands flowers, say what you
> will.
> Here it *never* rains.
> If we got some money, we *might* go to Germany for a
> bit—to the Black Forest.
> Knees of the Gods.
> Thank you very much for doing this for me. Send me
> the type bill.
> Wiedersehn to A.
>
> > > > D. H. L.

The "attractive money" consisted, according to the *Dial*'s records, of forty dollars for "Adolf" and fifty dollars for "Rex."

Although the writing of "Adolf" may be dated, for "Rex"
there are apparently no references in the letters and diary of

Lawrence or in the memoirs of his associates that suggest
when the sketch was written. "Rex" may be an early sketch by
Lawrence, and therefore important as the only work by Lawrence written before 1919 to appear in the *Dial*. Keith Sagar
believes that "Rex" was written in June 1920 because the entry
in Lawrence's diary appears to indicate that it was sent to
Aldington that month.[13] The letter of May 30 to Aldington
shows that Sagar's date is at least one month too late. Harry T.
Moore notices that the depiction of the uncle in "Rex" is similar to the portrayal of the uncle in "The Primrose Path," a
short story written before July 28, 1913 (*CL* 216).[14] The similarity suggests that both works were written at nearly the same
time; if so, Lawrence's work in the *Dial* represents a wide
range of his career.

After Aldington introduced Lawrence to the *Dial* and
handled the typing and payment for the first two sketches,
Robert Mountsier—then near the close of his work as Lawrence's American agent—assumed these duties and proceeded to
send his work to the magazine. In March 1921, the issue after
the one in which "Rex" appeared, the *Dial* published "Pomegranate," the first poem by Lawrence it printed. "Pomegranate" was first in another respect, for Lawrence later placed it
first in his collection *Birds, Beasts, and Flowers*. It was written
in the autumn of 1920 in Sicily, at Fontana Vecchia near
Taormina, as were many of the other poems in *Birds, Beasts,
and Flowers*. Along with other poems from that group, it was
first offered to J. C. Squire, then the editor of the *London
Mercury*, who refused it (Ted 92) and earned Lawrence's ire.

Subsequently, Mountsier sent the poem to the *Dial* staff;
they received it on October 21, 1920, and they too refused it
four days later. The editors changed their minds about "Pomegranate," however; when more poems from *Birds, Beasts, and
Flowers* arrived at the office, they reconsidered their rejection
in the light of this group entitled "Apostolic Beasts," an unprecedented action in itself for the *Dial* to take, and requested
"Pomegranate" back for publication in the issue of March
1921.

Apparently when the *Dial* received the group of four poems constituting "Apostolic Beasts," sent by Mountsier before February 1921, the editors realized that "Pomegranate" was integral to the total design of *Birds, Beasts, and Flowers;* their change of attitude showed that they recognized the unified scheme and general excellence of the volume. So Lawrence received twenty dollars for "Pomegranate," on its appearance on two pages of the *Dial* for March.[15]

The issue for April 1921 contained three poems of the "Apostolic Beasts" group—"Saint Luke," "Saint Mark," and "Saint John." The first poem of the group, "Saint Matthew," was not accepted and did not appear until two years later when *Poetry* published it in its issue for April 1923. The *Dial* refused "Saint Matthew" on several counts. Perhaps the editors decided their readers would be offended by the tone of the poem, by the comparisons that Matthew, the speaker, makes between himself and Christ, and by the assertion of men's power: "But even thou, Son of Man, canst not quaff out the dregs of terrestrial manhood" (*P* 181). Yet the most obvious reason for rejection is an aesthetic and historic one, for there are, indeed, only three "apostolic"— or more properly (as Scofield Thayer indicated to Lawrence), evangelic—beasts: St. Mark's lion, St. Luke's ox, and St. John's eagle. The symbol for St. Matthew's Gospel is a man, not a beast at all, and the editor of the *Dial* recognized that by placing the title of "Apostolic Beasts" at the head of this group of four poems, Lawrence was arbitrarily and indecorously imposing a title on the group in order to fit it into his general scheme of *Birds, Beasts, and Flowers.*

The *Dial* therefore accepted the second, third, and fourth poems of the group and paid to Mountsier on February 25, 1921, eighty dollars; as was the practice, although "Apostolic Beasts" did not appear until the April *Dial,* where it had a splendid spread of six pages, Lawrence was paid on acceptance. And although the *Dial* printed Lawrence's title as he gave it in the typescript he submitted, something of Thayer's uneasiness was evident in a query he put to the poet. In a letter

to Thayer on July 31, 1921 Lawrence replied, "I didn't answer
you about Apostolic Beasts. Of course I knew it should be
Evangelic Beasts—But then I loathe the word Evangel, and
prefer the Apostolic sense of the animals." [16] That the magazine preserved Lawrence's title, even though he did not reply to
Thayer's query until after the poems had been published for
four and a half months, shows, if nothing else, the care his
manuscripts received at the *Dial*.

The last poem from the *Birds, Beasts, and Flowers*
collection that the *Dial* published was Lawrence's masterpiece,
"Snake." Mountsier forwarded the manuscript of the poem to
the magazine, where it was received on February 23, 1921,
just two days before the staff accepted "Apostolic Beasts."
Again one senses that the staff recognized the contextual pattern of Lawrence's poetry being submitted and that the editors
desired to publish representative poems from the collection. It
is even possible to suggest that as the arrival of "Snake" preceded the payment for "Apostolic Beasts," the excellence of
"Snake" convinced the magazine staff of Lawrence's excellence
as a poet as well as a storyteller and led to the publication of his
other poems in the magazine. Certainly the submission of
Lawrence's poems came in an ascending order of excellence,
culminating in "Snake," for which the *Dial* paid thirty dollars
for publication in the issue for July 1921.

After the five poems from *Birds, Beasts, and Flowers*, the
Dial next printed in two issues in 1921 parts of Lawrence's
travel book, *Sea and Sardinia*. In the issue for October appeared excerpts from the first and second chapters, "As Far as
Palermo" and "The Sea"; and in the issue for November appeared excerpts from the next four chapters, "Cagliari," "To
Mandas," "To Sorgono," and "To Nuoro." The chapter heading "To Sorgono" was altered in the *Dial* to "Sorgono: The
Inn"; and parts of the chapter itself were transposed to appear
under the next chapter heading, "To Nuoro." [17]

The publication of these selections from *Sea and Sardinia*
signalized an important departure for Lawrence, and, although
his good relations with the magazine were not affected by the

change, it caused some confusion for the staff of the *Dial*. From his villa at Fontana Vecchia near Taormina, he answered an inquiry from the English firm of literary agents, Curtis Brown, in a letter of April 4, 1921, asking the head of the firm, "Will you undertake to place my stuff? And will you let me know your terms? If so, make it for not more than five years, so that we needn't be tied to one another." Lawrence named "three pieces of MS. in hand": *Birds, Beasts, and Flowers; Mr. Noon (Part I)*, a novel that otherwise does not enter this account; and the *Diary of a Trip to Sardinia*, given as a "provisional title." On the date he wrote his letter to Curtis Brown, Lawrence professed not to be aware that Robert Mountsier had not only submitted but had been paid for the five poems from *Birds, Beasts, and Flowers* that the *Dial* had accepted and that four of the five had already been published (the April issue, according to custom, had appeared around the middle of the preceding month). "No one," he assured Curtis Brown, "has seen any of these poems, save Squire's two"—a reference to his statement earlier in the letter that J. C. Squire's *London Mercury* had accepted "Hibiscus and Salvia Flowers" and "Purple Anemones." As for the "diary," which of course was *Sea and Sardinia*, Lawrence told Curtis Brown: "Am sending photographs of first part—hope to send other photographs shortly of Sardinia itself. Try and sell this book to periodicals—or part of it. And I don't care how much the editors cut it" (*CL* 647).

As Lawrence admitted to Curtis Brown in a second letter dated April 22, "My English things are not very tangled"—he had terminated his agreement with his English agent J. B. Pinker early in January 1920 (*CL* 611) and was dealing directly with British editors and publishers for the time being —but "my American business was the mess" (*CL* 649). Obviously Lawrence had already given to Mountsier instructions regarding *Sea and Sardinia* similar to those he gave Curtis Brown early in April; and Mountsier was to be regarded as American representative, Curtis Brown as British representative henceforth. Lawrence envisioned the new book as being serialized in the *London Mercury* and the *Dial* with color drawings by his friend Jan Juta illustrating the travel account. "About the pictures, I am afraid I let myself be a little too much influenced by Mountsier; who, of course, quite rightly takes the purely American point of view. . . . Perhaps we can manage that [J. C. Squire's] *Mercury* and the *Dial* print an extract with two or three pictures. That I leave to you. We must not have the English side of the business subordinated too much to the American." And then he added, revealing his consistent animus toward the medium he could not do without: "About magazines—I can't help feeling a hatred of their ways and means and all that. But still am grateful to you and your magazine manager for all the trouble you have taken. Somebody told me there was part of the *Whitman* essay in the *Nation*"—a reference to the publication in the *Nation and Athenaeum* for July 23, 1921 of a shortened version of the essay on Walt Whitman in *Studies in Classic American Literature* (*CL* 660).

So anxious was Lawrence to appear in the *Dial* with parts of *Sea and Sardinia* that he undertook to act as a salesman for it. This account of the Lawrences' ten-day trip to the island of Sardinia in January 1921 was written, said the author, because Scofield Thayer had requested another travel book from Lawrence similar to his *Twilight in Italy*. Lawrence's letter complaining about magazines and setting out his plans for serializing *Sea and Sardinia* was addressed to Curtis Brown on July 7, 1921. On July 30, Lawrence directly approached Scofield Thayer about the matter:

Villa Alpensee
Thumersbach
Zell-Am-See
Austria   Via Salzburg
   30 July 1921
Dear Thayer
   I asked Miss Monk to post to you c/o Brown Shipley, after she had typed it out, a copy of a story: "The Gentleman from San Francisco" translated from the Russian of I. Bunin by my friend S. Koteliansky, and by me rubbed up into readable English. Having experience of Naples and Capri,

I find the story extremely good, as a presentation of the unpleasant side of this picture. It is extraordinarily *it*. You may like to print it in *The Dial*. If so let me know. If you wanted any information about Bunin, you could write to: *S. Koteliansky, 5. Acacia Rd. St. Johns Wood London. N.W.* I would rather my name didn't appear: but make no serious objection if it would be of use to you. If you don't want the story, do you think anyone else in America might consider it? I want to help Koteliansky if I can.

Then I suppose Seltzer or Mountsier will send you the *Sardinia* travel book. You won't like it, probably, because, as somebody said, it lacks the quality of ecstasy which is usual in Mr. Lawrence's work. But I think it is pretty vivid as a flash-light travel-book. I hope Seltzer will do the colored illustrations by Jan Juta. They are good. You'll like *them*.

How long are you going to be in Europe? And are you ever coming this way? — or Italy? I should like to meet you. Probably we shall go to Florence end of August — then later to Taormina. I hate the word "probably."

I didn't answer you about Apostolic Beasts. Of course I knew it should be Evangelic Beasts — But then I loathe the word Evangel, and prefer the Apostolic sense of the animals.

What a cross, irritable paper *The Dial* is! Yet you all insist I shall be ecstatic — I'm glad Rémy de Gourmont's Sparrowdust is settled. It was rubbish. Otherwise the Dial is fun.

Yrs.,
D. H. Lawrence [18]

This letter was written during the Lawrences' journey north for a visit with Frieda's family at their schloss near Baden-Baden, to escape the dust and heat of summer in Sicily. Lawrence had taken a side trip in the Alps to an Austrian lake resort, Zell-am-See, and was attempting to attract Scofield Thayer out of Vienna for a first meeting. For Thayer, a comparative stranger, Lawrence modified the response to "The Gentleman from San Francisco" that he had expressed on June 16, 1921, to Koteliansky (*CL* 656). "Dear Kot," he had said, "Yesterday [arrived] 'The Gent. from S. Francisco' and the pen," a much needed gift he was writing the letter with and for which he sent "very many thanks. Have read 'The Gent.'—and

in spite of its lugubriousness, grin with joy. Was Bunin one of
the Gorki-Capri crowd? – or only a visitor? But it is scream-
ingly good of Naples and Capri: so comically like the reality:
only just a trifle too earnest about it. I will soon get it written
over," Lawrence promised; for the text would not need much
altering. And he applauded the phrase a "little carved peeled-
off dog"; it was too good to alter. Especially heartening to the
poverty-stricken Kot was his collaborator's opinion that "I
really think the *Dial* might print 'The Gent.' And if so, we get
at least 100 dollars. Good for us!" – a triumphant outburst that
was, as matters turned out, not justified by the price the *Dial*
eventually paid for "The Gent."

Despite its display of Lawrence's usual irritability toward
those who did him favors and admired his work, the letter from
Zell-am-See also shows an attempt to establish a *modus vivendi*
with an American magazine and its editor increasingly important to his career, his art, and his financial well-being. It is not
an easy letter. There is Lawrence's curt rejection of Thayer's
well-intended query, in a letter now lost, whether "Evangelic"
wasn't a more accurate descriptive term than "Apostolic," as
the title most fitting for the four poems of "Apostolic Beasts."
(Yet Thayer's objection to "Apostolic" rankled; over three
months later, Lawrence admitted to Catherine Carswell, in a
letter to her husband: "I know it should be Evangelic or Apoca-
lyptic. . . . representing the four beasts of the Apocalypse –
Man [*sic*], Lion, Bull [*sic*], and Eagle. – In mediaeval Missals
and Books of Hours and such, sometimes one comes across
fascinating diagrams of the four Beasts" (*CL* 676). There are
the combined abuse and praise of the *Dial* and its staff and
reviewers: "What a cross irritable paper the *Dial* is!" and yet it
was fun – except for its insistence that Lawrence be "ecstatic,"
a reference to Conrad Aiken's old review in Martyn Johnson's
Dial. One complaint pleased Thayer, Lawrence's relief that
Rémy de Gourmont's *Sparrowdust* was settled. Thayer vehe-
mently objected to his staff about the well-nigh interminable
serialization, from September 1920 through May 1921, of
Ezra Pound's English version of Gourmont's *Dust for Spar-*

rows. Lawrence's dislike of those hundreds of *aperçus* and adages reenforced the editor's own distaste and perhaps made palatable the brusque presentation of *Sea and Sardinia* and "The Gentleman from San Francisco." Yet this prickly pear of a letter contains, along with the prickles, Lawrence's quite positive response to Thayer and the *Dial* and attractively expresses curiosity to meet an editorial paragon who combined in himself the disparate traits of literary strong man and fastidious aesthete. Perhaps, accustomed as he was to the whims of rich patrons, Lawrence was hoping that if Thayer could not come to Mahomet, then the prophet might be invited, expenses paid, to come to Thayer. And with sympathy, one can understand the brusqueness of the letter: it expresses Lawrence's agonizing insecurity as no other attitude could, the wounded sensibility of a man so hounded and cursed that his approach to a powerful editor was a bared, ambiguous grimace of scorn and friendliness.

Thayer was unable to reply immediately; like his previous letter to Lawrence, this one also has been lost, but the fished-for invitation was forthcoming. And Lawrence's tone is much less aggressive and apprehensive, as he has become aware that he had reached one person who sincerely esteemed his work.

Villa Alpensee
Thumersbach
Zell-Am-See   Via Salzburg
   17 August 1921
Dear Thayer
   Ach no. Vielen Dank—but the North Sea, a storm, a cross editor at the end of an endless railway journey; ach nein, Süsser Herrgott, was hab' ich dann getan?—Jeh o Jeh, warum soll ich so gestraft werden Nimmer, nein—aber tausendmal Dank.
   No. It snowed on the mountains here and seven people fell down a glacier for ever and I foreswore the north. I loathe the smell of snow in my nostrils. I loathe the accursed white element grinning under heaven. I shall die if I don't eat yellow figs within a fortnight. I am going south. Yea, I am going imperially over the Brenner. I am going south

Gott sei dank, ich reise fort. Ich habe genug—satt satt. Bin
schon vier monat hier in den teutonischen Welt ertrunken,
jetzt schwimm' ich heraus, kletter wie ein Meerneckar über
Stein und Fels aus, heraus, Weg. I am going South. No
more snow.

But why don't you make a detour? Go to Augsburg on
your way to Wien, and come to Florence on your way back
to Paris. Come to Florence. I shall be there certainly till
October 1st, and will stay on a bit if you are appearing. We
leave here next Monday.

32 Via dei Bardi
Florence

Send a line there.—Or we"ll meet in the spring.

Mountsier said he thought you had seen Sardinia [that
is, *Sea and Sardinia* in manuscript] & didn't like it. Well, you
probably won't like it. Yet it was partly your asking for
travel sketches à la Twilight in Italy which made me write it:
half an eye on The Dial. So live up to your responsibility.

'And then he took a Dial from his poke
And looking on it with lacklustre eye
Said very wisely: "Tis now ten oclock." '

The Gent from San Francisco will probably have reached
you. If I can wring the English MS. of Sea & Sardinia out of
Curtis Brown, 6 Henrietta St., London W.C. 2—you shall
have it. Send him a line yourself and ask him for it, if you
wish.

I shall go to Taormina for the winter: then if I have
enough dollars to my name, so that I can face New York
with calm equanimity, knowing I can leave it on the next
train for anywhere if I like, then in the spring I too shall
come to AMERICA. Needless to say my knees lose their
brassy strength, & feel like chocolate fondants at the thought.

D. H. Lawrence [19]

Lawrence's assertion that he had written *Sea and Sardinia*
actually at the suggestion of the editor of the *Dial* and that
therefore the *Dial* really had an obligation to take at least a
portion of the book—it worked! And Thayer had invited the
Lawrences for a visit where he was spending a few weeks with
his friends the von Erdbergs on the island of Sylt, on the
German Baltic shore. It was an invitation easily refused, if only
because the journey was long and the host's generosity did not

extend to paying railroad fare to Sylt. But more important for
Lawrence was Thayer's acceptance of the story that *Sea and
Sardinia* was the fruit of a brilliant editorial suggestion.

Now Thayer well may have suggested that the *Dial*
would welcome further travel sketches in the manner of *Twilight in Italy*, Lawrence's first travel book that both Gerald
Duckworth and Ben Huebsch had published in 1916; but only
Lawrence's impudent suggestion exists to assert the fact—exists, that is, until one finds the editor of the *Dial* accepting, in a
resigned spirit of irony, his contributor's assertion. On September 19, 1921 Scofield Thayer in Berlin sent his associate editor
in New York, Gilbert Seldes, a query: "Please let me know
what you accepted from Mr. Lawrence's *Sea and Sardinia*
which, as The Dial has I suppose been informed, was written
largely at my instigation. I trust you took at least two or three
chapters." (The comment "I suppose" was querulously added
in holograph, as a fastidious afterthought, onto the typewritten
letter.) Apparently Brown, in good faith, relayed Lawrence's
line about not caring "how much the editors cut" to Mountsier,
who in turn instructed the *Dial*, for the same letter besought
Brown as the newest Lawrentian agent, "Please work absolutely in unison with Mountsier." Although the *Dial* was indeed selective in its choice of excerpts from *Sea and Sardinia*
and did so on the authority of the author as transmitted by
Curtis Brown when he eventually sent along the typescript of
the book, the execution of the editing is so smooth that the
quality of the two articles fairly represents the work as a
whole; moreover, Lawrence's original sequence is followed.
The gaps in Lawrence's narrative that result from the editing
performed at the *Dial* become apparent only when one compares the magazine's version with Lawrence's original version.

But the author of *Sea and Sardinia* was most dissatisfied.
When he received a copy of the *Dial* issue containing one of
the two compilations of excerpts, he noted in his diary that he
"had Dial with scrappy *Sea and Sardinia*—hate it that they
mauled it about. A vile Sunday" (Ted 93). After the appearance of the second essay in the November 1921 issue, Law-

rence complained to Earl Brewster that "I haven't got *Sea and Sardinia* yet, but the *Dial* published mutilated bits in Oct. and Nov." (*CL* 678). For these mutilations he was paid one hundred and ninety dollars. There were no accompanying illustrations; obviously someone at the *Dial* either had not "liked *them*" or had decided they would not reproduce well in half-tone plates. Doubtless someone on the staff other than Thayer rejected these illustrations, for Thayer had met Juta when he was at Oxford and had arranged to publish a portrait of Lawrence by Juta as early as October 1921, the month of the issue that contained the first installment of *Sea and Sardinia*. A year later Thayer recalled that the portrait had not been published and in a letter on October 31, 1922 to Gilbert Seldes, inquired: "Did Richard Offner never send you the photograph after a portrait of D. H. Lawrence by Jan Juta of which he wrote me over a year ago that he was sending it? If you have the portrait and if it is halfway good I suggest that it be run the next time we run anything of Lawrence in The Dial. Indeed I do not understand why you did not run it with The Fox. I knew Jan Juta at Oxford and he is said to be at present Lawrence's most intimate friend." So the issue for February 1923, which contained Lawrence's essay, "Indians and an Englishman," also contained Juta's portrait and identified the artist in its "Notes on Contributors": "Jan C. Juta is the son of Sir Henry Hubert Juta, and was born in South Africa. Recently he accompanied Mr D. H. Lawrence on his trip through Sardinia; and he will be recalled as the artist who provided the illustrations in colour to Sea and Sardinia." The portrait of Lawrence was the only work by Juta to appear in the *Dial*, and the illustrations touted in its "Notes on Contributors" were those in Thomas Seltzer's edition of *Sea and Sardinia*, one of Lawrence's handsomest books. The omission of those accompanying pictures in the *Dial* was another cause for Lawrence's complaint against the magazine late in 1921.

His disappointment over the mutilated bits the *Dial* published undoubtedly had some effect in forcing a gradual realization that he could not rely on the magazine publication of his writing to earn much money—not unless he compromised with the demands of popular taste in the 1920's. The *Dial* was a glittering showcase for the writers of the vanguard, but it never pretended to provide them with steady incomes. And a steady income for a couple as peripatetic as Frieda and Lorenzo was to be earned only by writing for a wider audience than the *Dial*'s or, for that matter, than was available to his American publisher, Thomas Seltzer. The appearance of *Sea and Sardinia* in the *Dial* and the rather difficult negotiations over the publication of the Bunin-Koteliansky-Lawrence version of "The Gentleman from San Francisco" mark the climax of Lawrence's attempt to establish Thayer and his magazine as a patron and a secure source of income from America, which, despise it as he would, was also, as he recognized, the major possibility for the exploitation of his art. Yet the parts of *Sea and Sardinia* that the magazine printed opened a door, a door to a life Lawrence had dreamed and written about. Those two essays brought him, so to speak, to America, to Taos, and thus constituted the ground of his only experience of Rananim.

Even though *Sea and Sardinia* was written partly at Thayer's request—a piece of flattery graceful at best, hypocritical at worst—another work by Lawrence exemplifies still more pointedly than does the travel book both the relationship of writer and editor and the cosmopolitanism of the *Dial*. In January 1922 the *Dial* published, at Lawrence's urging, the translation he had rubbed up for his friend, S. S. Koteliansky, of Ivan Bunin's story "The Gentleman from San Francisco." The subject of publishing this famous piece of fiction was introduced in Lawrence's letter to Thayer of July 30, 1921 in which the project of publishing *Sea and Sardinia* also was broached. Like *The Waste Land*, which the *Dial* published later in 1922, "The Gentleman from San Francisco" was ultimately to become its author's most famous single work and to constitute an important element of his claim to his Nobel Award. And, like *The Waste Land*, "The Gentleman from San Francisco" caused a good deal of trouble at the *Dial*.

The story, with a page missing, was sent by Mountsier to

Scofield Thayer some time in September 1921. The editor of the *Dial* liked it, recognized its value, and wrote either to Mountsier or directly to Koteliansky, asking for a guarantee that "The Gentleman from San Francisco" would not appear in any other magazine or book form before its publication in the *Dial*. On the first of October Koteliansky assured Thayer that the story would not appear in England before the middle of December 1921.[20] Thayer replied on October 6,

> I have just received your letter of October 1st in regard to "The Gentleman from San Francisco."
>
> As Mr. Mountsier has called to your attention, a page from this story was missing when it was sent to me last month. I have only just received this missing page from Mr. Mountsier.
>
> You say that you can undertake not to have any translation of "The Gentleman from San Francisco" published in periodicals or any book form in England before the middle of December, you say that presumably we can publish it in either the November or December number of the "Dial." Unfortunately this missing page of the story has reached me so late that it is already too late for me to get the story to New York in time for the December number. The December number goes to press upon October 25th.
>
> I therefore cannot accept "The Gentleman from San Francisco" unless you can undertake not to have the story published in England before the middle of January. I trust I shall hear from you directly whether I may accept the story on these terms or whether I should return the manuscript to you.
>
> Should the story be accepted your translation will be paid for from the New York office upon its receipt there.

On October 15, 1921 Thayer sent the typescript of "The Gentleman from San Francisco" to Gilbert Seldes in New York, with a letter of explanation.

> I enclose a story which I got through D. H. Lawrence and Mountsier. The translation was made by S. S. Koteliansky of 5 Acacia Road, St. John's Wood, London, N. W. 8. I have informed Mr. Koteliansky that you will pay for the story immediately upon its receipt at the rate of one cent the

word. In this case we apparently shall not have to pay the
original author, a Russian, whose name appears upon the
manuscript. I presume that from Gregory Zilboorg or from
some other Russian in New York or from your own family
recollections you can educe an appropriate Contributor's
Note. I regret that Koteliansky has neglected to give me the
appropriate information for which I had asked him. Lawrence
rewrote Koteliansky's translation and that accounts for its
value. But payment is to be made to Koteliansky—and you
need not bother about Lawrence at all unless you desire to
state in publishing the story that the translation is made by
D. H. Lawrence and S. S. Koteliansky. Either use both these
names or neither. Since this story will appear in England in
January, I have agreed with Mr. Koteliansky that the story
shall be published by the "Dial" in the January number.
This is imperative.[21]

Reassuringly, Seldes wrote Thayer on November 5, 1921
that "the Lawrence-Koteliansky-Bunin story has arrived
safely." "Kot," as his Bloomsbury friends called him, was not
at all an orderly person, but he expected order and promptness
from the *Dial* and complained to Lawrence about Thayer's
apparent failure to pay for acceptance of "The Gentleman from
San Francisco" even before Gilbert Seldes could have received
a complete copy of the manuscript. On November 10, 1921,
writing from his villa at Fontana Vecchia near Taormina,
Lawrence acknowledged Kot's letter about Scofield Thayer
and asked, "Did he ever properly acknowledge yours? And he
ought to have paid you by now. I wonder if you are hard
up"—a remark immediately recognizable as an ironic joke;
Koteliansky, an expatriate Russian economist, racketed around
Bloomsbury pretty much living by his wits and on the kindness
of friends such as Lawrence, often not much better off than
himself. "If you are, you won't hesitate to tell me, will you. My
English money is at the last crumbs, but thank goodness I've
got some dollars in America—when Mountsier will put me into
touch with them. So just let me know if you are in need." And
after complaining as usual about his American agent, Lawrence asked what Koteliansky was doing "about the rest of the
Bunin book? Who is working over your translation? Perhaps

[Leonard] Woolf. If it isn't very long, I'll do it if you wish me to" (*CL* 672–73). But it was Woolf who helped rub up the rest of the Bunin stories into acceptable shape, and this act of kindness was to become later still another point of contention.

In other ways America bulked large in Lawrence's letter and in his prospects both personal and professional. He was so tired of Europe, "a dead dog which begins to stink intolerably. Again I entertain the idea of going to America. A woman offered us a house, an adobe cottage in Taos, New Mexico, on a mountain with Indians near." His reference was to Mabel Dodge Sterne (as then she was); the invitation had just been forthcoming, she was determined to draw Lawrence to her, to persuade him to "give a voice to this speechless land" of the American Southwest.[22] But Lawrence's climactic phrase "on a mountain with Indians near" sounds, surely, like the excitement of a nine-year-old fresh from reading Karl May. "Really, I want to go," he told Kot. "I will go to the States. Really, I think the hour has struck, to go," a typical Lawrentian rationalization. "*Basta la mossa!* I hope we can go in January. I hope we can get a merchant ship from Palermo or Naples to New Orleans or to Galveston in Texas. You will say it is just my winter influenza which makes me think of America. But finally I shall go. But don't tell anybody." He was in a funk and hated England because Philip Heseltine was threatening to bring suit against *Women in Love*, which, Heseltine alleged, libeled his wife and himself. Let his English friends strive as they might, said Lawrence; and he paraded his independence of England, that "dead dog that died of a love disease like syphilis": "I did a second volume to *Psychoanalysis and the Unconscious*, and sent it to America. Nowadays I depend almost entirely on America for a living. I think Seltzer has just published at five dollars the slight travel book, *Sea and Sardinia*. If he sends me copies I will send you one" (*CL* 672–73).

By December 14, Koteliansky had received payment for what Lawrence occasionally referred to as "The Gent." and had sent half the sum, twelve pounds and a shilling, to his cotranslator.

Not all difficulties were swept away, however. When the story appeared in the *Dial* for January 1922 Ivan Bunin was sent copies of the issue. Five months later, on May 20, 1922, Scofield Thayer wrote Bunin from Vienna, asking for more stories.

> I trust you received the copies of the January Dial which were sent you from New York containing the English translation made by D. H. Lawrence and S. S. Koteliansky of your masterpiece "The Gentleman from San Francisco." You may be interested to hear that this story has in The Dial roused much admiration both in America and in Europe.
>
> I have just read in Die Neue Rundschau a German translation of your story entitled "Kasimir Stanislawowitch." I am enthusiastic over it.
>
> Can you let us have it for The Dial? If so could you send the Russian manuscript to me here? I should then forward this manuscript to New York where it would be translated into English and where it would appear in The Dial in the course of the autumn. We pay for matter that has already appeared in a foreign journal at the rate of one cent the word.
>
> In the case of the previous story "The Gentleman from San Francisco" we bought from Mr. Koteliansky direct who said that he in turn had obtained the English rights from you. In this case I prefer to deal with you directly if you yourself find this not disadvantageous.
>
> I admire your work very much and should be glad to hear from you of any other fiction of yours which has appeared in either German, French or Italian and not yet in English which I might take for The Dial. I am sorry that the fact that I do not understand Russian makes it impossible for me to read your work in that tongue.
>
> I trust I may hear from you before I leave Vienna the latter part of next month.[23]

From the context of his letter, one gathers that Thayer was not aware that Koteliansky and Leonard Woolf had already translated the particular story that *Die Neue Rundschau* for April 1922 had published in a German version. Indeed, the very month Thayer wrote to Bunin, Leonard and Virginia Woolf published Bunin's *The Gentleman from San Francisco and Other Stories* as "Translated from the Russian by S. S. Koteliansky and Leonrad Woolf," and Lawrence's name as a collaborator was omitted from this English edition issued by the Woolfs' Hogarth Press. According to the errata slip, Lawrence's name was omitted from the title-page through an error; Seltzer's American edition of 1923 correctly listed Lawrence as Koteliansky's collaborator for the translation of what Thayer wisely regarded as Bunin's masterpiece.[24] So Lawrence finally received full credit for having rubbed up the story in relation to which he had told Thayer, "I would rather my name didn't appear; but make no serious objection if it would be of use to you." As for "Kasimir Stanislawowitch," Gilbert Seldes did purchase the story from Bunin, and the English version appeared in the *Dial* for July 1922.[25] It was, after all, the Koteliansky-Woolf version, and the magazine's records reveal that the cotranslators were jointly paid thirty dollars for their work.

Lawrence's kindness to Kot served still further. In the issues for June, July, and August 1924, the *Dial* published his translation—this time with Katherine Mansfield as collaborator—of Maxim Gorki's "Reminiscences of Leonid Andreyev." Bunin also was rewarded by Lawrence's help in translating "The Gentleman from San Francisco" and in getting it published in the *Dial*. In the issue for February 1927 Alyse Gregory respectfully reviewed Madeleine Boyd's translation of Bunin's *Mitya's Love;* she prized Bunin's ability to create a mood even above that of Arthur Schnitzler, the great modern Austrian master who was one of the *Dial*'s most valued contributors. Finally, in the issue for October 1927 appeared Bunin's "Reminiscences of Tolstoy" in Alexander Karin's English version.[26]

When the *Dial* wished to take advantage of its prescience in publishing "The Gentleman from San Francisco," it ran into difficulties with Thomas Seltzer. It so happened that Scofield Thayer sank about one hundred and twenty-five thousand dollars of his own money in a publishing venture in 1923 and persuaded his treasurer for the *Dial*, Lincoln MacVeagh, also to become the director of the new Dial Press. From its incep-

tion in January 1924, the Dial Press was a separate firm from
the Dial Publishing Company, which published the *Dial;* but
the two firms shared the same building in Greenwich Village
as well as certain officers and stockholders, and Lincoln Mac-
Veagh published a good many works by contributors to the
Dial. As might be expected, works the *Dial* had published originally were hospitably received at the Dial Press, and it advertised in the magazine lavishly in every issue. As early as the
spring of 1923, Thayer started to make plans for the Dial Press
to bring out an anthology of *Stories from The Dial*, which
would include "The Gentleman from San Francisco." The correspondence of Thayer and Seldes reveals that their old difficulties over the story persisted, for Thomas Seltzer was re-
luctant to permit the *Dial* to include the story in its anthology
and thus compete for sales with *The Gentleman from San
Francisco and Other Stories.*

A second story the *Dial* wanted to include in its anthology, "Hungarian Night," by its Paris correspondent Paul Mor-
and, was also a property of Seltzer, and he refused outright to
permit the magazine to reprint it. From Europe, where he was
not only working for Thayer and scouting for the Theatre
Guild but, more importantly for himself, was writing *The
Seven Lively Arts*—for which he is known most widely—Gilbert Seldes wrote "Sco" on April 23, 1923:

> Will you bend your mind for a moment to these matters. It
> is an affair I undertook and think of great importance as
> publicity and I ought not to bother you about it only you
> ARE, aint you? the editor of the Dial and the Dial is involved.
> I will therefore note the position and say what I propose to
> do, rather than ask your advice. And you will say yes or no,
> hein?
>
> Seltzer is making a bloody nuisance of himself in regard to
> the Stories from the Dial. He has (a) the Bunin as we
> published it; regrettably I have with my own eyes seen
> Bunin's written repudiation of that translation as unauthorized;
> (b) another translation of Morand's Hungarian Night which
> *is* authorized but is not ours. Neither of these does Seltzer
> make available for our book.

Now it happens that the authorized Bunin is in Knopf's
hands and a moderately good translation is made. Also it
happens that Morand has publicly advised me to go ahead and
republish our own translation of Hungarian Night. It comes
down to this then, that at the risk of enraging Seltzer (and
his advertising) I can publish our own Morand and the other
Bunin—wait, I know it is difficult—and can pacify Seltzer
by noting the existence of his book versions of both.

Of course we published the good translation of Bunin and it
is absurd to republish another. The thing to do in the case
is to publish a note with it saying that "out of courtesy to the
author we are printing here the version of this story which
appears in his collected and authorized book, The Dial having
previously published, with full authority, another translation."

I incline to do that—a drastic remedy for a preposterous
publishing situation. Everybody concerned up to this time
has been a bit shady in the matter. And this seems one way
out. The alternative is to threaten Seltzer that we will do
this and force him to let us use the original one. I can try that
first.

If we have to drop the Gentleman from San F. we'll put in
Timmermans [a story by Felix Timmermans, "The Very
Lovely Hours in the Life of the Beguine Symforosa," that the
Dial had published in April 1922]. And get the Gent into a
later one. But I think it would be absurd not to claim the
credit for the Gent which is making a vast hit in book form
and over which 2 publishers are scrapping and for which
there is publicity, in our first vol. The Morand affair is small
in comparison.

From his flat in Vienna, Thayer asked in his reply of
April 26,

> Can you not see Bunin and explain that his story came
> to me from D. H. Lawrence and explain that we paid for the
> original author as well as for the translator (did we not?)
> and so obtain his intercession? You might at the same time
> get one or two more stories from him if he has anything
> publishable on hand. I wrote him a year ago c/o his publisher
> in Berlin for the second of his stories which appeared in the
> Dial and which at that time you had not yet bought. I had

seen it in the Fischer publication Die Neue Rundschau. He
didn't answer my letter. I don't know whether he received it.

I should think it would be better if you publish The
Gentleman from San Francisco at all to publish the translation
we had in the Dial. No other could be so good and no other
could have the name Lawrence. But I leave the whole matter
to your good judgment and to your superior knowledge of
the details.

The records of the *Dial* do not indicate how the problems
with Lawrence's translation and Morand's story were eventually solved; but the solution, however arrived at, earned prestige for the magazine anyway: both "The Gentleman from
San Francisco" and "Hungarian Night" appeared in *Stories
from The Dial*, as well as Lawrence's popular "dog" story,
"Rex." Lawrence's short story and his translation appeared as
the third and fourth stories, respectively, in the impressive
anthology. Moreover, "Rex" did not appear in any other anthology except *Stories from The Dial* until *Phoenix*, the first posthumously published anthology of Lawrence's uncollected writings.

In several respects the publication of "The Gentleman
from San Francisco" is representative of Lawrence's entire
relationship with the *Dial*. First, Lawrence obviously understood the magazine as eclectic, cosmopolitan, and avant-garde
and as publishing only the best art and literature, "old" or
"new." That Lawrence's taste and Thayer's coincided is evident from their agreement regarding Bunin's great story. They
disagreed, to be sure, as when the *Dial* refused to reproduce Jan
Juta's illustrations for *Sea and Sardinia;* and here Lawrence
was the uninstructed, Thayer the professional. (Lawrence had
a curiously old-fashioned weakness for pictures that tell a story
or gloss a text; Thayer's preference for the decorative and
abstract is of course the more "modern," the more widely
accepted today.)

Second, Lawrence's confidence in the *Dial* manifested itself in his recommendation of what was primarily another writer's work. One recalls his letter to S. S. Koteliansky a month before he wrote to the *Dial* about Bunin's story: "I really think

the *Dial* might print 'the Gent.' And if so, we get at least 100 dollars. Good for us!" Wrong as he was about that payment— it was only thirty dollars that Kot received—Lawrence's optimism stemmed, it is clear, from the respect the editors of the magazine extended to his abilities as an artist and his aesthetic judgment. Lawrence carped and grumbled when Scofield Thayer accepted the option of placing the Lawrentian seal upon the translation of "The Gentleman from San Francisco": "My dear Kot," he wrote on January 14, 1922, "I had the *Dial* by the same post as your letter. They are impudent people. I had told them not to put my name. Of course they did it themselves. But I really don't care. Why bother. . . . I am glad you like 'The Gent' when he was done" (*CL* 684). But Lawrence's lying about the *Dial* and the "impudence" of Thayer, Watson, and Seldes was mere swagger, to show off his own importance to that glamorous journal and his importance and his kindliness to dear Kot.

Finally, the publication of "The Gentleman from San Francisco" in the *Dial* made Lawrence in effect an agent for the magazine and resulted, directly or indirectly, in the publication of five works by two major Russian writers, Bunin's "The Gentleman from San Francisco," "Kasimir Stanislawowitch," and "Reminiscences of Tolstoy," and Gorki's "Reminiscences of Leonid Andreyev" and his "Russian Letter." It was through his publication of Koteliansky's translation of Gorki's reminiscences that Thayer was enabled to approach Gorki personally and, as a result of this successful strategem, could announce the appointment of Maxim Gorki as Russian Correspondent in the editorial "Comment" of the *Dial* for June 1925. Further, through this chain of circumstances, four translators were brought to the *Dial*, at least two of whom—Koteliansky and Woolf, if not Karin and Lawrence himself—would probably not have appeared, except for Lawrence's original suggestion, as translators in the magazine.

Additional proof that Lawrence occupied then a central place among *Dial* contributors is evident from his next writing that Thayer published. In February 1922 the *Dial* contained part of the fourteenth chapter of *Aaron's Rod*. Only one other magazine ever published a part of another of Lawrence's novels: in its issue for September 1913, the *Forum*, like the *Dial* an American magazine, published the fifteenth and final chapter of *Sons and Lovers*. This particular publication coincided with the appearance, the same month, of *Sons and Lovers* in its first American edition; by no coincidence, the editor of the *Forum* and the publisher of *Sons and Lovers* in America was Mitchell Kennerly.[27] In contrast, the publication in the *Dial* of *Aaron's Rod* was a disinterested act, prompted by the admiration of Thayer and Watson for Lawrence's writing, dissociated completely from any commercial interest as the publisher of Lawrence's books.

Publishing in a magazine a portion of any of Lawrence's full-length novels was quite a feat. Despite his unsuccessful effort to have *The Lost Girl* published serially in 1920, Lorenzo usually voiced a strong aversion to having his longer novels serialized or allowing the excerpting of parts of them in magazines. Toward the end of his life, in a letter of May 28, 1927, he confided to Mabel Dodge Luhan that he was holding back the manuscript of *Lady Chatterley's Lover*—"not even having it typed. Much better if I print only periodical stuff" (*CL* 982). That is to say, periodicals to Lawrence existed for the sake of printing his slighter writing, of paying him while he kept the pot boiling both for them and for his own long-range survival as a novelist.

Despite this difficulty, at the instigation of the *Dial* Thomas Seltzer permitted a portion of *Aaron's Rod* to be published in the magazine two months before his American edition appeared in April 1922. Negotiations took a good deal of time. Early in August 1921, just two months after Lawrence had sent the first part of the manuscript to Mountsier, the *Dial* got in touch with Seltzer about the novel. A letter to Thayer from James Sibley Watson, Jr., on August 14, 1921, suggests that the editors had considered serializing the entire novel and reveals a surprising move by Richard Aldington to woo Lawrence away from their magazine:

> *D. H. Lawrence novel:* Called up Seltzer and was told
> novel was 100,000 words—i.e. over 200 Dial pp. They said
> they would be able to let us know in 2 wks whether they
> could offer it to us; implying not that they were offering it
> elsewhere but that they had not received instructions as to
> its disposal. The thing sounds too long, though possibly we
> might take pieces from it. They said they were bringing it
> out about April. It seemed to me that under the circ's and
> after reading extract from Aldington's letter we could scarcely
> trust him (and his stated disposition to give us the least
> salable material), in case it was a question of giving the
> rights to us and not to some better-paying magazine; while
> if there were no question of this sort, Seltzer would let us
> have the novel shortly anyway. In other words Aldington
> would choose the Century, if it were between The Dial and
> the Century, and would advise Lawrence to do likewise.
> Pound might be a better man to cable on that account. If
> you think it best, could you not cable him directly from
> Edgartown [the summer home of Thayer's mother, where
> he often went for the sailing]. I have only stated the
> information about the novel that we have been able to gather.
> Will you decide?

In the copy of the letter in the *Dial* papers, Thayer penned
marginalia, among them one advising either himself or Watson to "see [the novel] first, then cable Lawrence if
necessary."

Between August 14 and December 15, 1921 the feeling at the *Dial* about *Aaron's Rod* altered, presumably as
the misleading information the staff received from Thomas
Seltzer concerning the novel was rectified. That is to say, his
enthusiasm was received with reservation. A letter from Gilbert Seldes to Scofield Thayer of December 15, 1921 concluded
by mentioning that "for literary interest" Seltzer had been
mistaken: "*Aaron's Rod* is not the completion of a trilogy with
The Rainbow and *Women in Love* as the first two members of
it. It has nothing to do with the Brangwyns and what is more,
although Lawrence announced that it was to be a 'safe' book,
Mountsier reports that it is nothing of the sort. Portions of it
have been offered to us and are now in our hands." [28]

So Thayer did not cable either Ezra Pound or Lawrence,
and the staff—Thayer or Watson—made its selection of a chap-

ter from *Aaron's Rod*. The hesitation was, as usual, over the moral "safety" and the libelous portraiture of the novel. Lawrence recognized the problem. In a letter to Donald Carswell, dated November 15, 1921, he acknowledged that "Everybody hated *Aaron's Rod*—even Frieda. But I just had a cable from Seltzer," he added defensively, "that he thinks it is wonderful. Maybe it is just a publisher's pat. Anyhow it is better than a smack in the eye, such as one gets from England for everything" (*CL* 676). Just over two months later, he told Curtis Brown that he hadn't been able to force himself to alter any passages "for the sake of the 'general public' ([Seltzer] didn't say *jeune fille*). I sat in front of the MS. and tried: but it was like Balaam's Ass, and wouldn't budge. I couldn't do it, so I sent it back to Seltzer to let him do as he pleases. I would rather Secker [Lawrence's London publisher] followed the true MS. if he will—and *vogue la galère!*" (*CL* 689). Under the circumstances, one does not wonder that the Dial selected a "safe" passage describing contemporary Italian politics.

Chapter 14 of *Aaron's Rod*, the excerpt the *Dial*'s staff chose to print, is a central chapter of the novel, the description of a Fascist march in Milan and the reprisal by the police. Entitled not very helpfully "An Episode," the incident is a digression inserted by Lawrence to reveal the turmoil in Italy in 1921, and the episode occurs out of the main action of the novel. The entire account filled only four pages of the issue for February 1922, and for it Lawrence was paid only thirty-five dollars.

The longest work by Lawrence the *Dial* published was not a major novel but a novella, *The Fox*, which ran for four installments in the magazine from May through August 1922. *The Fox* was first written in November 1918, revised extensively in 1919, and completed with a new ending in November 1921. From the beginning of his composition, Lawrence liked it. He called the first revision "odd and amusing" (*CL* 468); and when he completed the final revision, he wrote to his friend Earl Brewster that he had "put a long tail to 'The Fox' which was a bobbed short story. Now he careers with a strange and fiery brush." Then he added for the benefit of Brewster, who had spent much time in the Orient and had studied Oriental thought, "I hope you will read him some time, because then you will see that I am not really drawn Buddhawards, but west" (*CL* 678). Little of those philosophical overtones comes over in the popular cinematic adaptation (1968) of *The Fox*, noted mostly for its "frank" depiction of a lesbian affair; it even has a different locale for its action, Canada. Its advertising traded, of course, on Lawrence's wide if undeserved notoriety as an old master of arty pornography. In his diary Lawrence noted that the novella was about thirty-five thousand words long (Ted 94); aesthetically and financially this length proved fortunate. The long tail he added to the bobbed short story was the account of the necessary death of one of the two feminine protagonists, Nellie March, an incident that gives the work its further meaning. The records of the *Dial* do not reveal the date on which Lawrence submitted the novella or the dates on which Lawrence was paid, but that payment is recorded as five hundred dollars, the largest sum he ever received from the *Dial*.

The serialization of *The Fox* closes Lawrence's early period of association with Thayer, Watson, and their magazine; after the last installment in the issue for August 1922, five more issues intervened before another work of his appeared in the *Dial* for February 1923. During these months from August 1922 to February 1923, the Lawrences arrived in North America, met Mabel Dodge Sterne, went with her to live in the Indian pueblo of Taos, and established themselves, like the Indians, at the foot of the sacred Taos Mountain.

In a less material but surely no less significant sense, D. H. Lawrence had arrived in America by the autumn of 1922. His writing was a staple feature of the leading literary journal of the vanguard, the *Dial*, and the publishers of New York were beginning to scramble to secure his work. He had traveled a long way since those years of furious despair in 1917–18, and the New World, so welcoming yet somehow so obstinate, was his to ponder and describe.

3

LAWRENCE, *THE DIAL,* AND
MABEL DODGE LUHAN, 1921–1925

H AD A LETTER from Mabel Dodge Sterne," Lawrence
noted in his diary, "asking us to go to New Mexico—to
Taos. Want to go" (Ted 93). The date was November 5, 1921;
and for almost four years thereafter, he was on his way to Taos,
or living there and using it as headquarters for his restless for-
ays to Mexico, to Europe, to the East and West Coasts—or, toward the close of his long visit, impatiently prognosticating his
departure from that heavy, stubborn continent so lacking in
natural joy (*CL* 850). Disorganized though they were, the
American years affected his point of view just as they influenced his choice of subjects. A reading of Lawrence's contributions to the *Dial* bears out this assertion; and, equally to the
point, so do Lawrence's letters. Damn America and Americans
for their manifold failings he did, and did often, but the ranch
and Taos and New Mexico were just as often recalled with romantic nostalgia. In the last few weeks of his life, as he lay dying of consumption in Beau Soleil, the small box of a villa in
the south of France where he spent the fall and most of the
winter of 1929–30, he told Mabel Dodge Luhan, if only he
might get back to Taos, he should begin to feel well again:
"Europe is slowly killing me, I feel" (*CL* 1230). And three
weeks later, on January 24, 1930, he sounded a desperate note
to Dorothy Brett, the young Englishwoman who had followed

him all the way to Taos and who, unlike Lawrence, made her home there: "I want so much to get well enough to be able to start for New Mexico. I feel I'd get better there, and I get worse here. . . . I was wondering if it would be best to sail on your Dollar Line from Marseilles right to San Francisco, and land there. Landing might be easier, and the long sea voyage might do me good. But I shall see what Mabel says. But by the end of March, surely, I shall be well enough again —I pray the gods. But I'm bad this winter; much worse than last" (*CL* 1237).

Lawrence never returned to the mountains and his horses and his cow Susan; he died in Vence on March 2, 1930.

It was through his writing for the *Dial* that Lorenzo was led to Taos. The *grande dame* of the town, Mabel Dodge Sterne, drew him there, along with the less enthusiastic Frieda. Mabel Sterne had traveled out to New Mexico after the United States declared war on the German Empire in 1917. As perhaps the leading hostess for the young liberals and radicals of Greenwich Village, she could hardly have been expected to support with any enthusiasm the American participation in the First World War. Interested as she was in artists and the art of the vanguard—she had helped sponsor the Armory Show in 1913—Mabel Sterne might well have been expected to enter into the life of the group of artists who had come to New Mexico. But actually she went there because her third, and at that time latest, husband, the sculptor Maurice Sterne had suddenly left her to go West, to visit friends, also artists, in Taos. Taos was millennially removed from the fervors and the lovers, the parties and desertions of Greenwich Village where Mabel Dodge had played friend or mistress or Lady Bountiful to John Reed, Walter Lippmann, Hutchins Hapgood, Isadora Duncan, Lincoln Steffens, Emma Goldman, Carl Van Vechten —all among the crowd drawn to her town house on lower Fifth Avenue by the food and liquor and luxury to be enjoyed there. Carl Van Vechten said she was a woman, but a new kind of woman, or else the oldest kind; he wasn't sure which. Everyone went to 23 Fifth Avenue, and occasionally someone like John Reed stayed for a while.[1]

Ensconced in Taos, Mabel Dodge Sterne nevertheless followed the former pattern of her life amid the mountains, the desert, and the Indians. She was gregarious, she liked novelty, she liked intelligent and creative men, and she was very rich. Instead of retiring to Taos to live in bohemian simplicity, she made it fashionable. True, artists and invalids had been going to New Mexico since the 1870's; it was by all odds the most exotic milieu to be discovered within the United States. In particular, Taos was not expensive to live in, and it had the added advantage of pure, dry mountain air. Willa Cather, for example, had visited her brother in northeastern Arizona in the spring of 1912, and on her third visit to the Southwest in the summer of 1916, she settled in Taos for a longer stay.[2] Two more dissimilar books than *Death Comes for the Archbishop* and *Lorenzo in Taos* are difficult to imagine. Yet both are impossible to imagine apart from their environment of the Southwest, and whatever their differences of quality and of dedication, both spring from one of the major aspects of the New Movement in arts and letters after the turn of the century, the fascination of writers, painters, craftsmen with the Southwest as the raw material of their arts and as a good place to live and work. One cannot entertain any serious comparison of *Death Comes for the Archbishop* and *Lorenzo in Taos;* yet for all the intellectual shoddiness of the latter, it does have the merit of portraying at first hand the new fashion among the vanguard of living not on the coast of bohemia but in the shadow of Lobo Mountain.

For Mabel Sterne, life in New Mexico brought a fascination with the primitive, with Indian arts and crafts and religious cults, and with the Indians themselves, specifically with one Indian, Antonio Luhan or Lujan, a head man of the pueblo at Taos and now her lover supplanting Maurice Sterne. (After furiously ordering the poor fellow out of her house, she pensioned him off at a hundred dollars a month.) Still, the sun-kissed charms of pueblo and desert did not rout Mabel Dodge Luhan's old involvement with the vanguard out East in Greenwich Village, and she remained a leader there as in Taos. From its inception she was interested in the refurbished *Dial* of

Scofield Thayer and Sibley Watson. She subscribed to it and read it regularly; moreover, she lent it pictures from her collection to be reproduced in its pages, and her story "Southwest" appeared in the *Dial* for December 1925.

Her interest was reciprocated; not only was the *Dial* attuned to herself, it publicized the Indians of the Southwest and their arts and traditions. The first issue of the monthly *Dial*, for January 1920, published an essay on "The Art of the American Indian," by Walter Pach, a member in good standing of the Taos and Greenwich Village groups. He proclaimed that there was "more than one voice crying out in the world to-day that in the earlier forms of society values were attained that our present proud condition has lost." So well received was Pach's essay that the issue of March 1920 reproduced three Indian watercolors—Fred Kobotie's *"Na-Ka-Vo-Ma": Hopi Snake Dance*, from the Sia Pueblo *The Legend of the Deer*, and, also from the Pueblo Indians of New Mexico, a depiction of the Corn Dance. "Notes on Contributors" for the issue stated that the three pictures were from the collection of Mabel Dodge Sterne. A flippant gloss on them is Marsden Hartley's article "Vaudeville," in the same issue, in which the artist introduced his topic by confiding that he had but recently returned from "the vaudeville of the centuries. Watching the kick and the glide of very ancient performers. I have spent a year and a half down in the wonderful desert country of the Southwest. I have wearied, however, of the ancient caprice, and turn with great delight to my old passion, vaudeville." And Hartley's appreciation is appropriately followed by the three Indian watercolors from Mabel Dodge Sterne's collection. In his essay in the slightly earlier issue of the *Dial*, Walter Pach had introduced the subject of these watercolors by "untaught young Indians," which were "Primitives in the true sense of the word, their form and content deriving from an immediate response to the scenes they depict, the simple means of execution being suddenly raised to their intensity of effect by the intensity of conviction and enthusiasm of the artists." [3]

Thus in its quest for the primitive, the *Dial* followed the fashion for the Hispanized Indians of the Southwest both in choice of subject and choice of style. This combination of art and anthropology and fascination for the exotic and novel is one of the consistently maintained interests of the *Dial* throughout the 1920's. In its most famous single issue, the one in which *The Waste Land* was published (November 1922), Edward Sapir's review, "A Symposium of the Exotic," exemplifies the taste shared by Mabel Dodge Luhan and the *Dial*. Sapir here discussed the collection by various hands, *American Indian Life*, edited by Elsie Clews Parsons. Sumptuous though the volume was with its full-page plates in color, Sapir found the pictures disappointing; he was right of course, for they were elaborate in design and uninspired in execution, an incomplete fusion of late nineteenth-century naturalism and *art nouveau* quite lacking freshness. Yet disarming as the collection itself was in its amateurishness, the book gave "more than a hint of how compelling an imaginative treatment of primitive life might be." Sapir was interested in the question, to what extent can we penetrate into the vitals of primitive life and fashion for ourselves satisfying pictures on its own level of reality? And, to an extent, so was the *Dial*. The limitation was its self-imposed limitation of the aesthetic, for the *Dial* treated the primitive artifact primarily as an art object.[4]

Artistically the finest and historically the most significant example of Indian art the *Dial* published in its illustrations was the great Mayan Chac-Mool now in the national anthropological museum in Mexico City; it was reproduced in the magazine's half-tone plate from a replica which had been molded from the original sculpture and which was housed then at the American Museum of Natural History. The picture of the Chac-Mool was the frontispiece in the issue for October 1920, and describing it, "Notes on Contributors" asserted: "Chac-Mool is said to be the Drunken God or Dionysus of the Mayas, who flourished in Yucatan about 500 A.D." When Gilbert Seldes drew up an important publicity brochure featuring a dozen or so objects and pictures that had been reproduced by the *Dial*, he selected the Chac-Mool along with work by Picasso

and Demuth and other leaders of the time, as representing the
art that the magazine was reproducing in its pages. In October
1921 the frontispiece was a photograph of another replica, a
Head in Diorite also labeled as from the American Museum of
Natural History. "Notes on Contributors" said that "The Head
in Diorite was found in the Valley of Mexico. Its precise significance and origin are matters of conjecture. The original of
the Head is in Mexico City." Although scholarly opinion today
might hold such art as the Chac-Mool and the *Head in Diorite*
to be the sophisticated votive art of civilized peoples, the staff
of the *Dial* in the early 1920's classed them as "primitive"
along with Mabel Dodge Sterne's three watercolors by the
untutored young Indians.

The *Dial* also published creative work by writers and
artists involved with the "primitive" Indians and Mexicans of
the Southwest. Preeminently it published much of D. H. Lawrence's writing about New and Old Mexico; but he was one of
a good many who used this regional material. The American
historical novelist Mary Austin, for example, reviewed at
length, in the issue for July 1921, two volumes by Frank
Hamilton Cushing, *Zuni Folk Tales* (also the title of her review essay) and *Outlines of the Zuni Creation Myth*. The
issue for December 1925 featured Mabel Dodge Luhan's story
"Southwest," the very title redolent of the region. The May
1926 issue contained Elizabeth Shepley Sergeant's "The Wood-
Carver," two scenes from a play in nine scenes entitled *Sangre
de Cristo*. The significance of the play lies in the author's attempt to portray the psychological process by which a native
wood-carver who lives at the head of a remote canyon in Mexico
carves his images; thus the aesthetic fashion for the primitive
santos is exploited along with the more scientific curiosity
about primitive peoples—their crafts, customs, beliefs, attitudes. Henry J. Glintenkamp illustrated that life in the issues
for April 1924 and April 1926 with his linoleum cuts of Mexican genre scenes, among them two with such indicative titles
as *Blind Woman and Boy* and *Group of Mexican Boys*. In a
similar vein were Lowell Houser's linoleum cuts done in the

manner of the Mexican school of Diego Rivera and his fellow
artists, then becoming popular in the United States. Reproduced in June 1928 and April 1929, Houser's *Christo* [*sic*],
The Fisherman, and *Guadalupe Dancers* must have seemed as
novel as Cubist or primitive works. In the final issue, for July
1929, appeared Katherine Gorringe's account of the tribal celebration of some Californian Indians, "The Ukiah Big-Time."

The play by Elizabeth Shepley Sergeant and the linoleum cuts by Lowell Houser obviously were concerned with
Indian and Mexican subjects, but the artistic techniques in
both cases were brought into being by European-American culture. In one case, however, the *Dial* printed a group of pur-
ported translations of Indian poetry that actually were by Amy
Lowell, "Songs of the Pueblo Indians": "Women's Harvest
Song," "Basket Dance," "Women's Song of the Corn," "Prayer
for a Profusion of Sunflowers," "Prayer for Lightning," "Flute-
Priest Song for Rain." [5] When Ezra Pound protested the publication of Amy Lowell's poems, Scofield Thayer replied on
September 26, 1920: "The Amy Lowell I disliked as much as
you. The stuff was accepted because we are considered un-
American and Indian songs are American, so is Amy. The public who love to be humbugged fell for said songs flat." The
Dial thus took advantage of the new fashion for collecting and
admiring the primitive; nevertheless by exploiting that fashion,
the magazine did influence American taste in the arts. Perhaps
not in poetry or in fiction and memoirs: the artists, the poets,
the novelists would have written from and about Taos and
Taxco regardless of what the *Dial* advocated. But in the fine
arts—painting and sculpture mostly—the *Dial* achieved something more positive than the mere exploitation of the fashionable. It helped make primitive art, in a very real sense, "respectable," by taking it out of the American Museum of Natural
History and endowing it with the status of a painting by
Picasso or a poem by T. S. Eliot.

Closely related to the new awareness of the American
Southwest was the spiritual aridity Eliot expressed through his
metaphors of the waste land and the "cactus land"—the latter

in "The Hollow Men," a version of which the *Dial* published in
its March 1925 issue. Eliot's denigration of the desert and the
mountains is the very partial view of an expatriate who had
become a Londoner by adoption. Precisely the opposite attitude
toward the same Southwestern locale was being expressed by
artists and writers who looked upon the high desert plateau as
a purifying quiet retreat far from the miasmic swamp of modern urban culture. In Carl Van Vechten's novel of 1928, *Spider
Boy*, the protagonist, a young playwright named Ambrose
Deacon, has sought refuge in Santa Fe from the unwelcome
attentions of moving-picture financiers, and breathes a sigh of
relief: "He remembered that he was in a haven, hundreds of
miles from the spot where playwrights were seduced to become
prostitutes for the motion pictures." [6] If this is remarked with
tongue in cheek, the sentiment expresses nonetheless a heartfelt
truth for thousands—artists and writers, invalids and just
plain people escaping from the rat race—who came to New
Mexico in search of peace and quiet and, in many cases, some
solution to the besetting problems of mankind in those postwar
years.

With the same urges and for the same reasons, thousands
had flocked a decade or two earlier to Capri. Just as Carl Van
Vechten laughed at the pretensions of Americans being primitive in Santa Fe and Taos during the 1920's, so a few years
earlier had Norman Douglas and Ivan Bunin satirized the
pretensions of those outsiders who came to Capri in search of
rest and solace and the good life. In *South Wind* and "The
Gentleman from San Francisco" Capri was both Nepenthe and
an idyll of mad pursuit. In *Spider Boy*, Santa Fe was both a
haven for the pure in heart and a more sinister resort where a
spinster might go native and, in the words of one cynical
observer, take a toothsome male "off to her mountain fastness
[to] eat [him] up." Eden or *Walpurgisnacht*, the New Mexico
of the artists and intellectuals and bohemians provided their
answer to the question posed by the modern city, by modern
democracy, by modern capitalism. To a high-minded few, it
provided an answer to the final question posed in *The Waste
Land:* "Shall I at least set my lands in order?"

And so it happened that in the very months when Eliot was attempting to set his own lands in order through the creation of the most famous poem of the century, Mabel Dodge Luhan, under much the same compulsion, wrote to D. H. Lawrence. Unlike Eliot, she had discovered in the peace of Taos by the edge of the desert her means of ordering her lands. The difficulty was that she did not trust herself to express her message with the needed force and beauty.

Reading the *Dial* for October and November 1921, Mabel Luhan came upon that astonishing frontispiece, the Mayan Chac-Mool, and then read the mutilated bits of *Sea and Sardinia* the editors had elected to publish. Her response was entirely different from Lawrence's anger. When she read him in Taos, "especially *Sea and Sardinia* and *Tortoises* and *Birds, Beasts, and Flowers*," she thought: "Here is the only one who can really *see* this Taos country and the Indians, and who can describe it so that it is as much alive between the covers of a book as it is in reality." For Taos had something wonderful in it, like the dawn of the world. When he came out there, Lawrence always called it pristine, she said. And she was sure she had been right about one thing in him: "He *could* see and feel and wonder."

She repeated that it was after reading *Sea and Sardinia* that she wrote to Lawrence inviting him to come to Taos. To her, it was one of the most actual of travel books, for in it, in that queer way of his, Lawrence gave the feel and touch and smell of places so that their reality and their essence are open to one, and one can step right into them. "Perhaps it is because, when he is writing, the experience is more actual to him than when it occurred. He is in the place again, reliving in retrospect more vividly than he was able to do at the time it happened. Lawrence couldn't live, with pleasure, in the real moment. He lived afterwards." [7] Truer words were never written: however pleasant his current situation, however charming his hosts, Lawrence invariably complained or at least found a bluebottle in his soup. Afterward he would look back on the experience with nostalgia.

In some respects, Mabel Luhan's recollection is faulty.

When Lawrence wrote the first note about her in his diary, not one of the books she cited as having influenced her decision to write him had been published: Thomas Seltzer brought out *Tortoises* on December 9, 1921, and *Sea and Sardinia* on December 12, 1921; he brought out *Birds, Beasts, and Flowers* on October 9, 1923; and all three books he published were the first editions. Clearly, Mabel Luhan read the poems from *Birds, Beasts, and Flowers* and the two installments from *Sea and Sardinia* as they appeared during March, April, October, and November 1921 in the *Dial*. Also she must have read other poems later included in *Birds, Beasts, and Flowers* as they appeared during 1921 in the *New Republic:* "Medlars and Sorb Apples," "The Revolutionary," and "Humming-Bird." [8] But her impression of *Sea and Sardinia* is the key to her invitation to Lawrence to come to Taos; after reading the second installment in the *Dial*, she sent her letter off to him at Fontana Vecchia, where he received it on November 5, 1921.

Her letter was a long one, in which she told him all she could about Taos and the Indians—and about Tony Luhan and herself. She told Lawrence how much she wanted him to come and know her land before it became exploited and spoiled, before good roads would let in the crowds. She tried to tell him every single thing she could think of that she felt would draw him, simple things as well as strange ones. She described a lofty, pastoral land far from railroads, full of "an almost heard but not quite heard music, and where the plainest tasks took on a beauty and significance they had not in other places." This was an effective sales pitch—true, explained Mabel Luhan, "but not for me, for I had no tasks." She used to sit most of the time, "sort of listening," before Lawrence came. After he arrived, he persuaded her to all sorts of tasks, washing floors—shades of Gourdjieff! and Lawrence detested Gourdjieff!—and making bread and wearing aprons for a while.

In her long letter, Mabel Luhan told Lawrence how a woman of Taos would come to the door and stand smiling toward the Sacred Mountain, after she had put her cake in the oven. For the life there was all a unity: "The mountain and the fields were not separate from one's life. One did not go *out* to things, one was a part of them. The mountain, if anything, came to one, came into the house; one ate it with the cake." At least life there seemed that way to herself. In *Lorenzo in Taos*, she added from the perspective of 1932 that after Lawrence had lived in Taos for a while, he upbraided her for being too cluttered up by things. But in the blissful ignorance of her initial excitement, off she sent her letter, so long it was rolled like a papyrus, enclosing an Indian necklace to Frieda that might carry some Indian magic in it, to draw them both to Taos. And in the letter "I put a few leaves of *desachey*, the perfume the Indians say makes the heart light, along with a little *osha*, the root that is a strong medicine—neither of which are in the botany books, but both of which are potent." [9]

Lawrence's acceptance, written immediately upon the arrival of her invitation, bubbled with his own dangerous magic. Hers had worked, of course: he had smelt the Indian scent, like a wistful herb it was, and had nibbled the medicine tasting like licorice root. Truly, Frieda and he would like to come to Taos, and it seemed feasible. He thought he had enough dollars in America to get the two of them to Taos. Then came a rapid barrage of questions. How much would it cost by the month to keep house in Taos? They were *very* practical and did all their own work—washing, cooking, floor-cleaning—because he loathed servants creeping around poisoning the atmosphere, and anyway he *liked* doing things. Second, was there a colony of rather dreadful sub-arty people about? (Of course there was, but Lawrence learned about them only after he arrived.) Third, were Mabel Luhan's Indians dying out, and was that rather sad? Fourth, what did the sound, *prosperous* Americans do in her region? (One thing they didn't do was gad about with the Luhans. Tony was an important local politician, but Mabel was too *outré* for the middle class.) Finally, how did one get to Taos, what was the nearest port? He seemed to have heard of it and even to have seen photographs of it at Leo Stein's house in Settignano. And was this Mabel Dodge Sterne who wrote him—after explaining, presumably, all about Tony and herself, she had unaccountably signed herself as Sterne without further ado—was she a relative of the artist Maurice Sterne?

Replying to Mabel Luhan's *cri du coeur*, Lawrence assured her that he believed what she said: "one must somehow bring together the two ends of humanity, our own thin end, and the last dark strand from the previous, pre-white era. I verily believe that. Is Taos the place?" And again Lawrence assured his hostess-to-be about their coming to Taos and asked her to advise and instruct him, by return mail, as she deemed necessary. "I want to leave Europe. I want to take the next step. Shall it be Taos?—I like the *word*. It's a bit like Taormina." [10]

Diana Trilling has made the classic summation of the relation thus begun between Mabel Dodge Luhan and D. H. Lawrence. Lawrence, according to this account, knew what he was getting into and must be assigned a good portion of the responsibility for what occurred to abort their relationship, for choosing Mabel Luhan as an intimate, and then for moving in on her at the point where she was most vulnerable. "From their first contact, Mabel had shown her hand. Her invitation to Lawrence to visit her in Taos was patently the communication of a woman any sensible man runs a mile from, enclosing strong Indian medicine to draw Lawrence to America and assuring him she was willing him in her direction." If Mrs. Trilling misquotes *Lorenzo in Taos*—actually, Mabel Luhan said that the strong medicine was sent in the form of a necklace for Frieda, to draw "them" to Taos—few will quibble with that interpretation of the invitation. From the prospective hostess' point of view, Frieda Lawrence had to be included as a social necessity but for no other reason. And Mrs. Trilling acutely adds that "instead of answering no thank you very much, I'm busy in Europe, Lawrence acted coy, he was flattered and he stimulated Mabel to persist until she had thoroughly entangled him and then, when he was living on her hospitality, he behaved abominably; he criticized everything she did—the way she dressed, the way she ran her house, the

way she treated her husband—all the while paying himself out
to her on a long sexual line which he was jolly sure was firmly
in Frieda's keeping!" [11]

As subtle as he was about women, Lawrence knew what
he was letting himself—and Frieda—in for. But he preferred
big, dominating women in life and avenged himself on them in
literature. The fruit of his revenge on Mabel Luhan ripened
only when the *Dial* serialized "The Woman Who Rode Away"
in its issues for July and August 1925. Here he accomplished a
good deal in return for her kindnesses to him: he ridiculed in
the figure of the mineowner Lederman, the kind of permissive
spouse Mabel Luhan's husbands seem to have been; he demol-
ished Mrs. Lederman's "vulgar excitement at the idea of ancient and mysterious ways" of the Indians; and he concluded
his story by depicting the lady drugged and bound and about
to be disemboweled by the Indians as a sacrificial victim. [12] In
the same spirit, he had abused his benefactress Lady Ottoline
Morrell in *Women in Love*, if not so fatally; and he even
satirized Frieda on occasion.

Perhaps because Lawrence knew full well what he was
getting himself into, he delayed the physical meeting with
Mabel Luhan as long as he could by taking a leisurely voyage
east to America, stopping off en route at Ceylon to visit with
his friends Earl and Achsah Brewster and then staying for
several months in Australia, where he worked up his novel
Kangaroo. He professed, he believed he wouldn't go to America (*CL* 685); yet hint by seductive hint, letter by letter,
league by league he came. From Palermo in the last week of
February 1922 the Lawrences sailed, and by Labor Day of
1922, he was lodged safely in the Palace Hotel in San Francisco
and writing "Dear Mabel Dodge." One notes the preservation
of a minimal formality; he had entered their correspondence
with "Dear Mrs. Dodge."

Lawrence's agent, Robert Mountsier, was meanwhile la-
dling out funds for travel and then for settling down in Taos,
where Frieda and Lawrence arrived on September 11, 1922.
They met there a woman rather like a Zorach female nude—

stocky, not swift in movement, with a broad sensual mouth and
a round face that the lovely eyes, long-lashed, dominated; her
hair was dark, worn in a Liberty bob. She dressed as she felt
suited her, mostly in those years in long shapeless dresses and
rebozos about the house; but she liked to ride—a true Amazon,
she must dominate—and then she wore a chic habit consisting
of hat, loose jacket, figured silk scarf, white shirt, gloves, and a
charming sort of knickers over knee-length, soft-leather boots.
In her early forties, with a grown son whom she was in the
process of settling down nearby, she was a glamorous person-
age; except for the riding habit, she was hardly the arrested
postdebutante of "The Woman Who Rode Away." For Lawrence, however, she was emphatically youthful. In an untitled,
abandoned manuscript, he once more noted Mabel Luhan's air
of youth and observed her as sturdy with a round face "like an
obstinate girl of fourteen," yet approaching forty, at first
glance full of candor and naïve-looking, at second glance somehow dangerous (Ted 51).

When Mabel Luhan met Lawrence, she saw a man tall
but so slightly built and so stooped that he gave the impression
of being small. His head, which hung forward, seemed too
heavy for his very slim body; the whole expression of his figure
was of extreme fragility. His movements were quick and sure.
His hair was a very heavy, ash-colored crop, cut around in a
bang and falling in rather Greeklike locks; in contrast, his
beard was soft, silky, bright red in hue. His eyes were large
and set wide apart in a long, slender face with a chin dispropor-
tionately long, a defect perhaps intentionally concealed by the
beard. His under lip protruded from the surrounding hirsute
decoration in a red so violent it made the beard look pink.
Above it was a nose very podgy, almost vulgar, and certainly
undistinguished. Thus Lawrence appeared to the only girl
with whom, so Frieda once confided, he was ever unfaithful to
her; and Mabel Luhan vouched for the vividness of the portrait
—sent her by Lawrence's inamorata.

At the conclusion of their first conversation, Mabel
Luhan felt surging within her a great desire to save Lawrence

—most immediately and specifically, from Frieda—and she announced silently to herself, "I *would* save him!"

That day, however, he had the final words. Walking toward the Luhans' house, his eyes shining blue and seeming to be assuaged, Lawrence paused an instant and said: "The burden of consciousness is too great for a woman to carry. She has enough to bear with her ever-recurring menstruation." [13]

The Lawrences ate, slept, wrote, had their domestic battles, gave parties, made their American acquaintances and friends in Taos much as they had elsewhere. At first they lived in a small house close by the Luhans' large house, built for Tony, and later at Kiowa Ranch, 160 acres on the slope of Lobo Mountain, which Mabel Luhan gave to Frieda. In return, Frieda sweetly presented Mabel with the manuscript of *Sons and Lovers*, to the considerable annoyance of the erstwhile landlady. Lawrence also gave advice to his hostess but would not let himself be seduced by her. In his fresh enthusiasm for America, Taos, and his new friend, he proposed collaborating with her on a novel expressing the life, the spirit of America. He wanted to compose it around the figure of Mabel Luhan—her life from the time she left New York to come out to New Mexico, from civilization to the bright, strange world of Taos and her renunciation of the sick old world of art and artists for the pristine valley and the upland Indian lakes. As Harry T. Moore has pointed out, one reason the novel was never completed is that Frieda was jealous: "I did not want this," she said, and she achieved her aim by constantly interfering with the two collaborators (*CL* 724). Even though Lawrence abandoned this plan after a preliminary scene, it did bear fruit eventually (and with his encouragement) as the four volumes of Mabel Luhan's *Intimate Memories*.

Always, he was gathering to himself his impressions, trying to unify them, trying to dominate this alien milieu. It was not Europe, where in one fashion or another he had been if sometimes a foreigner, always a European. It was not Ceylon or Australia or Tahiti, where he had been confessedly and

professedly a passerby. From the outset of his journey he had
expressed a detestation of Americans and their cult of liberty
and democracy. Also from the outset he had expressed his
belief in Taos, in the Indians—though they must do half the
believing: in Lawrence as well as in the sun. And from the
outset he had written shockingly, jarringly to Mabel Luhan,
wandering on about conscious-automatic control, cursing the
"arty" set whom he prophesied he should have to contend with
once he came to Taos. A week after he arrived in Taos, he
found the Apaches picturesque but not very *sympatisch* (*CL*
715).[14]

   While Lawrence was revising his impressions of the New
World and its primitives in the light of reality, the *Dial* re-
ceived nothing from him during those latter months of 1922.
Robert Mountsier sent only the manuscript of *Kangaroo* to
Gilbert Seldes before the managing editor of the *Dial* sailed for
Europe aboard the *Manchuria* on January 9, 1923. The author
disapproved. In a letter to his publisher Thomas Seltzer, Lawrence expressed his displeasure over learning that Seldes had
carted off to Berlin the English copy of *Kangaroo*, which
Mountsier had sent to the *Dial* instead of to the London agent,
Curtis Brown. Brown it was whom Lawrence wanted to take
care of the publication of *Kangaroo*, and he was growing tired
of Mountsier, who apparently was beginning to take over the
British business as well as the American. The letter to Seltzer
emphasized that "whatever Seldes decides, I don't really want
the *Dial* to publish a *bit* of the book" (*CL* 737–39). The most
probable explanation of that prohibition is that Lawrence preferred not to undergo a repetition of his experience with the
"mutilated" publication of sections from *Sea and Sardinia*. One
notes, in this connection, the ambiguous emphasis on the word
bit. And he was done, said Lawrence, with Mountsier, save for
winding-up trifles. But the *Dial* occupied his attention. "Did
you see this month's Dial?" he asked Seltzer. The reference
was to Jan Juta's portrait of the master and to "Indians and an
Englishman," both in the issue for February 1923.

   The same month, the business arrangement with Mountsier was closed out. On February 24, 1923, along with proofs of "Model Americans," a book review of Stuart Sherman's *Americans* Lawrence was writing at the invitation of the *Dial*, he received a letter from Seldes (*CL* 740–41). The next day, in a reply that was detached but cordial, Lawrence asked Seldes to return *Kangaroo*. "Let Curtis Brown have *Kangaroo* as soon as you can, will you? (Not *The* K.) I don't really mind if you mention it before it is published. It is usually publishers who have feelings about these things." And after expressing his general attitude toward America ("there is a vast unreal, intermediary thing intervening between the real thing which was Europe and the next real thing, which will probably be in America, but which isn't yet, at all"), Lawrence returned to business: "I got proofs of the Prof. [Stuart] Sherman criticism along with your letter. Hope it will amuse you," he added with reference to his only book review for the *Dial*. So the dissatisfaction with Robert Mountsier probably did not extend to the *Dial;* in the letters of 1922–23 in which Lawrence attacked Mountsier, he did not link his American agent with the magazine.

The first report of his encounter with America Lawrence published in the New York *Times Magazine* for December 24, 1922; "Certain Americans and an Englishman" is his brief account of the effect upon the Pueblo Indians of the Bursum Land Bill, and of course he took the part of those certain Americans who were Indians. Lawrence published both the second and third reports of his encounter with America in the *Dial* for February and March 1923; these two impressions are much more personal than his piece for the *Times*. "Indians and an Englishman" is the first of the two *Dial* descriptive essays. The typescript in the *Dial* papers indicates that, taking advantage of the link with the *Times*, the editorial staff retitled the essay, which originally had been called, rather less appositely, "Pueblos and an Englishman." The third essay about Indians, entitled "Taos," appeared in the next issue of the magazine in March 1923, and it may be that again the staff gave the second essay its title. The magazine's records indicate that "Indians

and an Englishman" was a first installment and describe
"Taos" as the second installment of "Indians and an Englishman." Hinting at Lawrence's disagreement with his American
agent, Tedlock suggests that Mountsier's office did not prepare
the typescript for "Taos" and notes that his address is not on
the manuscript (Ted 181). Yet, as the record shows, the *Dial*
mailed the check for "Taos" to Mountsier. In the confusion over
who was responsible to whom, Lawrence may have blamed the
Dial for an inefficiency that it wasn't responsible for.

Certainly he was the star of the February 1923 *Dial*. The
issue not only reproduced his portrait by Juta—which made
him look like one of those Russian mystical vegetarians whom
he disliked—but also introduced his essay in "Notes on Contributors" with a flourish: "D. H. Lawrence is now visiting
America, and living on a ranch in New Mexico. Under the title
Indians and an Englishman *The Dial* will publish at varying
intervals Mr Lawrence's impressions of the Southwest." The
importance of "Taos" and "Indians and an Englishman" in
Lawrence's thought and work is great indeed. Oddly enough,
these two "key" essays remained uncollected until their inclusion in the posthumous edition of similar pieces in 1936, *Phoenix*.

Yet it is deceptively simple to view Lawrence in a new and
different light as just another *Dial* contributor, albeit a very
distinguished one, who was following the fashion of setting
down his impressions of the primitive Southwest. To be sure,
the *Dial* was, mainly, interested in the pleasant fact—it did
seem an established fact in the winter of 1922–23—that a
regular and major contributor was now concerned with a topic
that also preoccupied the magazine and its readers. It thus
would continue to receive acclaim for its consistent support of a
controversial artist, and granted the generosity and the altruism of Scofield Thayer and Sibley Watson, surely one sym-
pathetically understands the categorizing by "Notes on Contributors" of Lawrence with Mabel Luhan, Marsden Hartley,
and other members of the coterie in and about Taos. Lawrence's own assessment of the situation was quite different.

He informed Curtis Brown, in a letter dated February 10, 1923, that he had asked the *Dial* to send his British agent a copy of the February issue, containing the first installment of his article "Indians and an Englishman." Had Mountsier sent Curtis Brown a copy of this piece? It might well have been acceptable to several English periodicals. "I think," he added, "the *Dial* publishes the next—and I think the final—instalment in April." That is to say, the Southwest was, like the rest of the world, mere grist to his mill. "It has a different thing by me for March. You could," he advised his British agent, "get the complete MS. from them" (*CL* 737).

The "thing" Lawrence mentioned as having written at Taos was one of his most notable book reviews, his sole such work indeed for the *Dial*. In it he locked horns with Professor Stuart Sherman of the University of Illinois, one of the most formidable academic critics of the day, a professed antagonist of the vanguard, and therefore a man the *Dial*'s staff regarded with suspicion. In *Americans*, the book under review, Sherman considered some of the same American authors Lawrence had written about in *Studies in Classic American Literature*, and the two books, so widely different in their approach to what then was a novel subject not taught in most colleges and universities, were published less than a year apart, Sherman's at the end of 1922 and Lawrence's in late August 1923. Sherman returned the courtesy by reviewing *Studies in Classic American Literature* as "America Is Discovered" in the New York *Evening Post Literary Review* for October 20, 1923.

Lawrence's long review essay is a slapdash assortment of his quirky views about America, Americans, and the literature they produced. He liked certain aspects of Sherman's essay on Emerson but held that the Emersonian altruism led people nauseously astray, disagreed with Sherman's praise for Walt Whitman's identification of himself with everything and everybody, and in a well-known summation announced that "Whitman's 'you' doesn't get me." We've had enough democracy, opined Lawrence—and prophesied that when "Germany is thoroughly broken, Democracy finally collapses." It was an entertaining, idiosyncratic statement of prejudices and opinions and, although opposed to the prejudices and opinions usually aired in the *Dial*, considerably enlivened the issue for May 1923. Its publication also began a literary relationship that ended when Stuart Sherman died in 1926. While Sherman was editor of the Sunday *Books* section of the New York *Herald Tribune*, he reviewed Lawrence's *St. Mawr* under the title "Lawrence Cultivates His Beard." Lawrence responded with a cordial offer to review a book plainly and from the moral point of view. He was amused by the references to himself and his beard and respected this man who cared about the deeper implication of a novel (*CL* 846).[15] Again, the *Dial* proved a helpful catalytic agent.

For the two impressions of New Mexico and the review essay of *Americans*, Lawrence received more than he thought he had been paid by the *Dial*. In his diary for March 3, 1923, he indicated that when he broke with his American agent Robert Mountsier, he would allow Mountsier to keep "the $105 from *Dial*; $70 for Indians article, pub. Feb. $35 for Sherman criticism, published March (?)" (Ted 97). The diary entry for March 9 indicates that Mountsier agreed to these terms but corrected his client's figures, explaining that "$70 and $35 were for Indian article, and $65 for Sherman—total $170" (Ted 97). Mountsier's figures tally with the records of the *Dial*, and the double payment for the "Indians article" is actually for both "Indians and an Englishman" and "Taos."

For two years, from May 1923 until April 1925, the *Dial* published nothing by Lawrence. Of all the aspects of his long relationship with the magazine and its staff, this is the most difficult to explain and clarify. Most immediately he may not have sent anything to the *Dial* because of the confusion that ensued after his dismissal of Robert Mountsier. The time spent in closing out the business arrangement with Mountsier—the settling of accounts and the return of manuscripts—suggests a delay of a month or two during which neither author nor agent would have submitted Lawrence's material to the *Dial*. Further, the adjustment of the new American agent—who was also the old British agent—to the American literary market, and more specifically to that portion of the American market available to Lawrence, may have taken some time. In paying off Mountsier and hiring Curtis Brown as agent for both America and Great Britain, indeed as his sole agent, Lawrence sought to reach a wider market than Mountsier could get for him; concomitantly, he sought a better-paying magazine outlet than the *Dial* and a more stable publisher than Thomas Seltzer. The latter he achieved when Curtis Brown brought him to Alfred A. Knopf; but there was no successor to the *Dial*. The record shows that Curtis Brown made a conscientious, ongoing effort to sell Lawrence's work to an ever wider range of magazines; yet if the importance of the *Dial* to Lawrence diminished in the later 1920's, his agent never found a satisfactory substitute, and to the end of his career Lawrence never established a similarly viable relationship with another American magazine.

About the time he left Mountsier, Lawrence may have felt that, after his quarrels and estrangement with Mabel Dodge Luhan, the *Dial* might not be so hospitable to him as it had been in former years. Under the whip of Frieda's urging, Lawrence returned to Europe—to London, Paris, Baden-Baden —for the fall and winter of 1923–24. He kept telling Mabel Luhan that he loathed both London where his former friends instinctively hated him and that place (it was Gourdjieff's sanatorium) near Fontainebleau where the inmates were playing their sickly stunt (so fatal to poor Katherine Mansfield). Germany, though, making a great change, was more interesting. Things might happen there, people might be as one wanted them to be (*CL* 778). The strain of the intense friendship between Lawrence and Mabel Luhan was aggravated not only by his bad health that winter but by her use of him as a combination lay confessor and psychiatrist. He begged that they keep a bit of a laugh going, that she keep her "horse" common sense. As soon as her infernal seriousness would heave up, like a greasy sea, everything would be lost. And he reminded her of the dangers to their friendship they had experienced at Taos. If only they'd kept up an honest laugh, then the vileness of 1923 need not have been (*CL* 770–71). But bent on divorcing Lawrence from Frieda, Mabel Luhan persisted in sending him lengthy Jungian analyses of herself and him and their acquaintance, complete with diagrams of the anima and persona. She merely succeeded in divorcing Lawrence from herself. After the Lawrences' arrival back at Taos in late March 1924, she never seemed to see him alone any more or to have him undividedly. Lawrence had both Frieda and Dorothy Brett in tow; life became richer for him but poorer for Mabel Luhan, who wished to admit only Tony and Frieda to their group. By September the tension had broken, at least for Lawrence, still attempting to cope with Mabel Luhan's emotional gropings after some stable relationship that would satisfy herself, Tony, Lawrence, and Frieda. Toward the conclusion of a letter to Mabel on September 22, Lawrence assured her that she need have no split between Tony and himself if only she would stick to what was *real* in her feelings in each direction (*CL* 809). But three weeks later he was on his way to Mexico, their "real" intimacy shattered. It may well be that he did not wish to encumber the *Dial*'s staff with the embarrassment of his estrangement from Mabel Luhan; yet it was during his winter in Mexico that he sent his story about her involvement with the primitive and with Indians, "The Woman Who Rode Away," to the *Dial*. All in all, nineteen or twenty months elapsed between the appearance of Lawrence's "Model Americans" in the *Dial* for May 1923 and the acceptance of "The Woman Who Rode Away" sometime in January 1925, in time enough, that is, for it to be puffed in the house advertisement in the March 1925 issue.

For this long absence, besides the change of literary agents and the estrangement from Mabel Dodge Luhan, one looks to still another cause: the change in editors at the *Dial*. During the sixteen months from January 1924 until April 1925 that Alyse Gregory worked as managing editor, none of Lawrence's work appeared in the magazine. Lawrence's letters and the biographies about him have almost nothing to say of any possible relationship with Alyse Gregory, her English husband, Llewelyn Powys, or Llewelyn's brothers John Cowper and T. F. Powys, all four of them novelists and contemporaries of Lawrence. Of T. F. Powys, Lawrence entertained no very high opinion; he told Charles Lahr that T. F. Powys was not a better writer than Thomas Hardy, for his was a wooden Noah's Ark world, all Noah's Ark—but amusing as such (*CL* 1144). Clearly he knew of the Powys family through mutual friends in England as well as by repute.

Also Lawrence was acquainted with Alyse Gregory as a frequent reviewer for the *Dial* both before and after her term as managing editor. On three occasions she reviewed Lawrence's work, always unfavorably. Her first of these reviews was a long and inopportune essay in the issue for January 1924 that may have alienated Lawrence from the magazine for a while.

In that same month—when she became managing editor and her unfavorable, lengthy review essay of Lawrence's recent work appeared—Alyse Gregory wrote to Lawrence soliciting his manuscripts for publication in the *Dial*.

> We should be so very glad if you would send us some of your recent work, either poetry or prose. We understand, of course, that your work must be very much in demand, yet we do not think that we are wrong in saying that you will find nowhere in this country at least, an audience more appreciative of your writing than is to be discovered among the readers of The Dial.

Alyse Gregory's letter reveals that the *Dial*'s staff were acutely aware that Lawrence's contributions had suddenly stopped, and it may even be regarded as a token apology for her review in the January issue. For Lawrence the letter effected nothing; at any rate, no reply exists among the *Dial* papers. And although "Notes on Contributors" in the issue for February 1923 announced that "The Dial will publish at varying intervals Mr Lawrence's impressions of the Southwest," "Indians and an Englishman" and "Taos" were the only essays in the series to appear in the *Dial*. Lawrence continued to record his impressions, but he sent them to other American magazines: the New York *Times Magazine, Theatre Arts Monthly,* even Spud Johnson's *Laughing Horse.*[16]

The reasoning that Alyse Gregory was a cause of Lawrence's temporary boycott of the *Dial* is further supported by the fact that about the time she resigned, Lawrence sent a story to the magazine and thus ended his neglect of so many months. Although Miss Gregory did not officially leave the magazine until the end of April 1925–the earliest date at which her successor, Marianne Moore, could leave her post at the New York Public Library to work for the *Dial*–she had made up her mind in January 1925 and had resigned effectively by the middle of February. The records of purchase at the *Dial* do not reveal when the magazine received and accepted "The Woman Who Rode Away," which appeared in July and August of 1925, but the house advertisements in the issues for March, April, and May 1925 all announced the forthcoming publication of this story. "The Woman Who Rode Away" was probably received in January 1925 and significantly was not published until after Alyse Gregory had left the magazine. The resumption of Lawrence's contributions to the *Dial* in the month of Miss Gregory's resignation and the publication of his work obviously intended for the *Dial* in other periodicals during Miss Gregory's term as managing editor may be due to other causes, but the sequence of events indicates Lawrence's aversion–whatever the reason–for Alyse Gregory.

The years of Lawrence's American experience conclude with the publication of "The Woman Who Rode Away" in those two issues in 1925. Originally Lawrence had intended that the long story would be published with another story, "The Princess," and a novella, *Saint Mawr,* all of which were written in Taos in 1924. The settings of all three stories are the Taos country or Mexico, and all three have similar themes and characters. At the beginning of July 1924, Lawrence showed a manuscript of "The Woman Who Rode Away" to Mabel Luhan; and about this time he made a trip to a cave near the Arroyo Seco, which supplied the scenery of the concluding episode of the story.[17]

As Mabel Luhan describes the excursion, it was a trip made on horseback by Lawrence and herself and perhaps Frieda, Tony, and Clarence Thompson, a young lodger at the Luhans'. The party went to visit a remarkable cave and waterfall high on the side of the mountain above the village of Arroyo Seco. They had to leave their horses and climb a nearly obliterated trail, along a thin stream descending through pines and cedars and tall grasses. Following the trail and stream, winding in and out and finally rounding some huge rocks, they approached the opening of the cave, a place the local Indians felt so strongly about that they would not camp near it for fear of the bad spirits there. The vast, pelvic-shaped aperture faced the west and yawned to the sky; and veiling it thirty feet across, the mountain water fell to a pool below. Inside the chill, damp, dark cavern, bears hibernated in holes in the rock walls, said Tony Luhan; and in the rear, at the right, a rude stairway cut into the rock led to a shelving ledge, over one end of which the ancients had painted a sun, still faintly visible. From this "high altar" one looked out at the clear fall of water across the opening, green and transparent. At the winter solstice, when the waterfall had turned to an icy column, as the sun turned to go south it shone through the erect, transparent pillar of ice and fell precisely upon the altar. For Mabel Luhan, the impressions of a visit to this cave crowded about, awesome and terrible, half-formed out of the past and not to be put into modern English.

Other experiences are pertinent to "The Woman Who Rode Away" besides Lawrence's and Mabel Luhan's moments in the ceremonial cave. The arduous climb up the mountainside Lawrence transmogrified into the long, dreamlike journey of the woman who rode away, up and up, led by the "wild" Indians to their hidden valley in the clouds of the high Mexican mountains. Lawrence's plan to ride with young Clarence Thompson into the desert on horseback and never be seen again, to get away, in Clarence's ringing words, from the women and the strangers and all the world of things he knew —this became the plan of "The Woman Who Rode Away." Lorenzo conceived Mrs. Lederman through his yearnings for escape from the bickering that was destroying his New Mexican utopia. Clarence and he would ride off toward Old Mexico, never to return. So if Mrs. Lederman is recognizably Mabel Luhan, she also is recognizably her creator. Lawrence killed off Mrs. Lederman and thus dealt his mortal blow at Mabel Luhan's ideology—her primitivism, her advocacy of Jungian psychology—but he also released something of his own insecurity and self-mistrust in the violent conclusion of his story.

"The Woman Who Rode Away" was not, after all, included with "The Princess" and *St. Mawr;* instead it was saved for a later book and appeared as the title story of a volume that Alfred A. Knopf published in 1928 and that included, among its eleven titles, the other four stories that Lawrence contributed to the *Dial* during 1925–27. It was well worth the compliment. When it was published in the *Dial*, the first installment of "The Woman Who Rode Away" was placed at the beginning of the issue for July 1925, sufficient indication of the value the magazine attached to it, for according to the house rules of the *Dial*, the most highly valued work in an issue led off that issue. The story concluded in the next number, for August, and for the thirty-six pages of "The Woman Who Rode Away" Lawrence received two hundred and seventy-five dollars from the *Dial*. The esteem of the *Dial*'s staff for "The Woman Who Rode Away" was justified almost immediately; after reading the second installment, Helmut von Erffa, of the German department at Rutgers University, asked permission to make a translation, and agreeing that Germany might well like it, Lawrence replied on August 18, 1925 granting Erffa the permission (*CL* 848). And Edward J. O'Brien admired it sufficiently to include the story in his collection, *The Best British Short Stories of 1925*. "The Woman Who Rode Away" constituted the Lawrentian *ave atque vale* to America, coming out when it did, at the conclusion of his second American stay from March 11, 1924 through September 24, 1925.

By one of life's little ironies, on September 15, 1925, the day after Lawrence and Frieda arrived in New York en route to Europe, the *Dial* received the manuscript of Mabel Luhan's tale of Indians and Mexicans, "Southwest," for which, on acceptance, she was paid seventy dollars. "The Woman Who Rode Away" had killed off the Mrs. Lederman who rode away from civilization in order to immerse herself in the primitive life of the wild, unconquered Indians of the American deserts and mountains. "Southwest" is a direct answer—to the extent that any story can constitute a direct answer—to Lawrence's violent criticism of Mabel Luhan's adopted way of life, her marriage to an Indian prominent in the pueblo of Taos, and her wholehearted, aggressive espousal of Indian causes along with her new husband. Here she suggests her disappointment at Lawrence's revulsion from the very primitives he had traveled around the world to encounter; also she expresses her faith in a way of life so close to the earth and to life's origins. There are no marauding and despoiling Anglos in "Southwest," but their historic role in New Mexican culture has its fictional surrogate in the story: the Mexicans of the region are, instead, the villains. That is to say, in the words of the author, "Although antipathy may exist between Indians and Mexicans, as between Indians and white people, there are always exceptions to the general antagonism, and each Mexican family has its friends among the Indians." In the Mexican family described in "Southwest," it is the wife who is antipathetic to Indians, specifically to her husband's friend Silverbird. Told by the wife to leave a wedding party at his friends' house, Silverbird does so but, in revenge, returns with two of his Indian *compadres*, dancing and chanting hypnotically and drowning out the Mexican wedding music. The guests and hosts all fall down in slumber, the Indians triumph: their "mild, united song . . . had overpowered the disjointed utterance that had poured from the big room, and there was silence." Silverbird and his friends feast on the Mexican wedding food and gaze on the helpless bridal party. Then Silverbird humorously says to his two companions: "The *señora* was cross to me for no cause. I think now we give a good reason to be mad." And he goes to the door, faces the east, and seems to speak a few words to the sky. "Come, friends," he says to Eagle Star and Stonepath, "the sun will wake them. I have told him to do it. Now we go and leave them to be cross with each other, not with Silverbird." [18]

The story is artless, even ridiculous, related as it is in Mabel Luhan's leaden style. It is a märchen without an iota of the redeeming wonder of the fairy tale. Yet in one vital respect "Southwest" is prophetic as none of Lawrence's fiction is. The entire argument of "Indians and an Englishman," "Taos," and "The Woman Who Rode Away" is that so-called civilized men cannot communicate with, cannot empathize with, and therefore cannot significantly share life with the so-called primitive Indians (and by extension, with any preliterate people). But "Southwest" argues that some Indians can and do communicate with and empathize with some Mexicans and that the fancied superiority of the so-called civilized person is really a life-in-death against nature, because that way of living ensures oblivion to many beautiful forms of life and thus fatally narrows one's sympathies. [19] The two Indians of "Southwest" do not bloodily sacrifice the Mexicans—who, having been corrupted by "white" culture, are already deadened—but, rather, put the wedding party to sleep as a gentle revenge. This action is of course a deliberate contrast to the sacrifice performed by Lawrence's Indians, who kill their victim; moreover, Mabel Luhan's fictional milieu is not fantasized but, as Lawrence himself acknowledged, is deliberately realistic in depicting the life of the pueblo and the country round about Taos. From its author's point of view, "Southwest" is life-enhancing and life-realizing precisely because it is true to the values and ways of the Indians among whom she chose to live; thus her story eschews the melodramatic violence, the gratuitous cruelty, the facile exoticism of "The Woman Who Rode Away." "Southwest" is strikingly attuned to the direction and development American social attitudes took in the succeeding decades, and here it contrasts with Lawrence's elitist bias. Both Lawrence and Mabel Luhan were, in the broad meaning of the term, Platonists, but his views were antidemocratic and Nietzschean while hers were democratic and Transcendentalist in the tradition of Emerson and Whitman. Lawrence's sympathies were with the German adulation of *Blut und Erde*, hers were with the Indians who lived in the here and now, free in their souls, not neurotic because they had not lost their vision of creation.

Their views were irreconcilably antipathetic. Mabel Luhan wanted Lorenzo to record the kind of life that exists where people possess the true gold for which the gold of industrial civilization is but a deceiving counterfeit. Taos she regarded as a little living oasis in a desert world in which gold had sterilized the very souls out of people. But Lawrence could not "get" the spirit of the region. She expressed chagrin that he actually had to go to Mexico—as he did, for two visits—in order to write down what he absorbed of Taos. Into *The Plumed Serpent*, with its modern Mexican setting, he put the facts of his Taos experience of Indians and drums and dancing, but of actual Indian life, Mabel Luhan asserted, there is very little told. She could recall only three direct writings about New Mexico, three essays first published in *Theatre Arts* and the New York *Times Magazine* and then collected in *Mornings in Mexico:* "Indians and Entertainment," "The Corn Dance," and "The Snake Dance." Unaccountably she omitted both the essays the *Dial* published: "Indians and an Englishman" and "Taos." Before quoting a major portion of "Indians and an Englishman" in *Lorenzo in Taos*, Mabel Luhan describes it as a part of an article Lawrence wrote after a trip to the Apache Reservation. She had the manuscript among her papers in an incomplete state, and if she had ever seen it in the *Dial*, she obviously had forgotten by 1932 whether Lawrence had ever published it. She had forgotten too that this same manuscript includes the first six paragraphs of Lawrence's essay in the New York *Times Magazine* for December 24, 1922, "Certain Americans and an Englishman." "It does not seem to me to be very good," she added. "Was it because Frieda was not along with him on that occasion?" In one complaint, however, she was surely right: "Even *The Woman Who Rode Away*, about the sacrificial cave, he gave to Mexico!" Her rationalization for the change of locality is that Lawrence "belonged to those centuries of civilization that come between the bright, true golden age of pure delight and the brilliant age of gold; between those two 'soulless' periods when men wandered pitifully wondering what was the matter with the world and with themselves that they should so unaccountably suffer." Moreover, although Lawrence believed he was through with what he called inessentials, they were not through with him; history never lost its importance for him. That was the reason Mexico mattered more to him than New Mexico, though, thought Mabel Luhan, maybe he would not have acknowledged his bias. "Mexico has some written 'history'; New Mexico has none." [20]

If her interpretation is acceptable, one more fully understands why Lawrence returned to Europe, that dead and stinking dog, and why Mabel Luhan, heading in an opposite direction, crossed her psychic bridge to a new life in Taos with Antonio Luhan, a life transcending history. History was concerned, she wrote, with the behavior of men turning somersaults in a vacuum. Lawrence envisioned that concern very differently. He returned to history when he went back to Europe in the fall of 1925. After four years of wandering among exotics and primitives—in Ceylon, Tahiti, and New and Old Mexico—he resisted the temptation of the occult, which is that a man may transcend the historical process into which he is born. Lawrence forsook much of what William York Tindall has described as his personal religion compounded of anthropology and theosophy, of animism and the occult. [21]

The abandonment, or disillusion, was gradual. First he recognized the gulf between such a civilized, modern, twentieth-century being as himself and the Sardinian peasant with a medieval face, *rusé*, never abandoning his defenses for a moment, "as a badger or a polecat never abandons its defenses." Then there was the revulsion in Ceylon from Buddhism; as Lawrence related to Mabel Luhan, "the nasty faces and yellow robes of the Buddhist monks, the little vulgar dens of the temples: all this makes up Ceylon to me, and all this I cannot bear. *Je m'en vais. Me ne vo'* " (*CL* 699–700). Then in Tahiti, Lawrence discovered that whatever else the "South Sea Islander is, he is centuries and centuries behind us in the life struggle, . . . we can't go back to the savages: not a stride. We can be in sympathy with them. We can take a great curve in their direction, onwards. But we cannot turn the current of our life backwards, back towards their soft warm twilight." [22]

In "Indians and an Englishman," Lawrence omitted even his tentative optimism about one's being able to take a great curve in the direction of the savage. Instead, he made public acknowledgment of his apostasy from the fullness of a faith the seductiveness of which he admitted he must battle against. Pondering on the Apache ritual that he had just witnessed, he concluded that he didn't want to live again the tribal mysteries his blood had lived long since: "I don't want to know as I have known, in the tribal exclusiveness. But every drop of me trembles still alive to the old sound, every thread in my body quivers to the frenzy of the old mystery. I know my derivation. I was born of no virgin, of no Holy Ghost. Ah, no, these old men telling the tribal tale were my fathers. I have a dark-faced, bronze-voiced father far back in the resinous ages. My mother was no virgin. She lay in her hour with this dusky-lipped tribe-father. And I have not forgotten him. But he, like many an old father with a changeling son, he would like to deny me. But I stand on the far edge of their firelight, and am neither denied nor accepted. My way is my own, old red father; I can't cluster at the drum any more" (*Ph* 99). Had Mabel Luhan's copy of "Indians and an Englishman" been complete, she would, no doubt, have recalled the article with positive disdain, so widely does its theme diverge from her own attitude.

When the *Dial* published "Southwest," Mabel Luhan mailed a copy of the story to Lawrence. Early in January 1926 he wrote her from the Villa Bernarda, at Spotorno on the Italian Riviera, that he and Frieda had received her Christmas Day letter, " with the little story, yesterday. The story gives one the feeling of the *pueblo* and the country very much." Not altogether sincerely, he added, "I liked it!" (*CL* 880). Yet he left Kiowa Ranch that Mabel Luhan had given Frieda; he left his horse Azul and his cow Susan, the pure dry air and the warm radium spring where the Lawrences and the Luhans companionably had bathed. And he never came back.

4

LAWRENCE AND *THE DIAL* OF MARIANNE MOORE

A FTER THE PUBLICATION OF Mabel Dodge Luhan's "Southwest," and throughout the final, European phase of his life and career, Lawrence kept up his pleasant relationship with the *Dial*. There was no longer the intimacy of former years, but the tone of the correspondence between the staff and their contributor is friendly. The *Dial* did not publish and apparently did not receive, from either the author or Curtis Brown's American representative A. W. Barmby, any of Lawrence's longer fiction, travel essays, or book reviews. As the editor of the *Dial*, Marianne Moore would have commissioned Lawrence to write a review; it is a loss to letters that there was no successor to "Model Americans." Still, in the three and one-half years, 1926 through July 1929, that remained to the *Dial* before it ceased publication, it brought out four stories and eleven poems by Lawrence.

At the beginning of 1924, about the time that Lawrence went to Alfred A. Knopf as an author through the good offices of Curtis Brown, Knopf backed H. L. Mencken and George Jean Nathan as coeditors of the *American Mercury*. Had Mencken been receptive to Lawrence's work, no doubt he would have appeared with some frequency in that periodical outlet. For the rest of Lawrence's career, Knopf was his principal though not his sole American publisher. He published, among other volumes, a book of short stories by Lawrence, *The Woman Who Rode Away and Other Stories*, in 1928, and of the eleven pieces composing the book, the title story and four others—in number of pages well over half the length of the volume—had previously appeared in the *Dial*. And from Knopf's edition of *Pansies*, the last book of poems by Lawrence published before he died, eleven poems appeared in the *Dial* in two of its three final numbers, for May and July 1929. So the magazine continued to remain a significant outlet for Lawrence's publication in periodicals; its diminished importance to him reflects, of course, his growing acceptance by American readers and constitutes a tribute to the service the *Dial* performed for writers and artists of the vanguard.

After "The Woman Who Rode Away," the next fiction Lawrence published in the *Dial* appeared also in two installments, a year later in the issues for July and August 1926. And as with "The Woman Who Rode Away," a story by Lawrence not only began an issue but initiated a new volume of the magazine. (Volumes of the *Dial* consisted of the January–June and the July–December numbers, on a semiannual basis: two volumes a year, each of six issues.) "Glad Ghosts" came to the *Dial* through a rather curious circumstance. Lawrence wrote it in the winter of 1925 at the request of Lady Cynthia Asquith, daughter-in-law of the wartime Liberal prime minister Herbert Asquith and his wife Margot, the famous political hostess and wit. Lady Cynthia wrote an occasional novel and frequented the London literary drawing rooms, and ever since she had stood by Lawrence during his vicissitudes of the war years, they had been friends. "Glad Ghosts" was at first meant for an anthology of ghost stories she was compiling, *The Ghost Book*.[1]

After Dorothy Brett finished typing the holograph copy, Lawrence had second thoughts about sending this particular story to Lady Cynthia. He had wondered to Brett, earlier, how Cynthia Asquith would swallow "Gay Ghosts," as it was then entitled (*CL* 882). Thinking better of his promise to contribute something to *The Ghost Book*, Lawrence sent it off instead

to Curtis Brown. "But they'll never find a magazine to print it,"
he glumly assured Brett. "They wrote that even 'Sun' was too
'pagan' for anything but a highbrow 'review': Fools!" (*CL*
886). Lawrence, for once, decided to be tactful and not to hurt
the Asquiths by asking Lady Cynthia to include in *The Ghost
Book* a story in which the two principal figures were modeled
on herself and her husband, Herbert Asquith the younger, and
in which the action is as much about sex as it is about ghosts.[2]
As his contribution to the collection, Lawrence submitted "The
Rocking-Horse Winner," a most satisfactory substitute, the
most popular of all his stories.

Curtis Brown mailed "Glad Ghosts"—as the firm had said
it would do—to that broadminded, highbrow review, the *Dial*,
which accepted it on March 22, 1926. By April 28, 1926 Lawrence was able to ask Brett rhetorically, "Did I tell you the
'Glad Ghosts' story is appearing in the *Dial*"—his indirect way
of pointing out to her the acuity of his earlier guess (*CL* 907).
And just after it appeared he reminded her again, though more
lightheartedly: "Did you see *Glad Ghosts* in the *Dial?* Amusing" (H 668). Although "Glad Ghosts" is longer than "The
Woman Who Rode Away," forty pages as opposed to thirty-
six, Lawrence received only one hundred and seventy dollars
for it, approximately a hundred dollars less than he had received for the earlier story.

Lawrence's estimate of the "pagan" quality of "Glad
Ghosts" was an opinion he continued defensively to hold, for
after the story had appeared in the *Dial*, he congratulated his
good friend Achsah Brewster as having been right to let her
daughter Harwood read "Glad Ghosts." The sooner the young
would read books that treat of sex *honestly* and with a bit of
sincere reverence, he asserted, the better for them. The danger
for adolescents was that they were flippant, impertinent, and
contemptuous to sex—"that secret, dirty thing—till they've
made a mess of it, and lost their chance" (*CL* 964). It was that
attitude in Lawrence's writing that, to the vanguard of the
1920's, seemed so liberating and so prophetic; and of course,
that attitude was welcomed by the *Dial* and its readers.

In the succeeding two volumes of the *Dial* for 1927, three of Lawrence's stories appeared in fairly rapid succession. The first, in the April issue, was "Two Blue Birds," which Lawrence had finished by May 13, 1926 at the Villa Mirenda near Florence and which he sent to Curtis Brown the same date (H 658). As its records attest, the *Dial* accepted the manuscript on November 24, 1926, counted the story as 5,779 words, and mailed to Curtis Brown a check for one hundred and twenty dollars. It may be that "Two Blue Birds" made the rounds for several months before alighting at the *Dial;* yet it is one of Lawrence's most easily acceptable stories, with the gloss and brittleness of fiction in the *New Yorker.* Either through the good work of Curtis Brown or by virtue of its appearance in the *Dial,* "Two Blue Birds" was included later in 1927 in a large anthology edited by Maxim Lieber and Blanche Colton Williams and published by Brentano's, *Great Stories of All Nations.*

The third of Lawrence's longer stories that appeared in the *Dial,* in addition to "The Woman Who Rode Away" and "Glad Ghosts," was "The Man Who Loved Islands," which led off the second volume for 1927, in the issue for July. Twenty-six pages long, the story was counted at 10,300 words, and for it, the *Dial* paid Lawrence two hundred and ten dollars upon acceptance on January 20, 1927.

As he had done so many times before in his novels and stories, Lawrence gave rein to his penchant for satirizing his acquaintances and friends in both "Two Blue Birds" and "The Man Who Loved Islands." He seems to have escaped the ire of his victim in the publication of "Two Blue Birds," but the same victim complained bitterly and, to some extent, effectively about the publication of "The Man Who Loved Islands." Perhaps because the butt of Lawrence's satire was British, the *Dial* escaped unscathed, and so did Alfred A. Knopf when he included both stories in his 1928 edition of *The Woman Who Rode Away and Other Stories.*

This victim was none other than Lawrence's good friend for the past two decades, Compton Mackenzie. By contrast

with Lawrence and his struggle for recognition, Mackenzie
rose quickly and gracefully to an early acclaim for his novels—
and, just as importantly, to respectful notice from Henry
James himself. In "The Younger Generation," his review of
the latest crop of writers—chief among them Joseph Conrad,
Edith Wharton, and Mackenzie—in the *Times Literary Supplement* for April 2, 1914, James praised *Sinister Street* and
Carnival for "Mr. Compton Mackenzie's literary aspect";
"though decidedly that of youth" and of "a great deal of young
experience," it offered "the attraction of a complexity defiant of
the prompt conclusion" and really charmed "us by giving us
something to wonder about." Of *Sinister Street* and *Carnival*,
James remarked that "we take [them] for a lively gage of
performance to come"; and he also described Mackenzie as a
successful and resourceful young discoverer and observer of
life. Such extraordinary praise from the greatest living master
of the novel in English only served to send the younger man
back to his typewriter.

   One day soon after the outbreak of the First World War
—it was late in August—Mackenzie took a day off from his
writing chores and went to Buckinghamshire to visit the Gilbert Cannans. Cannan suggested a call on Lawrence and
Frieda, who were living nearby at Chesham, and so Compton
Mackenzie and D. H. Lawrence met while the latter was scrub-
bing the floor of the ugly brick cottage he and Frieda had just
moved into. Lawrence, hot and dirty, was suddenly confronted
by the thin elegance of Mackenzie, worldly and already successful; the awkward personal situation was sharpened by the
larger national situation, in which Frieda and Lawrence found
themselves alienated from the preoccupations and prejudices of
his countrymen, newly gone to war against the Germans.
Reading Mackenzie's recreation of the scene, one observes
Lawrence placed on the defensive and then giving way to bad
temper, taken out as usual on Frieda. At any rate Mackenzie
seems to have found *her* charming.[3]

   At the very beginning of January 1920, the two writers
met again, on Capri where, after having been invalided from

active military service, Mackenzie was writing *Sylvia and Michael*, the sequel to his best seller *Sylvia Scarlett*. Again the contrast between the prosperity and relative content of Compton and Faith Mackenzie and the poverty and insecurity of D. H. and Frieda Lawrence eventually curdled Lawrence's temper, but not this time to the point of his openly losing it; Mackenzie was too important for Lawrence's well-being. Only in corresponding with Catherine Carswell was Lorenzo ironic about Compton Mackenzie's niceness, qualifying it by being condescending to the generations of actors behind him, poking fun at his being quite rich and as walking with a sort of aesthetic figure in a pale blue suit to match his eyes and a woman's large brown velour hat to match his hair. In an image out of some medieval romance, Lawrence placed himself among the Poor Relations at Mackenzie's hospitable board, at the other end of the table from the host and his Rich Relatives (*CL* 605–6). To Cecily Lambert Minchin and W. E. and S. A. Hopkin, however, Lawrence mentioned Compton Mackenzie as a good sport and a friend (*CL* 607, 610). They had in common their literary ambitions and a wariness about the British unofficial censorship—the bourgeois attitude toward art and morals —that they had already antagonized. Here one difference was that Mackenzie was busily working on another popular novel, *Rich Relatives* (hence Lawrence's quip), while Lawrence could write only for the few—or so it then seemed. It was Mackenzie who advised Lawrence about the economics of publishing *The Rainbow* and *Women in Love* with the firm of Martin Secker; Secker thus became Lawrence's British publisher as he already was Mackenzie's. And it was Mackenzie who served as courier, taking with him to London Lawrence's manuscript of his prize-winning novel *The Lost Girl* and delivering it to Martin Secker (*CL* 614–33 *passim*). Throughout those sunny winter days early in 1920, walking down the lanes of Capri, arguing Greek philosophy and the occult in taverns, Mackenzie remained sympathetic and understanding even though as a recent Catholic convert he could hardly share some of his friend's antipathies and beliefs. In a series of letters,

Martin Secker, Compton Mackenzie, and Lawrence reveal how friend and publisher slowly guided Lawrence into the harbor of an enduring relationship with Secker's firm at a time when no one else would touch *Women in Love*.[4]

Years passed; the two novelists went their very different ways, Lawrence writing in relative poverty to increasing critical acclaim, Mackenzie writing in sleek prosperity, well able to disdain the avant-garde that adulated Lawrence. In August 1927 their paths crossed once more, and tempers flared after Compton Mackenzie read the British publication of "The Man Who Loved Islands" in the *London Mercury* for that month. Although Mackenzie does not mention that he protested the publication of "The Man Who Loved Islands" to Martin Secker, the publisher wisely omitted the story from the London edition of *The Woman Who Rode Away and Other Stories*. But in 1929, when the London firm of Heinemann announced publication of an expensive reprint edition of the volume, Mackenzie told Charles Evans of Heinemann that if Evans included "The Man Who Loved Islands" in the forthcoming reprint, "I should injunct it." Except for Compton Mackenzie's inaccuracy about dates in his account of the incident, Lawrence's letters agree as to what went on. Heinemann withdrew rather than have a lawsuit—and to Pino Orioli, Lawrence remarked, "Aren't these little authors beyond belief, with their vanity!" (*CL* 1188). Some weeks later, he added, to S. S. Koteliansky, that Compton Mackenzie had descended on Heinemann "with a shriek, threatening a suit for libel," and they withdrew their plans for the reprint of the eleven stories.[5]

The war clouds Mackenzie sent up over "The Man Who Loved Islands" seem today largely unjustified. Apparently only the title and none of the situations in the story suggest that Mackenzie is the inspiration for Cathcart, the central character. From the very beginning the story is obviously an allegory instead of a pointed satire, and Cathcart is not a caricature but a typically Lawrentian figure who retreats into himself instead of reaching for someone who can fulfill him. Even the three islands in the story function symbolically as the self-imposed limits of Cathcart's diminishing involvement with other men. Moreover, in most of Lawrence's satires there is a quality so outrageous that it detracts from any more serious fictional purpose, as one observes in the offensive and yet inconsequential action of "Smile," a caricature of John Middleton Murry; but "The Man Who Loved Islands," recounted in an allegorical framework, is neither outrageous nor offensive and the serious intent is carried forcefully to the end.

According to Compton Mackenzie, Lawrence moaned, "But it's not meant to be Monty." Mackenzie recalled his reply as being to the effect that "I was well aware of that but that if Lawrence used my background of a Channel Island and an island in the Hebrides for one of his preposterous Lawrentian figures the public would suppose that it was a portrait. In any case Lawrence needed a lesson in botany. He had written too beautifully about flowers to be easily forgiven for covering a granite island in the Channel with cowslips; he should know that cowslips favour lime. I was in fact getting tired of Lawrence's caricatures of people against photographic backgrounds." A mutual friend, Francis Brett Young, wrote "to tell me that Lawrence was ill and that my injunction of his story was making him worse. So I withdrew the injunction and the lunatic story may be read to-day." [6]

Not the least strange aspect of the affair is that Mackenzie raised no protest at all against the even more offensive caricature of himself and his wife in "Two Blue Birds." Unlike "The Man Who Loved Islands," where only the title remotely suggested Mackenzie, in "Two Blue Birds" Lawrence included personal details, such as Compton Mackenzie's practice of dictating his novels, and severely treated Faith Mackenzie as a sexually frustrated and aggressive society figure. Yet Compton Mackenzie does not mention Lawrence's depiction of the Mackenzies in this story, except indirectly and rather confusingly when quoting Faith Mackenzie about a certain visit Lawrence made to their villa at Capri after his return from America in 1925. Lawrence asked Mrs. Mackenzie to dine alone with him, and she went, she says, gladly because she

enjoyed his company; and when they discussed her husband,
she allowed Lawrence to talk more frankly about Mackenzie
than she would have permitted anyone else to do, because, she
wrote in her diary, "I know he loves him." And she admitted
that she had talked freely, warmed by Capri wine and Lawrence's sensitive understanding and the glow of kindness in his
deep eyes. He seemed to her that night an angel, and guile-
lessly she confided some of the secrets of her heart that hitherto
had never been let loose. To her dismay, some months later a
short story appeared in one of the popular magazines—*Pall
Mall* for June 1928 must be what Mrs. Mackenzie was referring to, although the date seems awry—a story that Lawrence
could not have written had she not dined with him that night in
Capri. "A malicious caricature of Monty, and a monstrous
perversion of facts, yet the source of it clearly recognizable,"
she concluded. Of her account, her husband observed that
when she was upset by Lawrence's story, he thought she was
imagining a grievance, for he could not see the faintest resemblance to her or to himself, "and as there was no resemblance
to our background, which, as I told Faith, there certainly
would have been if Lawrence had been writing about her and
me, I urged her to give up worrying." [7]

Yet Faith Mackenzie's insight was accurate. When the
very young Kyle Crichton came to Kiowa Ranch in 1925 to
interview Lawrence, he asked the great man whether he dic-
tated his stories. There was amusement all around.

"It's a private joke of our own," explained Lawrence.
"Frieda and I were once staying with Compton Mackenzie and
at two in the morning we came on Compton in bed in silk
pajamas—eh, Frieda?—with Brett Young's brother, his secretary, taking notes and Mrs. Mackenzie two rooms away, playing softly and romantically on the piano. Ho! If I wrote like
that something fantastic would come out!" [8] That, precisely,
was the situation in "Two Blue Birds" except that the male
secretary suffered a change of sex for the sake of a fictional
triangle.

And, in fact, in her memoir, *As Much As I Dare*, Mrs.

Mackenzie does indeed give the game away when she describes how her husband's writing "absorbed our days and nights. Monty wrote and I played in the bower, which was the nicest room in the house in a small wing of its own." The bower was in their house in Cornwall, however, not in the villa in Capri; still, one envisions the setting of "Two Blue Birds" as English, not Mediterranean, so Lawrence did get his milieu right. Perhaps a bit of gossip about the Cornish bower—could it have been related by Martin Secker, a familiar visitor with the Lawrences as well as the Mackenzies?—led Lawrence to recall that exotic night on Capri and so made possible the yoking of the Capri adventure and the house in Cornwall that resulted in "Two Blue Birds." [9]

Sir Compton Mackenzie, knighted and elderly, informed Edward Nehls in 1953 that "You will find an impression of Lawrence in my novel *The Four Winds of Love* [1937–40]." In "*The South Wind* [1937] . . . and in *The West Wind* [1940] . . . I called Lawrence Daniel Rayner. . . . Apart from names and places most of it is factually and conversationally exact." [10] As Daniel Rayner is an ambiguous figure in *The Four Winds of Love*, Compton Mackenzie got his revenge. Just which one of these two adversaries had the last laugh is impossible to say; at any rate Mackenzie had the last word.

The final piece of fiction by Lawrence to appear in the *Dial* was "In Love?" Published in the issue for November 1927, it was one of Lawrence's stories that *Hound and Horn* mentioned as being among the few rewarding moments the *Dial* offered in the later 1920's. A letter from one of the members of the *Dial*'s staff is interesting because it shows that by sending Lawrence the galley proofs of his work for the *Dial*, the magazine kept open its line of communication with a valued contributor. On April 13, 1927 the magazine wrote Lawrence as follows:

> We are sending you proofs of THE MAN WHO LOVED ISLANDS and of MODERN LOVE. The enclosed copy of a letter to Mr. Barmby of Curtis Brown will explain the change in the title of the second story.

> We have queried several points of punctuation on the
> proofs but shall make no changes without your authorization.

Not only was the check to the author sent to Barmby as American representative for Curtis Brown, even the letter of inquiry
that accompanied the proofs was sent to Lawrence in care of
Curtis Brown, at the firm's London address. It is worth re-
marking that under the editorship of Scofield Thayer, no such
arbitrary action such as the staff now took in changing the title
of Lawrence's story would have occurred without first consulting the author.

From the Villa Mirenda, Scandicci (Firenze), Lawrence
replied to "Mrs. Thayer," on April 29, 1927:

> I'm sending back the proofs of *The Man Who Loved
> Islands* and *More Modern Love* by this mail.—I don't think
> one wants the comma always after the ejaculatory Well! It's
> spoken all in a breath.
>
> As for the title, *Modern Love* is so famous as Meredith's
> poem-suite, it seems unfair to take it; besides, sounds too
> important. The story is too trivial for such a wholesale title.
> Best keep the *More:* or perhaps call it just: *In Love.*
> Perhaps with a query: *In Love?*
>
> But I leave the final choice to you & thanks for the
> suggestions[.]

And Lawrence signed his holograph letter with "Yours sincerely"; again he got his way with a minimum of fuss through
his businesslike tact. What the *Dial* had said to A. W. Barmby
is pretty obvious from its exchange with Lawrence. On May
16, 1927 the staff replied to his suggestions:

> Thank you very much for your letter, and for the proofs
> which we received to-day. We shall be careful to make only
> the corrections which you have indicated—not checking the
> tempo of your phrase by placing a comma after the ejaculatory
> Well!
>
> The title which you suggest—In Love?—seems to us
> exactly right, and we are happy to have your permission to
> use it.
>
> We are hoping to publish THE MAN WHO LOVED
> ISLANDS in the July Dial.

The transcript of this letter in the *Dial* papers refers to changes in "In Love?" but does not identify these changes, as proof sheets accompanied the *Dial*'s letter. In view of the *Dial*'s respect for an author's text, certainly all the changes were as minor as the punctuation change Lawrence was specifically asked about. Since all printed versions of "In Love?" differ radically from Lawrence's early manuscript (Ted 63–64), the *Dial*'s version is the earliest revision to see publication.

It was Lawrence who bestowed on the story its original title of "More Modern Love," in the full knowledge that the title for some readers would constitute a significant allusion to George Meredith's famous sonnet sequence; the ladies at the *Dial* wished to drop the "More" in his title. His suggestion that it be changed to "In Love?" was followed by the *Dial*, but the question mark was deleted from the title in all the subsequent book publications and in the bibliographies. According to Tedlock, if little delay occurred between composition and first publication, the date of the manuscript falls in 1927 (Ted 63). The date of acceptance by the *Dial* is March 26, 1927, when a check for one hundred and ten dollars was mailed to Curtis Brown, who had submitted the story. The various time lapses not only involving trans-Atlantic mail but the typing of Lawrence's holograph manuscript suggest a date of composition in the latter six months of 1926, rather than any time in 1927. Moreover, the fact that Lawrence extensively revised the story —so extensively that the version in the Frieda Lawrence collection is almost unrecognizable as the printed story—suggests a longer period of composition. As Tedlock suggests, the revisions are too extensive to have been made in typescript. Lawrence deprecated "In Love?" as trivial, but he thought enough of its quality to include it in the Knopf edition of *The Woman Who Rode Away and Other Stories* (Ted 63–64).

Alfred A. Knopf published *The Woman Who Rode Away and Other Stories* on May 24, 1928; such was the favor with which reviewers and public received it that a second printing was issued in June. Meanwhile, Lawrence was manufacturing the literary bombshell of his career; he detonated it in July 1928. *Lady Chatterley's Lover* is not a masterpiece, but then Lawrence did not wish to create a masterpiece. What he termed "my naughty book" he concocted to sell in such a way that he should gain the competence his work had hitherto denied him. In order that he might market it most beneficially for Frieda and himself, he wrote the kind of novel that would sell on his reputation as a writer who had in years past brought down on his head the righteous, the confiscatory wrath of British censorship. That is to say, Lawrence published *Lady Chatterley's Lover* privately, through his friend, the Florentine bookseller Pino Orioli, and they both negotiated sales of the book person to person, bookseller to bookseller. In order to distribute it profitably, they must tout *Lady Chatterley* not by advertising, which was too expensive and too subject to various censorships, but by word of mouth. The scheme worked. In August 1928, answering Alfred Stieglitz's cabled request for a copy, Lawrence crowed that *Lady C.* (as he called the book) seemed to have exploded like a bomb among most of his English friends, and they were still suffering from shell-shock (*CL* 1076). To ensure that precise effect, Lawrence had written three entire, separate versions; the third achieved the special effect of a kind of shell-shock. But even the first was unacceptable, although it had "hardly any fucks or shits, and no address to the penis, . . . hardly any of the root of the matter at all" (*CL* 1167). In fact, not until February 1932 did Knopf and Secker—too cautious to sponsor that mild first *Lady Chatterley* the author thought right for them—publish an expurgated edition; and not until April 1944 did the Dial Press bring out the first version of the novel. Lawrence's relationship with the *Dial* at the end of the 1920's, specifically his correspondence with the editor Marianne Moore, can only be understood in the context of the glaring crude notoriety he and his novel were receiving by the end of 1928—the newspaper stories, the pirated editions, the verbal ribaldry, the estrangement from more tender-minded acquaintances, and, most harassingly, the attentions of customs, police, and censors on both shores of the Atlantic.[11]

Lawrence's final contributions to the *Dial* were eleven

poems Marianne Moore selected from the author's own typescript of *Pansies*. "When I Went to the Circus" appeared in
the issue for May 1929, and a group of ten poems distinguished
the final issue of the magazine in July 1929. All eleven poems
were chosen at the same time by Miss Moore, apparently from
an early, unbowdlerized manuscript of *Pansies*, a different
version of which Knopf published as a book on September 27,
1929.[12]

Getting the manuscript of *Pansies* to Curtis Brown had
been so difficult that, for the nonce, Lawrence gave up the task.
He had sent two manuscripts of the projected volume to his
agent on January 7, 1929, only to have Scotland Yard intercept
and confiscate them. Later the police turned the manuscripts
over to Martin Secker with the recommendation—which he
accepted—that fourteen of the poems be omitted; but Lawrence
eventually won that particular struggle by later having the
complete volume privately printed (*CL* 1114–15). During January and February 1929, however, he was frantic over the
confiscation of his poems and, much as he hated typing, himself retyped the entire manuscript not so much to have another
copy in his possession as to use that second copy to evade the
proscriptions of authority. By February 9, 1929 Lawrence confided to the young Welsh novelist Rhys Davies that he had
retyped *nearly* all the *Pansies;* the chore was proving a fair
sweat, as he was bad at it (*CL* 1129). By February 11, the
typescript was complete, if sloppily executed. And this particular typescript of *Pansies* was uniquely valuable, for in retyp-
ing, as Lawrence informed Earl and Achsah Brewster, he had
made the poems "better," that is to say, he had revised the
poems in the two manuscripts appropriated by the British
police (Ted 112). England's loss was to prove America's gain.
Lawrence sent off his packet, not to Martin Secker or Curtis
Brown, both in London, both under the supervision of Scotland
Yard. Instead, he mailed it, with a covering letter, to Marianne
Moore at the *Dial*. He took no chance that the American
customs might be more lenient than their British counterparts
and sent his manuscript directly to Marianne Moore, *dame
pure et sans reproche.*

The correspondence about *Pansies* that passed between Lawrence and Miss Moore is illuminated by her prefatory remarks to the two letters he addressed to her, explaining what he was attempting to do in these late poems. Rivaling the manuscripts received by the *Dial*—wrote Marianne Moore in her memoir, *"The Dial:* A Retrospect"—were the letters from contributors, "indivisible as art in some instances from their authors' published work. The effect of vacuum silence and naturalness in a note or two from D. H. Lawrence belongs for me with Mabel Dodge Luhan's statement, ' "Inessentials" seemed deadly to him who knew how to savor a piece of crusty bread on the side of a hill.' " [13]

11 Feb 1929

> c/o Signor G. Orioli
> 6 Lungarno Corsini
> Florence Italy

Dear Marianne Moore

I should have liked to see you in New York—but how was I to know you would like to see me!—many people don't. . . . We are staying here in Bandol near Marseille a little longer, then going back to Italy—so will you write me there, if you get the poems. And many greetings.—

Regarding my statement about the Pensées: there are lines in the book, that are the outcome of certain hurts and I am not saying that in every case the lines themselves leave no shadow of hurt.

Lawrence's reference to not having seen Marianne Moore in New York has to do with his final stay there in the latter weeks of September 1925. She had already assumed her editorial post at the *Dial;* still acting editor, not yet editor, she nevertheless was in charge of operations. Meeting the Lawrences, charming them both as she surely would have with her calm, gentle directness, would have cemented more firmly the relationship of author and magazine. That the meeting never came to pass is due to Lawrence's admitted shyness at the prospect of a possible rebuff. Was he fearful that his quarrel with Mabel Luhan would affect his reception at the offices of the *Dial*? Did he suspect that Miss Moore shared the qualified view of his writing and his ideas expressed by Alyse Gregory in the pages of the *Dial* itself? One can only regret that this particular encounter never occurred.

The same day Lawrence wrote Marianne Moore, he also wrote Mabel Luhan. One gathers that she was living at the time in Croton-on-Hudson, her eastern headquarters; the letter is a deliberate piece of strategy in which Lawrence asked for help not in pleading with the *Dial* to publish *Pansies* but, rather, in keeping the news of publication from the gossips of Greenwich Village and the publishers' offices. For if it were broadcast that selections from *Pansies* would appear in the *Dial*, the censors and would-be censors would begin pestering him: "Today I have sent to Marianne Moore a copy of the *Pansies*. It hasn't got my name on, or anything, because the police started a fuss in London over *Lady C.* and even confiscated two MS. copies of the *Pansies*,—said they were obscene —a *lie*," he shrilled. He announced he was suing for the return of the manuscript copies: "But don't mention it in New York please, not to anybody, it'll only start the smut-hounds bellowing again. But do let me know if the *Pansies* arrive safely at the *Dial* office—perhaps they might have a typescript copy made, and charge it to me." When he chose to do so, Lawrence maneuvered superbly. Not the least flattering aspect of this submission of his poems was that Marianne Moore would read *Pansies* in the author's own typed copy even before Curtis Brown saw it; Lawrence told Mabel Luhan that he wanted Miss Moore to send the manuscript over to his agent, who would have to place it with a suitable publisher, either Viking (if Ben Huebsch decided to do the *Collected Poems* in New York) or, as second choice, Knopf (*CL* 1129). Thus without disturbing Miss Moore's conscience, he used the *Dial* to evade any possibly lurking censors.

Lawrence was being persecuted for the alleged obscenities of *Pansies* and *Lady Chatterley's Lover;* he was hysterical over the baying of the smut-hounds; and by 1929, he was a slowly dying man. He fought the official censors, but he could not fight the gossip and backbiting of New York and New Mexican bohemians any longer. He wanted to take Frieda back to Taos, he told Mabel Luhan, if only for the summer. But he wondered whether she thought it quite safe for him. Wouldn't somebody or other begin doing him dirt? And he asked her not to wait in New York longer than she wished; for, really, it was New Mexico he wanted to go to.

In due time the precious manuscript of *Pansies* arrived at the *Dial*, and by March 1929 Marianne Moore notified Lawrence that the magazine had decided to accept certain of the poems.

> Dear Mr. Lawrence:
> By reason of the delay of one and another, it is only now that we have found that we may have the following poems:
> WHEN I WENT TO THE CIRCUS
> TO LET GO OR TO HOLD ON
> THINGS MEN HAVE MADE
> WHATEVER MAN MAKES
> WORK
> NOVEMBER BY THE SEA
> SEAWEED
> WHAT WOULD YOU FIGHT FOR?
> LIZARDS
> CENSORS
> ATTILA
> Next week we shall send a cheque for one hundred and sixty dollars ($160) to Miss Rowe Wright of Curtis Brown. Although it precludes our sending you proofs of WHEN I WENT TO THE CIRCUS, we have embodied this poem in the May issue (withdrawing something to make room for it) and are asking your permission to regard the enclosed typescript as proof. There is not even time, however, for it to be returned to us and should anything be amiss, please cable at our expense. Dialpubco, New York is the address. If for instance there ought to be space before the line beginning, "The elephants," the one word "space" would be sufficient; and if you objected to the title's being set in capitals, the word "low" would indicate the change. If, however, by April 15th, we have not had a cablegram from you we shall know we may proceed without changes. The other poems we should, as we think, like to publish as a group in November; they would appear about the middle of October, but we could publish them sooner if it were to your interest that we should.
> We admire exceedingly the sentences:

> *Pensées*, like pansies, have their roots in the earth, and
> in the perfume there stirs still the faint grim scent of
> under-earth. Certainly in pansy-scent and in violet
> scent it is so: the blue of the morning mingled with the
> corrosive moulder of the ground.

> Should the Foreword not have been published before we have
> brought out this group, might you accord us the privilege
> of prefixing these two sentences to our group?
> One can hardly express the enjoyment given by poems
> in this book, as feeling and as form of expression, and that
> we should have for The Dial what we have selected, is an
> eager delight. I admit, there are lines in the book, that are
> the outcome of certain hurts, and am not saying that in every
> case the lines themselves leave no shadow of hurt; one asks
> for the high beauty that you conceive, inviolateness from
> reprisal. But taken as a whole, there is an infection of beauty.
> Wishing you always the best,
>
> > Yours sincerely,
> > Marianne Moore

On April 18 Lawrence replied. As he had missed the
deadline of April 15 set by Miss Moore, he fell in entirely with
her plans for the publication of the poems from *Pansies:*

> Dear Marianne Moore:
> I like the little group you chose—some of my favorites.
> . . . I think I shall withdraw that introduction from the
> book form—so you just keep any part of it you wish, & use
> it with your group of poems, as you wish. . . .
> I knew some of the poems would offend you. But then
> some part of life must offend you too, and even beauty has
> its thorns and its nettle-stings and its poppy-poison. Nothing
> is without offence, & nothing should be: if it is part of life,
> & not merely abstraction.
> We must stay in this island a while, but my address is
> best c/ G. Orioli.
>
> > All good wishes
> > D. H. Lawrence

Unfortunately, the plans laid by Miss Moore and agreed
to by Lawrence did not reach fruition, at least as she had hoped
they would. Through a combination of factors, the owners of

the *Dial* decided to close down their operation. Dr. James Sibley Watson, Jr., was absent from New York for months at a time, and Scofield Thayer was unable to be active in the affairs of the magazine. Moreover, as Miss Moore has written, "what had begun as a spontaneously delightful plotting in the interest of art and artists, was becoming mere faithfulness to responsibility." [14] The news of the closing of the *Dial* was painfully given out and as painfully received. On May 16, 1929 Marianne Moore suddenly had to inform Henry McBride, the writer of the "Modern Art" chronicle for the magazine and a reviewer for it as well, that she had had to permit the Corn Exchange Bank to acknowledge his galaxy of reviews for the department of "Briefer Mention," for responsibilities had not come singly or lightly to those at the *Dial:* "After the July issue, *The Dial* is to be discontinued; so with the exception of a briefer mention of the book of woodcuts"—McBride's review of Roger Avermaete's *La Gravure sur bois moderne de l'Occident*, printed in the final issue—"we must plan for nothing further. We are hoping that our decision to close will not be known in general until the formal announcement in the June issue. . . . I cannot say how much I wish that instead of sending you these doleful items I could be enquiring of you respecting a free afternoon when you could have tea with us." [15]

Thus without being forewarned, Lawrence read his poems in the issue for July 1929 and read also, in the final page of text, Sibley Watson's brief message of farewell. On the evidence of his letters, he seems not to have read the little notice in the June issue that announced the cessation of publication with the issue for July; no one seems to have sent him the news about the *Dial*, printed in the New York *Times* for Memorial Day 1929. The end of the *Dial* was the "Announcement," signed with Sibley Watson's initials, "S. W.," on the last page of the issue for July 1929:

> Nine and a half years is a rather long time for one management in the present journalistic mêlée. On the edge of quitting we want to express our immense gratitude to the distinguished

men and women who, with us, have edited and helped edit
THE DIAL since 1920. These are: Stewart Mitchell, Gilbert
Seldes, Alyse Gregory, Kenneth Burke, Marianne Moore. We
are also grateful to our readers, always bearing in mind that
although a magazine can get along somehow without readers
it cannot exist without contributors—who were, however
indignantly, THE DIAL.

From Baden where he was visiting his indomitable old
mother-in-law, Lawrence advised Pino Orioli, in a letter dated
July 29, 1929: "Don't bother to send on the *Dials*. By the way,
those are the last numbers, it is now dead" (*CL* 1170). Who
had broken the news? At any rate, Lawrence took it, to judge
by the tone and content of his letters, casually; his comment to
Orioli is not repeated elsewhere in the published letters.

The remaining seven months of his life he occupied rather
fully in venting his fury on the British and American censors,
chiefly the former—they closed down a showing of his pictures
early in the very month his poems appeared in the final *Dial*,
and as if that were not harassment enough, Martin Secker
acceded to Scotland Yard's censorship of *Pansies* and brought
out an "expurgated" edition.[16] The scandal of *Lady Chatterley*
aroused further rages as well as a scornful delight that this
deliberately shocking novel would achieve the popular success
that until now had eluded Lawrence. But in these letters there
is a sick frenzy, the more material analogue of which is Lawrence's mortal bout of consumption. To Brett and to Mabel
Luhan he wrote yearningly of Kiowa Ranch, he wanted to
return to it. His restlessness consumed his remaining strength;
and not until the fall of 1929 did the Lawrences settle down in
their rented Villa Beau Soleil at Bandol on the French Riviera.
At the last, afflicted with what Aldous Huxley has termed a
terrible sadness, Lawrence submitted and went into the sanatorium Ad Astra. He wrote letters, made plans, posed for Jo
Davidson's bust of him, discontentedly moved on March 1,
1930 out of Ad Astra into the Villa Robermond—and died the
next day.

5

LAWRENCE'S FICTION IN
THE DIAL

L AWRENCE'S APPEARANCES IN the *Dial* seemed to make
his writing more attractive to other American magazines
than hitherto had been the case. From September 1920, when
his first work in the *Dial* appeared, until July 1929, the magazine's last issue, nineteen other American magazines published
his poems, stories, and essays.[1] The *Dial*, however, remained
his major periodical publisher; of contributions to American
magazines from September 1920 until July 1929, thirty of
seventy-nine titles of all his works published in American periodicals during that period, appeared in the *Dial*. For Lawrence's fiction the statistics are much more significant. Of
twelve stories and novels Lawrence published in American periodicals in the 1920's, eight appeared, in whole or in part, in
the *Dial*.

These figures do not adequately indicate the importance
of Lawrence's work in the *Dial*. No other magazine published
it in such variety; the various kinds of fiction—a translation, a
novella, a novel, and short stories—that appeared in those
pages provide a representative sampling of Lawrence's gift for
various kinds of writing within a major genre. Moreover, the
fact that both Lawrence's comparatively early fiction and his
late, mature fiction are contained in the *Dial* permits readers of
the magazine to trace the viability of his art and *Weltan-*

Georges Schreiber   *Frieda Lawrence*

Gaston Lachaise   *Scofield Thayer* (above)

Gaston Lachaise   *Gilbert Seldes* (upper left)

Gaston Lachaise   *James Sibley Watson, Jr.* (lower left)

Jan Juta   *D. H. Lawrence*

Marguerite Zorach   *Portrait of Marianne Moore*

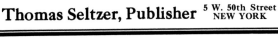
The Dial   March 1923

Chac-Mool (above)

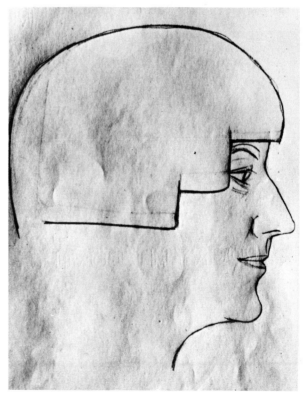

Attributed to Witter Bynner   *Mabel Dodge Luhan*

John Richardson   *D. H. Lawrence in Taos*

schauung. Finally, although Lawrence considered himself to be primarily a novelist and perhaps best expressed his themes in his fiction, the ideas he treated artistically in his novels and tales he stated explicitly and developed prosaically in his essays, so that one may profitably compare his fiction in the *Dial* with his work in other genres.

Lawrence's fiction in the *Dial* divides rather neatly into two distinct groups. Three works of the early 1920's were completed at nearly the same time. *Aaron's Rod* was completed in May 1921 (*CL* 655), and both *The Fox*, an earlier draft of which Lawrence had written in November 1918 (*CL* 566), and "The Gentleman from San Francisco" were completed in November 1921. The five later short stories were all published in *The Woman Who Rode Away* in May 1928.[2] Except for the title story, which Lawrence wrote at Taos in June–September 1924, the stories from the volume that earlier appeared in the *Dial* were written from December 1925 until autumn or winter 1926, while the Lawrences lived in Italy, at first at the Villa Bernarda at Spotorno and later at the Villa Mirenda at Scandicci, or while they traveled in Germany and, for the last time, in England and Scotland.[3]

Among the earlier group, "The Gentleman from San Francisco" would naturally seem to be the least characteristic of Lawrence's work, since he had merely, as he asserted, "rubbed up into readable English" Koteliansky's translation from the Russian of Ivan Bunin. Yet the story reflects perhaps what Lawrence himself would have written about rich Americans traveling in Europe. In his letter to Scofield Thayer recommending "The Gentleman from San Francisco," Lawrence remarked that the story was "extraordinarily *it*" as a "presentation of the unpleasant side" of traveling to Naples and Capri.[4] If only because "The Gentleman from San Francisco" exhibited to readers of the *Dial* a novel aspect of Lawrence's astonishing literary talents—quite unknown to American readers in 1922— the story, merely as translation, merits inspection in the context of its first appearance.

Stylistically, Lawrence's translation brings to the short

story an economy of phrasing and aptness of description. Some of the phrases that sound as if Lawrence might have written them are actually Bunin's conception; the description of Italy —"sweetly smells the earth in Italy after rain, and each of her islands has its own peculiar aroma"—recalls *Twilight in Italy*, but is actually the description as Bunin conceived it. Even such a phrase as "beatific love-tortures" (*G* 60), which sounds peculiarly Lawrentian, is Bunin's conception, otherwise translated as "blissful torment." [5]

"The Gentleman from San Francisco" resembles another story published in the *Dial*, Thomas Mann's "Death in Venice," and exemplifies an abiding editorial interest in highly colored but startlingly realistic stories about travel, especially in exotic places.[6] This same interest accounts in part for the *Dial*'s eager efforts, two years later, to publish Lawrence's essays about New Mexico. Like all the work in the *Dial*, however, the travel stories and essays were literary excursions and never pedestrian descriptions. In both "Death in Venice" and "The Gentleman from San Francisco," a wealthy man—in one story an artist, in the other a businessman—visits a warm, sunny climate; each protagonist finds the locale mysteriously ominous and feels strange things happening to him; and there, each finally dies. Mann and Bunin resemble each other also in technique: both evoke an atmosphere of impending doom by masterful descriptions of characters and landscape, and both understate the action to counterpoint their themes. The similarities of these two stories suggest that it was not only because of Lawrence's skill as a translator that the *Dial* purchased "The Gentleman from San Francisco"—even though Lawrence's ability convinced Thayer of its value—but also because of Thayer's admiration for the Russian and European masters' mastery of mood and characterization. At the same time, the publication of both stories in the *Dial* attests to the similarity of Lawrence's and Thayer's critical and aesthetic judgments.

The second work of fiction by Lawrence that appeared in the *Dial* was chapter 14 of *Aaron's Rod*. From the chapter the editors chose only eighteen paragraphs that describe a Fascist street demonstration, a part that is essentially a digression from the action of the novel.[7] The editors of the *Dial* thus avoided publishing those works by Lawrence that deal with themes of leadership and power, themes that were to occupy him for the next six years and find their voice in *Aaron's Rod*, *Kangaroo*, and *The Plumed Serpent*. Not until 1928 did Lawrence admit that "the leader of men is a back number" and "the leader-cum-follower relationship is a bore" and return to write of more private personal relationships.[8] The *Dial* did not publish any of *Kangaroo* or *The Plumed Serpent*, although it once considered publishing *Kangaroo* and reviewed both novels. The only one of Lawrence's stories in the *Dial* that reveals to some degree the themes of male comradeship and leadership is "The Woman Who Rode Away," which critics generally recognize as a short study for *The Plumed Serpent*, and in which the main character, Kate Leslie, is modeled after Mabel Dodge Luhan.[9]

In the issue for February 1922 the *Dial* not only published part of *Aaron's Rod* but also included information about the novel in its "Notes on Contributors." The first notice on the second cover of that issue recorded, "The observer in An Episode, by D. H. Lawrence, is the same Aaron who is the principal character of Mr Lawrence's next novel, *Aaron's Rod*, which has been announced for publication this winter." Although the publication in the *Dial* of part of chapter 14 and the accompanying "Notes on Contributors" helped to publicize the entire book, the *Dial* excerpted a portion of the novel that does not reveal the main action, the struggle of Aaron Sisson to learn from Lilly about submission to power. Doubtless the editors of the magazine recalled the suppression of Lawrence's two earlier novels, *The Rainbow* and *Women in Love*, and did not want to publish any part of *Aaron's Rod* that might lead to trouble with the censors.[10]

The *Dial*'s choice was a safe if not a happy one. Although chapter 14 of *Aaron's Rod* is one of the central chapters of the novel it is also one of the weakest and neither advances the relationship of Aaron and Lilly nor reveals any internal charac-

terization of Aaron. As the chapter opens, Aaron leaves Novara
and arrives in Milan in his pursuit of Lilly. In his hotel room
he hears noises from the street below and steps out onto his
balcony. He sees a crowd approach; as they near each building,
the flag on the building is taken down by someone inside. From
an untenanted building, a single flag waves and a young man,
cheered on by the crowd, precariously climbs onto a narrow
coping three stories from the street to haul down this last
banner. Suddenly soldiers appear; most of the crowd disperses,
calling epithets over their shoulders; and the young man is
ordered down and taken prisoner. Watching from another
balcony of the hotel are two young aesthetes whom Aaron
meets that evening at dinner. When he reveals that he is going
to Venice to see Lilly, the new friends advise him that Lilly is
in Germany and persuade him to go with them to Florence, for
a milder winter climate.

The part of the chapter that appeared in the *Dial* lends
itself naturally to publication as a self-contained excerpt. Even
the title which was used, "An Episode," is suggested by Lawrence's closing sentence of the section describing the incident,
"the scene was ended" (*AR* 183). The episode begins as Aaron
hears the crowd in the street beneath his hotel room window
and ends as the soldiers march away with the youth who
removed the flag. Within the incident are descriptions of the
crowd that reveal Lawrence's new interest in male comradeship and leadership, but they fit so naturally in a description of
any crowd that they pass unnoticed to a reader unfamiliar with
Lawrence's themes. The crowd, for example, consists only of
men who have "a demon-like fixed purpose and sharp will"
(*AR* 179). The descriptions of people and landscape in *Aaron's Rod* match Lawrence's depictions in the travel books,
Twilight in Italy and *Sea and Sardinia;* in "An Episode" Lawrence's felicitous phrases give life to the mob. As Aaron looks
down from his balcony, he sees "the packed black shoulders of
the mob below" and "the curious clustering pattern of a sea of
black hats . . . uneasily moving like boiling pitch" (*AR* 180).
When the soldiers appear, the crowd, "like drops of water . . .

seemed to fly up at the very walls themselves . . . on to window ledges, and then jumped down again and ran: clambering, wiggling, darting, running in every direction; some cut, blood on their faces, terror or frenzy of flight in their hearts" (*AR* 182). Thayer's admiration for Lawrence's travel books may account for the *Dial*'s publishing this descriptive portion of *Aaron's Rod*, as much as do the magazine's efforts to avoid censorship by selecting innocuous passages. Wrenched as this excerpted chapter is out of its context, what its reader misses is the symbolic significance of the crowd in relation to Lawrence's thesis.

The last work of Lawrence's early fiction to appear in the *Dial*, *The Fox*, is not concerned with the themes of *Aaron's Rod*, *Kangaroo*, or *The Plumed Serpent*, but with those of the earlier novels, *The Rainbow*, *The Lost Girl*, and *Women in Love*. The theme of personal relationships is embodied in the action of *The Fox;* a young man must destroy a young woman's Lesbian attachment in order to make her his lover and wife. Like the other earlier novels, *The Fox* has a symboliste quality that endows it with a unity that the novels about leadership lack. The symbol of the fox represents, as Eugene Goodheart in his study of Lawrence points out, "natural sexual vitalities." [11] It operates as a constant reminder of those vitalities on the consciousness of one of the characters and serves as a continuous unifying force for both the action and theme of the short novel.

Various critics have pointed out that *The Fox* is representative of all of Lawrence's fiction.[12] Equally important, however, is the way in which this short novel, with its psychological framework, is representative of the interest of the *Dial* in the new psychology and its application to the arts. The action of the novella fluctuates between the level of reality and the level of dreams. March dreams twice about the fox and subconsciously identifies Henry Grenfel with the animal. The subliminal action of the dreams is analogous to the action that occurs in reality. In the second dream, for example, March imagines that Banford has been killed and her corpse wrapped in the skin of the fox; in reality Henry, the fox in her dreams, manages to kill Banford and accomplish March's subconscious wish. The interplay of symbol and fact provides richness and complexity as it alternates between the two levels of existence and meaning in the novella.

Lawrence was of course far from being the only writer of the 1920's to become interested in Freudian and Jungian theories about dreams, personality, and the levels of consciousness. Nor was he the only writer of fiction published by the *Dial* to explore such theories in his stories and novels. The magazine was one of the first and one of the few to publish part of Proust's *Remembrance of Things Past;* in the issue for October 1920 appeared an anonymous English translation of "Saint Loup: A Portrait." Incidentally, the *Dial*'s records indicate that Ezra Pound sent the sketch to the magazine; since the *Dial*'s translation is different from the standard translation by C. K. Scott Moncrief, it thus appears to be the work of Pound and the only source for Pound's translation.[13] Moreover, this attribution constitutes a significant addition to the Pound canon.

Two other great European masters of psychological fiction regularly appeared in the *Dial*. One was the Viennese playwright and novelist, Arthur Schnitzler, who—like Lawrence—was one of the relatively few contributors to have a long work serialized in the magazine. Thayer called him one of the two or three greatest writers then living.[14] Schnitzler's short novel *Doctor Graesler* ran in five issues from July through November 1922.[15] In addition, his stories were frequently featured; for example, "The New Song" appeared in the issue for November 1925, only three issues after the publication of another of his stories, "Lieutenant Gustl," in the issue for August 1925.[16] Thomas Mann was another *Dial* contributor who excelled in portraying the machinations of his characters' subconscious. In addition to eight "German Letters" which appeared a little oftener than annually from December 1922 through July 1928, Mann's "Death in Venice," "Disorder and Early Sorrow," "Loulou", and *Tristran* appeared in issues as early as April 1921 and as late as November 1926.[17]

All of these contributors, as well as others such as Maxim Gorki, Sherwood Anderson, Jean Giraudoux, and Alice B. Parsons, shared with Thayer and many other intellectuals of the 1920's a keen interest in psychology and its application to the arts. The *Dial*, by publishing the work of these writers, reflects both its own interests and the interests and tastes of the decade. In his editorial "Comment" for March 1921, Thayer revealed that he had inquired of Freud whether the psychoanalysis of artists impoverished or enriched their work. He quoted Freud's reply: "Our experience, although not very rich in the analysis of painters and poets, has regularly brought out the fact that these artists are through analysis helped in their work." [18] And in February 1923 the *Dial* actually acquired a long thirty-page article by Freud; but Kenneth Burke, who was given the task of translating the essay from the German, persuaded Thayer that the essay was too technical for the *Dial*.[19]

To be sure not all of the writers published in the *Dial* were disciples of Freud or Jung. Some may never have read any books by the two great leaders who established the new science, or perhaps—like Lawrence—they rejected Freud because he tended to reduce human actions to axioms of science. Nevertheless, writers of the 1920's, recalcitrantly or willingly, were caught up in one of the dominant forces of the century; they could no more escape Freud than they could ignore the First World War. Many of the younger writers recognized that the principles of Freud elucidated and objectified the very phenomena that literature sought to convey subjectively. In effect Freud seemed to offer an empirical verification for the motives and action of the characters they created, and his theories furnished a new and objective framework for the explication of their art. More importantly, this new psychology complemented and expanded the dominant tone of enlightened emancipation in the 1920's, the tone for which the *Dial* became a landmark and for which the name Lawrence became a synonym.

The publication of the last installment of *The Fox* in the *Dial* for August 1922 marked the end of Lawrence's fiction from the early part of his career that appeared in the magazine. The publication of "The Woman Who Rode Away" in the *Dial* for July 1925 introduced the short stories from the last volume of stories that Lawrence was to write. During the intervening years, when no fiction by Lawrence appeared in the magazine, Lawrence visited America and Mexico, an experience that suggested new landscapes and new themes for his fiction. Also during this period his fortunes improved, as his new novels appeared, as the older ones found a new market when the ban on them was lifted, and as more American journals began to publish his shorter works. The fiction that appeared shortly after these years reflects a more mystical Lawrence, and the shorter fiction especially reveals a writer of keener satire, although Lawrence had tried his hand at satire as early as 1916, when he was writing *Women in Love*. Lawrence's works after the visit to America and Mexico also show that he was returning to his old fascination with personal relationships and was abandoning, at least in some of the shorter works, the themes of leadership and power. Henry McBride's review of *The Woman Who Rode Away and Other Stories* in the *Dial* for August 1928 suggests that Lawrence's later short stories are not essentially different in subject matter from his early work, but technically they are distinctively different—keener, more brittle, more incisive, more assured—as the stories published in the *Dial* reveal.

The only story in the *Dial* that relates directly to Lawrence's American experience is "The Woman Who Rode Away." The setting of the story is Mexico, the main character is modeled after Mabel Luhan, and the point of view satirizes rather viciously her adoration of Indian cultures. Yet the story has a purpose much more significant than the caricature of Mabel Luhan. It expresses some of the views about civilizations and races which Lawrence held and which are central to an understanding of his work of this period. The action of the narrative is scanty but heavy with ulterior meaning: a woman who lives on a remote Mexican ranch quests after new adventure and goes alone to a tribe of "Aztec" Indians who take her, not against her will, as a sacrifice. The Indians live in a valley hidden behind almost impassable mountains and they believe that the woman's deliberate entrance is a sign that white men will return to them the power they have taken away.

In "The Woman Who Rode Away" Lawrence embodies two myths about the sun. In an essay, "New Mexico," which he wrote in 1928, Lawrence accepts the Aztec myth that men sacrificed their hearts to the sun in order to become "undauntedly religious" (*Ph* 142–43). In an earlier essay, *Fantasia of the Unconscious*, Lawrence advances as a "clue to the cosmos" his own theory about the sun's dependence on life below: "Instead of life being drawn from the sun, it is the emanation from life itself, that is, from all the living plants and creatures which nourish the sun" (*FU* 56–57). Fascinating as these theories are, for the *Dial* they possessed a greater relevance for the magazine's interest in the primitive.

In the last part of the story Lawrence develops the Aztec myth and his own concept of the sun as drawing energy from life below. An Indian explains that white people do not understand the significance of the moon and the sun which once belonged to the Indians but which now white men have. "We know the sun, and we know the moon. And we say, when a white woman sacrifice herself to our gods, then our gods will begin to make the world again, and the white men's gods will fall to pieces" (*CSS* 570). Because the Indians have lost their power with the sun, the white men have stolen it. When the woman is sacrificed to the sun, "the sun will leap over the white man and come to the Indian again" (*CSS* 575). The woman consciously wants to become the sacrifice that will restore the Indians' gods. After elaborate ritual preparations, she is led on the shortest day of the year to a cave, veiled behind a hanging shaft of ice from a pinnacle above. She is stretched out on the platform of the cave, as on an altar, and virile, naked priests, holding knives, surround her. The woman understands that at sunset the oldest priest will "strike home, accomplish the sacrifice, and achieve the power" (*CSS* 581). On the birthday of the solar heroes of classical mythology the Indians' sacrifice woos the life-giving energy of the sun to their lost, dead tribe.

"The Woman Who Rode Away" is similar to the other

short stories by Lawrence published in the *Dial*. "The Man
Who Loved Islands" has affinities for "The Woman Who
Rode Away," for although the motives of Cathcart in that story
are different from those of Mrs. Lederman, he, too, is bent on
nihilism and self-destruction. Both characters desire to escape
civilization, the woman ostensibly to find a purer religion, the
man to create and rule a utopian manor. In "The Man Who
Loved Islands" the progression of the self-annihilation which
the main character inflicts is systematic and discernible,
whereas in "The Woman Who Rode Away," the self-destruction of the protagonist seems immediate and unconvincingly
motivated. Both stories have about them the atmosphere of
fable, but in "The Man Who Loved Islands" the structure of
the story is more appropriate to the fabular genre, as Cathcart
moves successively to three islands, each smaller and more
remote than the one before.

The three islands provide a narrative framework for the
story; at the same time they function, in Eliseo Vivas's term, as
a "constitutive symbol" of the entire story, "a symbol whose
referend cannot be fully exhausted by explication, because that
to which it refers is symbolized not merely *through* it, but *in* it
. . . unlike the metaphor where tenor and vehicle are appre-
hended independently." [20] Each of the three islands works to
diminish and finally to destroy the protagonist: on the first
island his servants and the forces of nature work to destroy him
economically; on the second island an unsatisfactory sexual
experience diminishes him; and on the third island, where he
has completely withdrawn from civilization, three winter
storms complete the destruction.

In addition to the dominant symbolic framework Lawrence employs another symbol. On the third island a bird with
three dots on its feathers appears at the islander's cabin "as if
he had some mission there" (*CSS* 741). The islander wonders
"why this bit of trimming on the bird out of the far, cold seas"
(*CSS* 741) and fails to see it as an omen that three snowstorms
are approaching and that the third island will be his last.

The sequence dealing with the middle island contains the

most significant action and reveals the most typically Lawrentian situation. There Cathcart succumbs to "the automation of
sex" that drives him away from civilization to his destruction
on the third island. A servant girl wills herself to be Cathcart's
mistress, and, completely without desire, he undergoes a pas-
sionless experience with the girl. By submitting to the girl's
will, Cathcart violates his integrity; unlike the girl, he believes
that sex is "one of the great life-mysteries" (*CSS* 737). After
accepting sex in a mechanical, desireless fashion, he experiences a personal disintegration, the worst state imaginable for
Lawrence: "If we lose desire out of our life, we become empty
vessels. But if we break our own integrity, we become a
squalid mess, like a jar of honey dropped and smashed" (*RDP*
177).

One critic, Frederick R. Karl, suggests that "The Man
Who Loved Islands" is "Lawrence's classic statement of what
has gone wrong with civilized man in the twentieth century."
Cathcart is to be compared to Egbert, a character in another of
Lawrence's short stories, "England, My England." Each char-
acter "lacks Soul, the Female part that would complete him. It
is not enough for Lawrence that Cathcart does not hurt anyone
else; his type of passivity destroys the individual himself." Like
The Fox, "The Man Who Loved Islands" is a "true microcosm
of [Lawrence's] work, an epitaph on *The Rainbow*, *Women in
Love*, *The Plumed Serpent*, and a forerunner of *Lady Chatterley's Lover*, whose ideas it almost entirely encompasses."
Finally, Karl compares "The Man Who Loved Islands" to
Eliot's *The Waste Land* and "The Love Song of J. Alfred
Prufrock." Like Eliot, Lawrence strikes "to the heart of the
twentieth-century malaise, with Cathcart a kind of Prufrock
with money and position, but perhaps even less resolution." [21]

For the *Dial* the situation of Cathcart was typical, not
only generally for the twentieth century, but specifically for
members of the magazine's own staff and contributors. It was
not merely a condition of passivity, as Karl asserts, but a
necessary and active withdrawal from society that constituted
their dilemma. For Thayer all artists were in effect "marooned

individuals" like Cathcart. In his editorial "Announcement" of
the Dial Award for 1924 to Marianne Moore, Thayer wrote
that "the Imaginative Individual . . . is in our world always
the Marooned Individual . . . these have their being forever in
isolation, for ever shut and cut off." He admired the "admoni-
tory ascetisms" of Miss Moore.[22] His comments about Miss
Moore were echoed in his description of Army Lowell in his
editorial "Comment" for July 1925, six issues later: Miss Lowell was hailed as "cosmopolitan yet isolated." [23]

The paradox for Thayer was one that Lawrence presents
in "The Man Who Loved Islands": the necessity for the artist
to withdraw from society and his need at the same time to belong to a human community. Like Cathcart, the sensitive individual with idealistic goals, Thayer failed to strike a balance
between two worlds. Driven to his inward creative island by
the forces of his imaginative powers, he was ultimately marooned there.

Another story by Lawrence in the *Dial*, "Two Blue
Birds," is similar in at least one respect to "The Man Who
Loved Islands." A main character in each story is modeled
after Compton Mackenzie, who admired Lawrence's work and
persuaded Martin Secker to publish it.[24] In "The Man Who
Loved Islands" apparently only the title of the story suggests a
connection with Mackenzie, athough the inspiration for the
entire story may have come from a visit Lawrence made to a
villa in which Faith Mackenzie was living in February 1926.
Harry T. Moore records that when Lawrence called at the
villa, Mrs. Mackenzie told him that her husband was away on
a channel island he had rented. Soon after that conversation,
"The Man Who Loved Islands" appeared.[25] It was this coincidence that caused Mackenzie to take offense at the story and to
threaten a lawsuit if it were included in the English edition of
The Woman Who Rode Away. As for "Two Blue Birds," it is
difficult to determine whether Mackenzie recognized himself as
a male character, although the story deals rather pointedly
with a popular English novelist. Harry T. Moore quotes from a
letter Lawrence wrote to Mabel Luhan that "Compton Mac-

kenzie, after swallowing one story in which he appeared as a character, was mortally offended by another more recent one in which I used him" and identifies the other story as "Two Blue Birds." [26] In another study of Lawrence, however, Moore indicates that the Mackenzies were displeased by both stories. [27]

The satirical quality is evident throughout the narrative. There is a triangle of characters, as in *The Fox*, but the characters in "Two Blue Birds"—Mr. and Mrs. Gee and Miss Wrexall—are comically presented. A popular novelist, debt-ridden, is married to an extravagant wife, who is usually away in some romantic spot carrying on a "gallant affair" while her husband is cared for by a charming if spinsterish secretary and her family. Although Mrs. Gee does not desire her husband, she cannot enjoy other lovers as long as Miss Wrexall tends to her husband; paradoxically she wishes that Mr. Gee and his secretary were having an affair, but both of them are too sexless for that; comically she envisions the whole sterile relationship in sexual terms—the "dictating business" is "ten hours a day intercourse" (*CSS* 515). The central incident in the story is a verbal battle between the two women, after which Mrs. Gee stalks off, asserting that her husband has no room for "two blue-birds of happiness to flutter round his feet" (*CSS* 527).

Lawrence is of course designedly unjust to the domestic details of the Mackenzies' lives. In a letter to Harry T. Moore, Compton Mackenzie commented that Lawrence "had a trick of describing a person's setting or background vividly, and then putting into the setting an ectoplasm of his own creation" and that those who knew his victims recognized the stories to be falsifications. [28] Even if Lawrence has not followed with a biographer's fidelity the situations and events in Mackenzie's life, the satire directed at him is sufficiently bitter. Mr. Gee in "Two Blue Birds" is vain because "women made him so" (*CSS* 514). When his wife inquires about an afternoon's work at writing, he admits, "It was a piece of pure flummery. But it's what they want. Awful rot, wasn't it, Miss Wrexall?" (*CSS* 525). This surely is Lawrence's fling at the facility and popularity of Mackenzie's fiction. The crowning blow comes appropriately from Mrs. Gee, who says she has "suspected for a long time" that the secretary must write a good deal of her husband's books from his hints (*CSS* 525).

That the *Dial* identified the novelist being parodied as Compton Mackenzie is conjectural, but it is significant that both of Lawrence's stories burlesquing Mackenzie, "The Man Who Loved Islands" and "Two Blue Birds," were printed in the magazine. Furthermore, a glance at the reviews in the *Dial* of Mackenzie's work reveals the magazine's gradual disenchantment with his novels. The last essay which Thayer wrote for Martyn Johnson's *Dial* was "Compton Mackenzie," in the issue for November 30, 1918. Running for seven double-column pages, it was the longest essay Thayer ever wrote for the magazine except for a serialized tribute to Marianne Moore on the occasion of the 1924 *Dial* Award to her, which appeared in his "Comment" for the issues from January to April 1925.[29] In surveying Mackenzie's work he praised "the yet sprouting body of this world of Compton Mackenzie . . . so indubitably alive." Thayer liked especially Mackenzie's view of existence, for "in the past there is no vulgar and in the past there is no real," and his technique of presentation: "that sea haze which is almost poetry absorbs and obliterates all." [30]

Eighteen months later in Thayer's new monthly *Dial* for May 1920, Gilbert Seldes reviewed Mackenzie's *Poor Relations*. He entitled his review "Mr Mackenzie's Jest" and concluded, "It would be easier to think lightly of Mr Mackenzie's failure if one did not remember what Henry James said of him. Remembering that, . . . the brief story of Mr Mackenzie's career takes on some of the proportions of tragedy." [31] Finally, in the issue for January 1921 appeared a review of Mackenzie's *The Vanity Girl* in the "Briefer Mention" section of the magazine. The reviewer—probably Thayer himself—expressed the final judgment of the *Dial* about Mackenzie. "What was gracious in Mr Mackenzie has yielded to what is smart, and his new novel is as utterly captivating as the Gaiety Girl he writes about can be on stage. Unfortunately, in reading a book, one is not protected by the footlights and one has the sensation of

being asked to chop down the trees in the second act
backdrop." [32]

If the *Dial*'s staff were aware that Lawrence was writing
about Mackenzie, they must have been delighted when Lawrence had his main character admit his work was "awful rot"
(*CSS* 525). Beyond its value as a satirical sketch of Mackenzie, the story is important for the view it affords of a modern,
sophisticated marriage.

Mrs. Gee, for example, is the kind of woman Lawrence
writes about in *Fantasia of the Unconscious*. "The passions or
desires which are thought-born are deadly," Lawrence asserts,
and to "teach a woman to act from an idea" is to "destroy her
womanhood forever" (*FU* 121). Similarly, in another essay,
Lawrence condemns the "gallant affairs" of people like Mrs.
Gee: "All this horrid scramble of love affairs and prostitution
is only part of the freak, bravado, and *doing it on purpose*. And
bravado and *doing it on purpose* is just as unpleasant and
hateful as repression, just as much a sign of secret fear" (*AA*
119–20).

In another story which the *Dial* published, Lawrence explores, again satirically, the relations of a couple about to be
married. Unlike Mrs. Gee, who has been left numb by too
many experiences, the girl of "In Love?" is afraid to submit to
her fiancé. The setting of "In Love?" is a farm her Joe has
bought as their first home, and the action occurs one night
when the girl, Hester, goes to the farm to spend the weekend.
From the beginning the reader is aware that Hester is upset; he
soon learns that she is distraught at discovering that Joe has
suddenly "made the wretched mistake of falling 'in love' with
her." Before their engagement "there would never have been
anything messy to fear from him," but "once he started cud-
dling and petting, she couldn't stand him" (*CSS* 649). That
night at the farm, she resists his advances by asking him to
play the piano and then sneaking outdoors. When Hester's
younger sister unexpectedly stops by, Joe becomes angry and
forces a confrontation. The sisters denounce his love-play, he
confesses that he did it because it was expected of him, and the

couple effect a reconciliation. After that Hester detects for the first time in her fiancé "the honest, patient love for her in his eyes, and the queer, quiet central desire" and submits to him (*CSS* 659–60).

Although "In Love?" is a light satirical piece, in it Lawrence seems to be offering a genuine description of modern affairs as he observed them. The title Lawrence originally gave his story, "More Modern Love," focuses better perhaps on its function of describing a fairly typical courtship of the 1920's. The tale develops artistically the situation Lawrence described in an essay written in 1929, entitled "Men Must Work and Women As Well."

> The young today have the fastidiousness, the nicety, the revulsion from the physical, intensified. To the girl of today, a man whose physical presence she is aware of, especially a bit *heavily* aware of, is or becomes really abhorrent. She wants to fly away from him to the uttermost ends of the earth. And as soon as women or girls get a bit female physically, young men's nerves go all to pieces. The sexes can't stand one another. . . .
>
> And this means, when we analyze it out, repulsion. The young are, in a subtle way, physically repulsive to one another, the girl to the man and the man to the girl. And they rather enjoy the feeling of repulsion, it is a sort of contest. It is as if the young girl said to the man to-day: I rather like you, you know. You are so thrillingly repulsive to me.—And as if the young man replied: Same here!   (*AA* 165–66)

The couple in the essay are identical to Hester and Joe in "In Love?" Hester asserts that "Nothing is so awful as a man who has fallen in love," Joe replies, "anyhow, you're mistaken . . . I'm not in love with you, Miss Clever," and Lawrence comments, "they knew each other so well" (*CSS* 657–59). After expressing their mutual hatred for each other, the couple decide that perhaps they are indeed "in love." It seems that Lawrence, accurately observing modern love and its paradoxes, discovered and wrote about the doctrine of "cool" almost forty years before it had a name.

"In Love?" and "Two Blue Birds" are the only two light comic stories in *The Woman Who Rode Away*. They present better than many of Lawrence's longer, serious stories, an accurate picture of modern love and marriage, and their publication in the *Dial* makes the magazine more important as a representative and eclectic source for Lawrence's work. Furthermore, both of these tales by Lawrence belong with a group of stories in the *Dial* that portray modern love, courtship, and sexual experiences. Although such stories strike many readers as being amusingly "period" in the 1970's, they are precisely the "advanced" fiction that gave the *Dial* its reputation, in the 1920's, of publishing what was explicit and rather daring—*pas pour les enfants*.

Three notable examples of such stories, other than those by Lawrence, are Sherwood Anderson's *Many Marriages*, which the *Dial* serialized in the issues from October 1922 through March 1923, Virginia Woolf's "Miss Ormerod" in December 1924, and Alice Beal Parsons' "Love at 42 Altgeld Avenue" in September 1925.[33] Irving Howe has devoted an entire chapter in his study of Anderson to analyzing the influence of Lawrence on Anderson. By comparison, according to Howe, Anderson is a failure; putting *Many Marriages* beside Lawrence's *The Rainbow* or *Women in Love* is "like a bad joke, a beating of failure with the nailed stick of genius."[34] Nevertheless, the fact that other writers in the *Dial* were influenced by Lawrence suggests both the degree to which Lawrence exemplifies the tastes of the magazine and his value as a contributor.

Alice B. Parsons' story, "Love at 42 Altgeld Avenue," is uniquely reminiscent of Lawrence's "In Love?" A girl who is not really attracted to her male friend decides to accept his appeals to romance. Like *The Fox* and "In Love?" the Parsons story ends tenuously; the girl merely decides "without knowing where it would lead her . . . to let herself be caught up into life." "Love at 42 Altgeld Avenue" also has a supernatural touch, faintly reminiscent of "Glad Ghosts": the young man takes his girl to a "spiritualist meeting" to ascertain whether another girl, now dead, whom he had once thought of marrying, would approve of his new friend.

Finally, Virginia Woolf's "Miss Ormerod" suggests at

least in part the kind of sophisticated, offbeat fiction dealing
with love and sex for which the *Dial* was famous. The story is
a fictional biography of an English entomologist, Eleanor Ormerod, whose life Mrs. Woolf traces with keen and idiosyncratic irony. One passage especially reveals the perverted psy-
chosexual aspect of the chief character:

> Ah, but Eleanor, the Bot and Hessian have more power
> over you than Mr. Edward Ormerod [her husband]. Under
> the microscope you clearly perceive that these insects have
> organs, orifices, excrement; they do most emphatically, copu-
> late. . . . Never did her features show more sublime than
> when lit up by the candour of her avowal. "This is excrement;
> these, though Ritzema Bos is positive to the contrary, are the
> generative organs of the male. I've proved it." Upon her head
> the hood of Edinburgh most fitly descended; pioneer of purity
> even more than of Paris Green.

It is interesting to note that Clive Bell in an essay, "Virginia
Woolf," which immediately preceded "Miss Ormerod," compared Mrs. Woolf's style to Lawrence's and found that Lawrence's prose, "though it is sometimes witty besides being fan-
tastically humorous, is never, or rarely, pointed." [35] Three
years later five stories by Lawrence in the *Dial*—"The Man
Who Loved Islands" and "Two Blue Birds" satirizing Compton Mackenzie, "The Woman Who Rode Away" burlesquing
Mabel Luhan, "Glad Ghosts" poking fun at Herbert and Cynthia Asquith, and "In Love?" satirizing the typical young lovers of the decade—were to prove Clive Bell wrong. One wonders further whether Lawrence clipped Bell's comment for
Compton Mackenzie when Mackenzie saw himself clearly as
the subject of Lawrence's prose.

   In another and completely different way, "Two Blue
Birds" and "In Love?" are important in Lawrence's relationship with the *Dial*. The magazine may have provided Knopf
with the manuscripts of the stories for their publication in *The
Woman Who Rode Away* in 1928. Tedlock reports that the
manuscripts in the Frieda Lawrence collection are different
from the published versions of the stories; yet the stories in the

Dial correspond to those in print today. Since the *Dial* first published the two stories and since the manuscript versions in Lawrence's collection have never appeared in print, it seems safe to conjecture that Knopf followed the *Dial*'s versions or used the proofs from the *Dial* that were sent to Lawrence for approval. A less likely conjecture is that Lawrence sent to Knopf typescripts identical to the ones he gave the *Dial*. In any case, in the Lawrence collection of manuscripts there is no holograph or typescript of the stories as they appear in print; in the *Dial*'s collection of Lawrence's papers are typescripts, for "In Love?" perhaps the only one extant, of the later versions that Lawrence made of the two stories.[36]

Also important to Lawrence's relationship with the *Dial* is "Glad Ghosts" a tale unlike any of the other four published in the *Dial* and collected in *The Woman Who Rode Away*. In "Glad Ghosts," Lawrence relates the tale in the first person, as Mark Morier; all the other stories are presented in the third person by a narrator outside the story, and in them Lawrence speaks his ideological message either through the omniscient narrator or one of the characters. Like "Two Blue Birds" and "In Love?," "Glad Ghosts" also presents Lawrence's views on sex and marriage, but in this story the action is recounted within a supernatural framework. Lawrence, of course, is one of the modern masters of the supernatural in fiction, as best exemplified in his often anthologized short story, "The Rocking-Horse Winner" (*CSS* 790–804). In "The Man Who Loved Islands," Lawrence demonstrates briefly his powers in conjuring up a world of supernatural forces, as the souls of the dead past sweep over the consciousness of the islander at night. In "Glad Ghosts" he again vivifies the world of souls, but this time in a quasimystical sexual union with the living.

Mark Morier, the narrator and also the mouthpiece for Lawrence, visits the ancestral home of an old classmate, Carlotta Lathkill, and her husband, Lord Luke Lathkill. He is lodged in the bedroom of the manor that is presumed to be haunted by an ancestral ghost and is told that if he can invoke the ghost, the streak of bad luck dogging the family will end.

That evening at dinner he meets other guests, Colonel and Mrs. Hale, a December-and-May couple, and Lord Lathkill's mother. The dowager Lady Lathkill, it turns out, is a spiritualist, who invokes the first wife of Colonel Hale. Although the first Mrs. Hale has told her husband to remarry, she forbids him to make love to his new wife.

Mark Morier acts as a superman-psychologist. Colonel Hale receives his dead wife in a physical-mystical union; she is finally satisfied and disappears. In the ghost room that night the family ghost comes to Morier in another physical-mystical, but more suggestively sexual, union. As a result Carlotta Lathkill bears a son, "ghost-begotten" and therefore incapable of inheriting the family's misfortunes, while Mrs. Hale bears a daughter.

"Glad Ghosts" is unique in the *Dial*, for the magazine did not favor ghost stories. Its acceptance can probably be explained by the prestige of Lawrence or by the unusual nature of its subject matter. Certainly it is a story as much about sex as about ghosts, and conceivably one could place it with the other avant-garde stories about sexual experiences which the *Dial* published, except that the union of spirits and living people moves in a direction of sexual freedom that is, to say the least, unsatisfactory.

On close inspection of the evidence, arbitrary classifications of the fiction in the *Dial* tend to break down; stories such as Lawrence's "Glad Ghosts" resist being squeezed into any one category without bulging out somewhere. Eventually the stories in the *Dial* are best classified merely as "unusual." An example of a story that, like "Glad Ghosts," defies easy categorizing, is Padraic Colum's "The Sad Sequel to Puss in Boots" in the issue for July 1921.[37] Here the narrator meets a cat who tells him that he once belonged to the Marquis of Carabas and that he was forced to flee the Marquis when his master demanded his eye. Such fantasy is at the opposite end of the literary spectrum from the expressive realism of "In Love?" It is difficult, consequently, to comprehend any principle of selection encompassing the range of fiction in the magazine; one finally is left with the only standard that Thayer suggested: the pleasure a specific work gave the editors.[38]

Despite its unique character, Lawrentian themes are evident in "Glad Ghosts." The most evident of these is Lawrence's insistence that the concept of sex goes beyond a physical relationship. Colonel Hale's first marriage was unsatisfactory because it was merely physical; as proof of his love, he can offer only his children, the products of a physical union. In other stories by Lawrence in the *Dial* the same theme dominates. The failure of Cathcart in "The Man Who Loved Islands" begins when he enters a union without desire for his partner; the problems of the characters in "Two Blue Birds" and "In Love?" stem in part from their failure to experience what Lawrence called "the normal sex sympathy" (*AA* 117–18).

The range of characters in "Glad Ghosts" is also representative of the range in its companion works. The sensual qualities of Mrs. Hale are symbolically represented in Lawrence's description of her as "like a black she-fox," a simile recalling the symbolism of *The Fox*. One finds much the same hierarchy of characters in "Glad Ghosts" as in *The Fox* and *Lady Chatterley's Lover*, but in "Glad Ghosts" the hierarchy is more complex. In all three works a "central" character is attracted by two others, who represent respectively life and death. In "Glad Ghosts" the most obvious central character is Carlotta, torn not only between her husband and Morier but also between Morier and Lady Lathkill. Similarly, Mrs. Hale is the character caught between her husband, who could offer life, and her husband's first wife, who denies life; but she may also be seen as pulled between the opposing forces of her husband and Lady Lathkill, her husband and Morier, and even her husband and Lord Lathkill. In the last two struggles her husband becomes the negative force, and Morier and Lathkill the positive forces; the narrator notices that she looks toward Lathkill, and he thinks, "Myself or him, it was a question of which got there first" (*CSS* 683).

Finally, in *The Fox* and in all of the stories by Lawrence

in the *Dial* there recurs a certain kind of character, one who is dominated by will and whose will makes her fail to achieve a consummation she needs and desires. Among the stories in the *Dial* the most striking example of such characterization is found in "The Man Who Loved Islands"; at least five times Lawrence insistently blames the failure of Cathcart's sexual experience on the fact that the wife "willed" the union, that it was "driven from the will," that "only with her will had she wanted him" (*CSS* 737). In "Glad Ghosts" Lathkill remarks that it is just as well his children are dead, because "they were born of our will" (*CSS* 690); Hester, the main character of "In Love?" cannot love Joe naturally because she feels that her emotion should be governed by her will. The wife in "Two Blue Birds" does not love anybody; instead she wills a series of "gallant" affairs, flirtations rather than fully consummated liaisons. The woman who rode away becomes the sacrifice she desires to be only because her will is drugged and she is power-less. Lastly, *The Fox* presents most clearly a struggle between the will of March that keeps March bound to Banford and her subconscious desire that Banford die so she might marry Henry.

The basic conflict in all the stories is that of a struggle in at least one character, sometimes in several, between conscious will and subconscious, natural tendencies. In *Fantasia of the Unconscious*, Lawrence writes of the two kinds of will:

> We can quite well recognize the will exerted from the lower centre. We call it headstrong temper and masterfulness. But the peculiar will of the upper centre—the sort of nervous, critical objectivity, the deliberate forcing of sympathy, the play upon tenderness, the plaintive bullying of love, or the benevolent bullying of love—these we don't care to recognize. (*FU* 80)

Earlier in the essay Lawrence explains that the will is at birth a "purely spontaneous control-factor of the living unconscious" (*FU* 47) but that it can be corrupted in two ways. If the free psyche collapses, the will can become part of the automatic response it is designed to check, and then paranoia results. The other danger is that the will becomes, instead of a free agent, "an instrument of the mind" (*FU* 48). Whenever Lawrence speaks of the will in any of his stories in the *Dial*, he is referring to "the will of the upper centre," or the will corrupted into egoism and forcing desires that should flow naturally.

In most of Lawrence's writing—whether in the *Dial* or not —the struggle of the will is essentially the basis of all conflict. Interested as Lawrence was in psychology, his works tend to explore beneath the surface of physical conflicts downward into the profundities of the psyche. It is significant that almost all of Lawrence's fiction in the *Dial* reveals his interest in psychological motivations; the fact that this particular kind of fiction by Lawrence appeared in the magazine suggests that Lawrence was aware of Thayer's interest in the new theoretical psychology and that Lawrence was aware also of the particular market for fiction in the *Dial;* alternatively, one is free to conjecture that the *Dial* chose from Lawrence's work those stories revealing the writer's artistic development of certain psychological principles that fascinated him.

In any case, the five stories from *The Woman Who Rode Away* that appeared in the *Dial* have about them a kind of unity of psychological pattern. Moreover, all of them may be understood as an artistic development of ideas that Lawrence had already written about in essays such as "The Crown" or in *Fantasia of the Unconscious.* Beyond this unity, though, the stories represent eclectically the range of Lawrence's writing, from a depiction of primitive culture and myth to a unique ghost tale to a moral fable to comic sketches. The variety of Lawrence's stories in the *Dial* is attributable simply to the fact that the magazine published more of his fiction than any of its American counterparts; and this range may well indicate, further, a rather careful selection by Lawrence, by his literary agent, or by the *Dial*'s staff of his work for the magazine. In any case a discerning reader of Lawrence's stories in the *Dial*, even if he had not read other work by Lawrence, could understand the common psychological pattern underlying his characters and at the same time would recognize his talent for weaving several kinds of tales.

For the early fiction by Lawrence the *Dial* occupies a

unique place among American magazines as the only one of the period to publish one of his translations, a part of one of his novels, and a novella. When these three contributions are added to the stories published later, the *Dial* becomes in effect as eclectic an anthology of Lawrence's fiction as anyone would wish to read.

6

LAWRENCE'S NONFICTION PROSE
IN *THE DIAL*

ALTHOUGH LAWRENCE IS remembered primarily for the fiction he produced, he also wrote biographical and auto-biographical sketches, long travel essays, literary criticism, a book-length essay on psychoanalysis, and short essays on many general subjects. Critics, among them some reviewers for the *Dial*, have asserted that for much of his life Lawrence was not a novelist but a philosopher who used novels as well as exposi-tory writing to develop his ideas didactically.[1] William York Tindall even suggests that after *Sons and Lovers*, Lawrence's first important novel, "his talents were misdirected by his the-ory" and that "his later works contain only hints of what he might have done."[2] Although Lawrence's essays may be sec-ondary to his fiction, they nevertheless become important as an explanation for much of that fiction and as a revelation of his ideas that he could not as successfully embody in his novels and tales.

Appropriately, the *Dial* reflects Lawrence's significance as a writer of fiction by its having published more of his stories than any other American magazine. It also published nonfic-tion by Lawrence, including two autobiographical sketches, a book review, and three travel essays, but in contrast to the quantity of his fiction that it published, the *Dial* printed only a small proportion of Lawrence's essays. Other magazines published thirty-five examples of his nonfiction that appeared in American periodicals during the period 1920 through July 1929; and *Travel* and *Laughing Horse* each published seven essays by Lawrence—one more essay apiece than did the *Dial*.[3] As of course the articles in *Travel* are travel essays, they do not reveal the range of Lawrence's nonfiction that the pieces in the *Dial* do, and the same holds true for Spud Johnson's *Laughing Horse*. The *Dial* thus remains the most representative periodical source in America in which to find not only Lawrence's fiction but his work in other genres.

For autobiographical sketches by Lawrence, the *Dial* is exclusively the American periodical source. Indeed "Adolf" and "Rex" are his only autobiographical accounts to be found in English except for sketches, all posthumously published, in periodicals, collections of his work, and Edward Nehls's composite biography of 1957–59.[4] These sketches are concerned with pets Lawrence and his sister owned when they were children. The titles of both narratives are also the names of the children's pets: Adolf was a rabbit Lawrence's father once brought home, and Rex was a dog that belonged to Lawrence's uncle and that the Lawrence children once tended. As the first two works by Lawrence to appear in the *Dial*, they form a strikingly appropriate introduction not only to the total body of his writing in the magazine (and its reviews of his work) but, for Lawrence's work, to the entire *oeuvre*. "Adolf" especially provides a poignant glimpse of Lawrence's family, in its account of the family's uneasiness over the father's return home after a night "down pit," the father's happiness at walking through dewy fields between the mines and his house, and the mother's fondness and pride for such amenities as lace curtains in a miner's cottage parlor, in sharp contrast to the father's rough habit of drinking tea from a saucer. On the part of Lawrence, the narrator of the sketch, there is a discernible attachment to his mother, whom he treats almost as a sibling; more distant is the affection for his father, a lone figure with a dry humor who in the short sketch makes his way between the coal fields and a rather alien family.

The second sketch, "Rex," reveals not only Lawrence's

mother and father but his maternal Uncle Herbert, after whom
Lawrence was named. The black sheep of the Beardsall family, Herbert operated a public house on the corner of Robin
Hood and Lamartine Streets at the bottom of Blue Bell Hill,
which figures so prominently in *Sons and Lovers*.[5] Rex, the dog
which the Lawrence children tended, belonged to this uncle,
and Lawrence briefly describes the trip he made to the public
house in Nottingham to fetch the puppy. The uncle himself
presented an enigma to Lawrence—"Strange to think he was
my mother's brother, and that he had his bouts when he read
Browning aloud with emotion and éclat" (*Ph* 14)—and Herbert Beardsall later blamed the Lawrence children for their
affection for Rex, which ruined him as a show dog. Lawrence
agreed with his uncle that "He [Rex] should have stayed outside human limits, we should have stayed outside canine limits"
but nevertheless concluded the sketch by commenting, "My
uncle was a fool for all that" (*Ph* 21).

The next nonfiction Lawrence contributed to the *Dial*
consisted of excerpts from five chapters of *Sea and Sardinia*.[6]
The *Dial* staff selected from the chapters which comprise about
three-quarters of the book—one hundred and fifty pages of the
Compass Books edition—a total of twenty-one pages for the
magazine. Although most of the descriptions of various scenes
and localities are omitted from the passages the magazine
printed, the editors chose eclectically some of the most telling
descriptive phrases and some of the most important digressions
Lawrence is provoked to make by what he sees. Moreover, the
sequence of Lawrence's narrative is faithfully followed and all
of the first chapters are represented, so the gaps in the *Dial*'s
excerpts are no more noticeable than are those in the original,
as Lawrence changes his descriptive focus from one subject or
episode to another. Instead, some of the superfluous and rather
confusing details, such as the episode of the American girl who
goes to the ship with the Lawrences when they sail from
Palermo, are omitted from the essay in the *Dial*, and the
account there is perhaps more unified than is the work itself in
its entirety.

From the first chapter, "As Far As Palermo," the *Dial*

omits the first five introductory paragraphs that relate Lawrence's restlessness and begins instead with the question,
"Where does one go?" Lawrence decides on Sardinia, "which
has no history, no date, no race, no offering" and which prom-
ises, like Russia, to break outside the tattered net of European
civilization (*SeSa* 3). Next the *Dial* version describes the day
of departure and gives Lawrence's digression on Sicilians as he
waits for the train for Palermo. All the remaining details of
chapter one—the train trip, a stroll through the streets of
Palermo—are omitted. From the second chapter, "The Sea,"
the *Dial* staff chose passages that depict the boat lying before
dawn in the harbor, Lawrence's exultation over Mount Eryx,
the island of Levanzo, where the boat stopped, and finally—the
last three paragraphs—the approach to Cagliari. The first installment ends as the Lawrences prepare to leave the ship.

The second installment of *Sea and Sardinia* reads as
though it were continuous with the first. It begins by describing the harbor at Cagliari and goes on to portray the multifar-
ious array of carriages and "marquise," and the commoners
and peasants around a parapet in the city. Then the account
moves dramatically from a colorful panoramic view of a great
square to a closeup conveying the forced intimacies of a train
ride to Mandas and shifts to a short anecdote about a large,
vociferous Sardinian who misses the train. The *Dial* eliminates
completely Lawrence's account of the night he spent at an inn
in Mandas, the train trip the next morning to Sorgono, and his
rage in Sorgono over the difficulty of finding a suitable hotel
and the indifference of the innkeepers to his plight. The account focuses briefly instead on the evening in the inn where
the Lawrences are forced to settle, and then skips to the ride by
bus and car to Nuoro. The excerpts in the *Dial* end with
Lawrence's ruminations, as he rides in the car, on the necessity
of discovering the past and thereby discovering oneself.

Unlike *Twilight in Italy*, which Scofield Thayer had read
and which led him to suggest that Lawrence write something
of the same kind, this second travel book by Lawrence has an
immediacy—probably because he writes in the present tense—

that the first does not have. A feverish pitch of description is sustained throughout *Sea and Sardinia;* a kind of lightning discharges throughout the entire essay. Cagliari is described as "a naked town rising steep, steep, golden-looking, piled naked to the sky from the plain at the head of a formless hollow bay . . . withal rather jewel-like: like a sudden rose-cut amber jewel naked at the depth of the vast indenture" (*SeSa* 52). Characters come to life with Lawrence's deft portraitive touches: "So his face all bright, his eyes round and bright as two stars, absolutely transfigured by dismay, chagrin, anger and distress, he comes and sits in his seat, ablaze, stiff, speechless" (*SeSa* 73). Even the routine of leaving a house for a trip becomes a ritual charged with excitement as it mingles with Lawrence's description of an early Mediterranean morning:

> Under the lid of the half-cloudy night sky, far away at the rim of the Ionian sea, the first light, like metal fusing. So swallow the cup of tea and the bit of toast. Hastily wash up, so that we can find the house decent when we come back. Shut the door-windows of the upper terrace, and go down. Lock the door: the upper half of the house made fast.
>
> The sky and sea are parting like an oyster shell, with a low red gape. Looking across from the verandah at it, one shivers. Not that it is cold. The morning is not at all cold. But the ominousness of it: that long red slit between a dark sky and a dark Ionian sea, terrible old bivalve which has held life between its lips so long. And here, at this house, we are ledged so awfully above the dawn, naked to it.   (*SeSa* 4)

Aside from its descriptive passages *Sea and Sardinia* contains digressions—important for an understanding of Lawrence's ideas and themes—on such topics as races, civilizations, and history, and most of these digressions were included in the excerpts in the *Dial*. When Padraic Colum reviewed *Sea and Sardinia* in the *Dial*, he noted that Lawrence's trip to Sardinia was really a secret quest, that Europe had become too feminine, and that in Sardinia Lawrence hoped to find "a survival of the old male civilization."[7] Passages from *Sea and Sardinia* suggest that Colum acutely assessed Lawrence's intention. At the beginning of the essay Lawrence decides to go to Sardinia because, although Sardinia is like modern Italy "with its railways and its omnibuses," there is "an uncaptured Sardinia yet" (*SeSa* 3). At the railway station at Catania, an episode which the *Dial* includes, Lawrence observes that "humanity is, externally, too much alike" (*SeSa* 6). In that respect Sicily resembles the mainland, and he comments ironically on Sicilian men who are "terribly physically all over one another," as they "pour themselves one over the other like so much melted butter over parsnips" or "smile with sunny melting tenderness into each other's faces" (*SeSa* 7).

Once in Sardinia, Lawrence contrastingly emphasizes the "maleness" of the men of that island. In Cagliari he describes peasant men with a rather excessive rapture, crying, "How beautiful maleness is, if it finds its right expression" (*SeSa* 61). The excitement produced in Lawrence by the sight of the peasants owes much to their garb, which emphasizes their bodies: "How fascinating it is, after the soft Italians, to see these limbs in their close knee-breeches, so definite, so manly, with the old fierceness in them still. One realizes, with horror, that the race of men is almost extinct in Europe" (*SeSa* 62). For Lawrence, though, the excitement at seeing the Sardinian peasants comes not from any physical desire for them but from the realization that had he lived in some civilization of the past, he too might have worn the peasants' costumes—"the uneasy sense of blood familiarity haunts me. I *know* I have known it before" (*SeSa* 62).

For the conclusion of the excerpts, the editors chose a passage, central to the entire book, which shows Lawrence's quest for the past, for a male civilization. On his way to Nuoro, Lawrence begins to realize how old Italy is, as he thinks of civilizations from the ages of the past that lived on Sardinia:

> Man has lived there and brought forth his consciousness there and in some way brought that place to consciousness, given it its expression, and, really, finished it. . . . The land has been humanised through and through: and we in our own tissued consciousness bear the results of this humanisation. So that for us to go to Italy and to *penetrate* into Italy is like a

most fascinating act of self-discovery—back, back down the
old ways of time. Strange and wonderful chords awake in us,
and vibrate again after many hundreds of years of complete
forgetfulness." (*SeSa* 122)

Through *Sea and Sardinia* runs the theme of the secret quest
for a survival of the "male past," and the selection by the *Dial*'s
staff of passages that reveal the theme, to the exclusion of
descriptive passages, suggests the abiding interest of the magazine in primitive civilizations and cultures, and points up Lawrence's own fascination with the subject.

In this respect, *Sea and Sardinia* relates thematically to
the two shorter travel essays by Lawrence that appeared in the
Dial. "Indians and an Englishman" and "Taos" grew out of his
early experiences in the American Southwest in 1922; like
Lawrence's trip to Sardinia, his visits in America had for their
purpose the discovery of a primitive civilization and the recognition of his rapport with the prehistoric past. Another purpose
of his visit was to find a setting for the ideal colony he hoped to
establish; but before he could found Rananim, the perfect
colony of the future, Lawrence had to experience vicariously an
older civilization. In *Sea and Sardinia* he asserted, "There are
unknown, unworked lands where the salt has not lost its sa-
vour. But one must have perfected onself in the great past first"
(*SeSa* 123). For America, the "great past" was not European
civilization, which was dead and which Americans must aban-
don, but the civilizations of Indians in America before the
white men. As early as 1920, even before he came to America,
Lawrence had decided that America should continue the civilization of Indians; in "America, Listen to Your Own," an essay
published in the *New Republic* for December 15, 1920, he
wrote: "They [Americans] must pick up the life thread where
the mysterious Red race let it fall. They must catch the pulse of
the life where Cortes and Columbus murdered. There lies the
real continuity" (*Ph* 90). After Lawrence had visited the
Southwest, he saw the impracticability of his proposal, as the
series of essays he wrote about Indian life reveals.

The *Dial* intended to publish several of Lawrence's essays

about the Southwest, but only two appeared in the magazine, perhaps because Lawrence did not care for Alyse Gregory, who became managing editor during the period when Lawrence lived in America and recorded his impressions of Indian life. Both "Indians and an Englishman" and "Taos" appeared respectively in the issues for February and March 1923, before Miss Gregory's appointment. "Taos" was written to describe the annual Fiesta of San Geronimo, which Lawrence visited in September 1922, but the essay reveals Lawrence's feelings about the Indians' culture more clearly than it describes the specific celebration he attended. At the opening of the essay, Lawrence is already aware of the distance that separates him from the Indians: "The Indians say that Taos is the heart of the world. Their world maybe" (*Ph* 100). He begins by writing of cities that give one a feeling of permanence, a reminder of their past greatness; Taos pueblo is like these cities, "the old nodality of the pueblo still holding, like a dark ganglion spinning invisible threads of consciousness" (*Ph* 101). For Lawrence there is about the pueblo a "dryness" and "weariness," and getting "into the Indian vibration" is "like breathing chlorine" (*Ph* 101). Although Lawrence's comments may be a criticism of Mabel Luhan's own "Indian vibration," they also constitute a valid statement of his inability to identify with the red fathers whose "life thread" he thought Americans should carry on.

Although "Taos" infers Lawrence's dissatisfaction with Indian life, the other essay in the *Dial*, "Indians and an Englishman," states it explicitly. When Lawrence first met an Indian, he explains, "something in my soul broke down, letting in a bitterer dark, a pungent awakening to the lost past, old darkness, new terror, new root-griefs, old root-richnesses" (*Ph* 95). He complains of the "unbearable sulphur-human smell" that comes when the Indians cluster and of the "endless plangent monotony" when they speak (*Ph* 95, 98). A feeling of sadness and nostalgia comes over him when he hears the warwhoop of the Apaches and recalls the time "when man was dusky and not individualized" (*Ph* 95). Between the Indians and the white men who watch them dance, Lawrence feels "a sort of unconscious animosity" (*Ph* 96). Finally, he decides that although in the great past he had belonged to the same race as the Indians, for him now there is no going back.

> We do not need to live the past over again. Our darkest tissues are twisted in this old tribal experience, our warmest blood came out of the old tribal fire. And they vibrate still in answer, our blood, our tissue. But me, the conscious me, I have gone a long road since then. And as I look back, like memory terrible as blood-shed, the dark faces round the fire in the night, and one blood beating in me and them. But I don't want to go back to them, ah, never. I never want to deny them or break with them. But there is no going back. Always onward, still further. The great devious onward-flowing stream of conscious human blood. From them to me, and from me on.
>
> I don't want to live again the tribal mysteries my blood has lived long since. I don't want to know as I have known, in the tribal exclusiveness. But every drop of me trembles still alive to the old sound, every thread in my body quivers to the frenzy of the old mystery. I know my derivation. I was born of no virgin, of no Holy Ghost. Ah, no, these old men telling the tribal tale were my fathers. I have a dark-faced, bronze-voiced father far back in the resinous ages. My mother was no virgin. She lay in her hour with this dusky-lipped tribe-father. And I have not forgotten him. But he, like many an old father with a changeling son, he would like to deny me. But I stand on the far edge of their firelight, and am neither denied nor accepted. My way is my own, old red father; I can't cluster at the drum any more.   (*Ph* 101)

In his earlier study, *Fantasia of the Unconscious*, Lawrence had described the kind of experience he was to undergo in his visits to the Indians. "Yet we *must* know," he contends, "if only in order to learn not to know" (*FU* 112). The process of learning "not to know" the Indian ways and his refusal to hear the tribal mysteries illustrate concretely not only Lawrence's relations with the Indians of the Southwest but also the situation central to "The Woman Who Rode Away" and, to a lesser degree, "The Man Who Loved Islands." In both short stories the principal characters attempt to assimilate themselves to primitive ways, the woman through the religion of the Chilchui Indians, and the man through the forces of nature; relentlessly pursuing such experience rather than rejecting it at the fatal point-of-no-return, both characters are destroyed in and through the process of knowing.

Lawrence's concept of acquiring knowledge only to reject it later was foreign to Mabel Luhan's understanding. She accurately remarks that Lawrence, "of all men alive, could perceive and record the peculiar vestiges of another mode of life that have miraculously survived in the undisclosed valleys of the Rio Grande River." She complains, though, that Lawrence "could not give himself to it," could not free himself "from his past or the past of his race" and thus reveals that she was oblivious to Lawrence's dual recognition that the Indian race was part of his past but that he had transcended that past, so to speak. For he held that in contrast to white men the Indians retreated into their past rather than surged onward. Mabel Luhan says of Lawrence's rejection of Indian life that "too much oxygen will burn out the lungs. He ran to save himself from purity and died in the old country." [8] Instead, for Lawrence, Indian life was "like breathing chlorine," and becoming a part of it brought a swifter death.

Lawrence's experience with the Indians was only one episode in the series of his attempts to recover the past. William York Tindall asserts that Lawrence belongs to the tradition of "romantic primitivism": "He detested reason, the machine, and science, and longed for a return to that religious, intuitive and visceral closeness to nature to be found in savage and archaic man." According to Tindall, Lawrence chose first the antediluvian world, secondly the world before 2000 B.C., and failing that, "the vestiges of glory which he discovered in the archaic societies of the Egyptians, Chaldeans, Hindus, and Mrs. Mabel Dodge Luhan's Indians." Tindall records what Mabel Luhan apparently never realized, that Lawrence did not want to return to the condition of savages, but felt "that the world might be reborn by a fusion with the past, by a return to the living worshipful universe of early man." [9]

Lawrence's involvement with the primitive is reflected in much of his writing in the *Dial—Sea and Sardinia*, "The Woman Who Rode Away," "Indians and an Englishman," "Taos," and "The Man Who Loved Islands." In at least two of these works, *Sea and Sardinia* and "The Woman Who Rode Away," Lawrence expresses his belief that a return to the primitive could serve as a catalyst for dying civilizations. In *Sea and Sardinia* Lawrence says that one can find new worlds only by reliving those of the past, and in "The Woman Who Rode Away" he exploits the primitive ritual in which human sacrifice is a means of obtaining the power of the sun and reclaiming tribal greatness. Of Lawrence's poems in the *Dial*, "Snake" most importantly reflects his concern with the primitive.

For the *Dial*, as for Lawrence, primitive art and cultures were a major preoccupation. For Lawrence primitivism was a vital part of the theosophy he developed in his essays, poems, stories, and novels; for the *Dial* the primitive possessed significance because writers and artists like Lawrence were discovering aesthetic and cognitive values in ancient and remote civilizations. The magazine reflected the aestheticism of the 1920's, of which primitive art was so integral a part, but of which it was, one must emphasize, one aspect of a complex whole. That the primitive was vital, in varying reasons for its essential importance, is basic to an understanding of the relationship of the author and his major American magazine outlet.

The last essay by Lawrence which the *Dial* published was his review of Stuart Sherman's *Americans*. Like his own earlier *Studies in Classic American Literature*, Lawrence's review of Sherman's book represents his unorthodox approach to literary criticism; it adds, too, another dimension to the range of his essays published in the *Dial*. The most obvious reason Lawrence wrote a review of *Americans* is that following its custom of commissioning reviews, the *Dial* asked him to do so. He was, after all, a likely choice for reviewing this particular volume; Sherman's book and Lawrence's *Studies in Classic American Literature* have several features in common, despite the completely different tastes, backgrounds, and styles of the two authors. One similarity the two works possess is that some of the authors they discuss are the same— Franklin, Hawthorne, and Whitman. A second similarity is that both books were anthologies, and chapters of both had been published before in magazines; Sherman's articles had appeared in the New York *Times Book Review*, *Bookman*, the New York *Nation*, and the *Step Ladder*, as introductions to the Modern Student's Library editions of *The Scarlet Letter* and *Leaves of Grass*, and as chapters in *The Cambridge History of American Literature*, of which he was later an editor; Lawrence's articles were published in the *English Review* and the *Nation and Athenaeum*. Finally, each author reviewed the other's book: Lawrence's condescending view of *Americans* was published in the *Dial* for May 1923 under the title, "Model Americans"; Sherman's more conventionally favorable review of *Studies in Classic American Literature* was entitled "America Is Discovered" and appeared in the New York *Evening Post Literary Review* for October 20, 1923.[10]

Beyond these similarities of subjects and dates Sherman and Lawrence stand in relation to each other as polar opposites. In 1922, when *Americans* was published, Sherman was a professor of English at the University of Illinois. He had been educated at Harvard and had been influenced by his association there with Irving Babbitt. The First World War affected his patriotism as profoundly as Babbitt encouraged his humanism, so that in *Americans* he selected ten American writers who revealed a tradition of Puritanism, which he labeled the "Religion of Democracy." From his experience at Nottingham University, Lawrence had acquired a dislike and distrust of college professors, and his experiences with censors and government spies had shattered not so much his love for England as his faith in the kind of blind religiopatriotic fervor that Sherman exuded.[11] Moreover, Lawrence disliked the pompous style in which Sherman asserted his convictions about American art and letters.[12]

The most ironic contrast between Sherman and Lawrence lies in the fact that both men had essentially the same purpose in writing their books. Both Sherman and Lawrence were trying to establish the spirit of American civilization as representative American writers revealed it; and both men, using as examples three of the same major writers, held divergent views of the climate or "spirit of place" that produced American writers. For Lawrence the American consciousness had "so far been a false dawn," a superficial cover of "idealistic clothes" that disguised the primal strength of the new country (*SLC* 303). For Sherman the American consciousness was not "a false dawn," but a disappearing sunset that modern writer-critics such as H. L. Mencken and Ludwig Lewisohn were rapidly losing sight of.[13]

In his review of *Americans*, Lawrence burlesques all of these qualities of Sherman that he finds repugnant as well as Sherman's theme that the representative men he has chosen for his study reveal the puritan tradition. In a letter to Gilbert Seldes, Lawrence indicated that he intended the review to be amusing rather than querulous; he acknowledged that he had received the proofs of the article from the *Dial* and added, "Hope it will amuse you" (*CL* 741). The plan of Lawrence's essay is to establish Sherman's purpose and technique and then to attack systematically Sherman's comments on each of the writers discussed in *Americans*—H. L. Mencken, Franklin, Emerson, Hawthorne, Whitman, Joaquin Miller, Carl Sandburg, Andrew Carnegie, Theodore Roosevelt, the Adams family, and Paul Elmer More.

In the introductory paragraph to the review Lawrence portrays Sherman as a powerless, rather effeminate man—the same portrait, astonishingly, that Sherman gives of Mencken in *Americans*.[14] With a nice doublehanded apology and attack, Lawrence defends Sherman while ridiculing all professors: "Well, Professor Sherman, being a professor, has got to be nice to everybody about everybody. What else does a professor sit in a chair of English for, except to dole out sweets?" (*SLC* 414). After establishing Sherman's character, Lawrence turns to the plan of the book, comments that Sherman "steers his little ship of Criticism most obviously between the Scylla of

Mr. Mencken and the Charybdis of Mr. P. E. More," and confesses—quite insincerely—that he had heard of neither, even though Mencken had just been made editor of the *Smart Set* when Lawrence's story "The Border Line" was published there (*SLC* 415). Lawrence's acerbity regarding Mencken, if nothing else, suggests he had heard of or had read Mencken's ridicule of *The Lost Girl*. In his review Lawrence next parodies Sherman's style by paraphrasing the message "To the Menckenites" in *Americans*. The introduction concludes with the observation that "The great arch is of course the Religion of Democracy. . . . If you want to trace the curve you must follow the course of the essays" (*SLC* 416).

Lawrence's comments on each of the writers discussed in *Americans* continue to burlesque Sherman's argument, but in dealing with some of these writers "Model Americans" does contain serious criticism. For example, Lawrence attacks Emerson's idealism with cogent force: the fault with Emerson's belief that he had direct contact with God is that "he cosily forgot that there are many messengers of God. . . . Ashtaroth and Ammon are gods as well. . . . But Ralph Waldo wasn't having any. They could never ring *him* up. He was only connected on the Ideal phone" (*SLC* 418). By urging Americans to listen to Emerson, Sherman was "really driving us nauseously astray" (*SLC* 418). For Lawrence the interest in transcendentalism is a "museum-interest," probably the most damaging comment one could make about Emerson (*SLC* 419).

As regards Hawthorne and Whitman, Lawrence reiterates the points he made earlier in *Studies in Classic American Literature*. There he wrote that Americans were never "truly *immersed* in *doing* something, with the deep blood-consciousness active." As a result "every time you 'conquer' the body with the mind . . . you cause a deeper, more dangerous complex or tension somewhere else" (*SLC* 350). He condemned *The Scarlet Letter* for "duplicity" because like all American artists, Hawthorne gave "mental allegiance" to a morality and at the same time passionately destroyed that morality (*SLC*

401). In "Model Americans" Lawrence echoes his own study
of *The Scarlet Letter:* the book is lurid and "makes one feel
like spitting" because "it is invented in the head and grafted on
to the lower body" (*SLC* 419). Commenting on Whitman,
Lawrence repeats in his review of *Americans* the belief he had
asserted in *Studies in Classic American Literature*, that no one
wanted "to be embraced in one of Waldo's [*sic*] vast promis-
cuous armfuls" (*SLC* 420).

As for the lesser lights of literature considered in *Americans*, Lawrence has only jibes to poke at Sherman's assertions
about them. The curious mixture of serious comment and playful burlesque in "Model Americans" may perhaps be explained
by saying that Lawrence treated seriously the major writers he
had read or had written of and that he relied on his sense of
satire and his dislike of Sherman's thesis for remarks about
those writers whom he had not read. Carnegie, for instance, is
"the sweetest example of how beautifully the *Religion Civile*
pays, in cold cash"; and as for the Adams family, even though
their aristocracy is "played out," they can still rely on Democracy (*SLC* 421). Lawrence's conclusion to the essay is equally
satiric. He asserts that Professor Sherman has served a dish of
cookies which he bids the reader eat and have: "The cookies
are Tradition, and Heroes, and Great Men, and $350,000,000
in your pocket. And eating 'em is Democracy, Serving Mankind, piously giving most of the $350,000,000 back again. 'Oh,
nobly and heroically get $350,000,000 together,' chants Profes-
sor Sherman . . . 'and then piously and munificently give away
$349,000,000 again.' " And impudently he adds a little coda:
"P.S. You can't get past Arithmetic" (*SLC* 421).

"Model Americans" was a coup for the *Dial*. As the major
literary journal of advanced opinion in America, it welcomed a
review in Lawrence's idiosyncratic style, especially the review
of a book on the same subjects and themes Lawrence had
written about. The *Dial*, moreover, agreed with Lawrence in
his dislike of Sherman's approach to literary criticism. As the
first critical review in America to advocate the objective analysis later known as the New Criticism, the *Dial* would natu-

rally have found Sherman's humanist approach and his insistence on the importance of background and milieu to be outdated and prejudicial to a correct interpretation of the writers' works.[15]

On the other hand, the *Dial* sanctioned at least the idiosyncrasy, the bluntness, the intensity of Lawrence's approach to criticism. Unlike Sherman's book, Lawrence's *Studies in Classic American Literature* would have been amenable to the *Dial* because Lawrence tends there to treat each work as an entity in itself, to analyze the characters of fiction according to his psychological theories and to get at the intention of an author. Although he is also concerned with evaluating the American literary climate, unlike Sherman Lawrence does so inductively and without forcing the works considered into a mold or selectively choosing authors to support a case already judged. Unfortunately for the *Dial*, all the essays of *Studies in Classic American Literature* except the study of Whitman had appeared before 1920, so that Thayer could not introduce readers to that major aspect of Lawrence's talent.[16] The review of *Americans* nevertheless reflects Lawrence's new and unorthodox approach to literary criticism and explores further some of the most significant ideas and authors found in *Studies in Classic American Literature*.

After the publication of "Model Americans," no other essays by Lawrence appeared in the *Dial*. Most of his later short articles and essays, collected in 1930 as *Assorted Articles*, appeared in English newspapers.[17] Lawrence preferred to publish his essays in newspapers, which sought them out and paid well for them but which refused his stories; so he resourcefully sent to avant-garde magazines like the *Dial* his short stories and poems (H 763). Despite the author's bias regarding markets for his writing, the importance of Lawrence's nonfiction prose published in the *Dial* from September 1920 to May 1923 can hardly be overstated. Consisting of autobiographical sketches, travel essays, and a book review, these pieces display a range of Lawrence's writing not found in any other American magazine. The *Dial* has the distinction of being the only magazine anywhere to publish, during his life, Lawrence's autobiographical sketches; it was one of the few magazines in America, and was the first of the few, to publish portions of Lawrence's travel books. More importantly, the interests of the *Dial* are reflected in the essays by Lawrence which the magazine published. Scofield Thayer suggested that Lawrence write *Sea and Sardinia;* "Indians and an Englishman" and "Taos" reflect the *Dial's* preoccupation with the primitive in general and the culture of the Southwestern Indians in particular; and the review of *Americans* is an instance of the *Dial's* rejection of humanism and impressionism for the methods of objective analysis. It is doubtful that any other contributor exemplifies the interests and sympathies of the *Dial* more brilliantly than Lawrence.

7

LAWRENCE'S POETRY IN *THE DIAL*

ALTHOUGH CRITICS TEND TO agree generally about the worth of Lawrence's various novels and short stories, about his poetry there is relatively little criticial agreement.[1] In 1954 R. P. Blackmur attacked Lawrence's poetry as a series of outbursts lacking discipline and restraint; in 1961 V. de Sola Pinto defended Lawrence, calling Blackmur's essay "one of those important wrongheaded pieces of criticism," and attempted to show that because Lawrence was writing in an "organic" or "expressive" form, his poetry could not be judged by the criteria used for traditional verse with conventional rhythms.[2] The disagreement of these two critics over Lawrence's poetry recalls the arguments of the *Dial* critics in the 1910's and 1920's.[3] The disagreement continues today; as late as 1966 Keith Sagar asserted, "The claim that Lawrence is a poet of real stature is still contentious." [4]

Either Pinto or Blackmur, as representatives of the extremes in praise and censure, could turn to the *Dial* for proof of his contention, for in its pages are found not only Lawrence's highest achievement in poetry, but also his weakest attempts. The masterpiece is "Snake" from *Birds, Beasts, and Flowers;* second in importance are four poems from the same collection, "Pomegranate" and three of the "Apostolic Beasts." All appeared in issues of the *Dial* from March through July 1921.

The other poems, which vary in merit, are from *Fansies* and were chosen by Marianne Moore from the first revised, complete manuscript of this major collection, the last volume of Lawrence's poems to be issued while he lived.[5] (Of the manuscripts of poetry he collected and revised for publication, only the posthumous *Nettles*, of 1930, is later.) In its May 1929 issue the *Dial* printed "When I Went to the Circus—," and in the final issue for July 1929 appeared a group of ten poems: "To Let Go or to Hold on—?" "Things Men Have Made—," "Whatever Man Makes—," "Work," "What Would You Fight For?" "Attila," "Sea-Weed," "Lizard," "Censors," and "November by the Sea—." [6]

Besides providing an eclectic range of Lawrence's poetry, the *Dial* is important historically as a major American publisher of his poems, second only to *Poetry*, which published twenty-seven, eleven more than did the *Dial*. *Poetry*, however, first began to publish in 1912, eight years before Thayer established the new *Dial*. From 1920 until July 1929 the *Dial* was the major American publisher of Lawrence's poems; of the twenty-six that Lawrence published in five American magazines during this time, sixteen appeared in the *Dial*. During this period only three poems by Lawrence appeared in *Poetry;* the publication of "St. Matthew" (the fourth poem of the "Apostolic Beasts" series) in the issue for April 1923 marked the end of Lawrence's relationship with Harriet Monroe's magazine, except for two prose pieces, one by Lawrence, another by Miss Monroe. The first was Lawrence's anonymous reply, in the Christmas 1923 issue of the little magazine *Palms*, to Harriet Monroe's article, "The Editor in England," which appeared in *Poetry* for October 1923. In *Poetry* for May 1930 appeared a memorial essay entitled "Comment: D. H. Lawrence" written by the editor herself. Moreover, in the period between April 1923 and March 1930, only three magazines in America published Lawrence's poems—Spud Johnson's little magazine *Laughing Horse* published "Mediterranean in January" and "Beyond the Rockies" in its April 1926 number; *Vanity Fair* posthumously published eighteen of Lawrence's poems from *Pansies* in the issue for March 1930; and then there were the eleven poems in the *Dial*.[7]

For the years from 1920 until Lawrence's death, the *Dial* is clearly the representative American periodical in which one finds Lawrence's poetry; for the early years the reader must go to the *English Review* and *Poetry*, both of which published poems from Lawrence's early volumes of verse. Before 1920 Lawrence published five volumes of verse—*Love Poems and Others* in 1913, *Amores* in 1916, *Look! We Have Come Through* in 1917, *New Poems* in 1918, and *Bay* in 1919. Also he contributed to Edward Marsh's anthologies of *Georgian Poetry* for 1911–12 and 1913–15, to the Imagist anthologies in 1915, 1916, and 1917, and to Harriet Monroe's anthology of *The New Poetry* in 1917.[8]

The poetry Lawrence wrote before 1920 one cites without lessening in any way the importance of the *Dial* to his career; the first issues of the new *Dial* appeared while Lawrence was writing *Birds, Beasts, and Flowers*, his most fully achieved collection of verse. Except for a few poems, such as "Piano" from *New Poems* and "A Doe At Evening" from *Look! We Have Come Through*, the early volumes reflect a poet struggling with influences he has not yet assimilated.[9] W. H. Auden, in an assessment of Lawrence's poetry, points out Lawrence's inability in the early poems to find "a distinctive style of his own": "it took him a long time to find the appropriate style for him to speak in. All too often in his early poems, even the best ones, he is content to versify his thoughts; there is no essential relation between what he is saying and the formal structure he imposes upon it." *Birds, Beasts, and Flowers*, on the other hand, "is the peak of Lawrence's achievement as a poet." [10] Auden's assertion is supported by Lawrence's own recognition of the quality of his book; in a letter to his agent Curtis Brown on February 10, 1923, Lawrence advised him of the forthcoming *Birds, Beasts, and Flowers*, "which I consider my best book of poems" (*CL* 737).

The first poem by Lawrence in the *Dial* reflects to some extent the weaknesses of the early poems, but it also reveals the

strength and originality of the *Birds, Beasts and Flowers*
collection. "Pomegranate" shows the influence of Whitman,
which Lawrence acknowledged in his essays.[11] The poem begins with an obviously Whitmanesque statement:

> You tell me I am wrong.
> Who are you, who is anybody to tell me I am wrong?
> I am not wrong.   (*CP* 123)

In addition to the influence of Whitman, "Pomegranate" reveals a debt to the Imagists: Lawrence catalogues in three
images "pomegranate trees in flower" in Syracuse; pomegranates "like bright green stone,/ And barbed, barbed with a
crown" at Venice; and in Tuscany "Pomegranates to warm
your hands at" (*CP* 123). The free verse and varying rhythms
and harsh images such as "gold-filmed skin, integument,
shown ruptured," also recall the poems of Whitman and the
principles established by the Imagists. The message of the
poem is presented intensely and seems peculiarly Lawrence's:
he insists that the reader see the "fissure," the sexual side of the
pomegranate, and be aware that "The end cracks open with the
beginning" (*CP* 123).

The reason that the editors at the *Dial* initially rejected
"Pomegranate" is suggested by Auden's criticism of Lawrence's early poems; in this instance there seems to be little
relation between the descriptions of the pomegranates and
Lawrence's insistently sounded theme. The influence of Whitman is so evident that the lines seem merely imitative, and the
clumsily dramatized discovery of the fissure—"And, if you
dare, the fissure!"—breaks the generally rich, warm tone of the
poem. Certainly it was not the Imagist quality of "Pomegranate" that caused its preliminary rejection by the *Dial*, as many
of the poets who appeared in the magazine belonged to the
Imagist group—for example, William Carlos Williams, who
received the Dial Award in 1926; Ezra Pound, the recipient of
the award in 1927; H. D. and Richard Aldington; Joseph
Campbell; Melville Cane; and Amy Lowell. Moreover, the
Dial's policy of choosing for publication each work aside from

the context of its production and according to its aesthetic excellence suggests that the editors judged the poem an artistic failure in comparison to other poems then being submitted to the magazine.

Such conjecture fails, however, to explain the subsequent acceptance and publication of the work. The *Dial's* records do not show the date that "Pomegranate" was accepted, but they reveal that "Apostolic Beasts," the next poems by Lawrence to appear in the magazine, were purchased on February 25, 1921. After the *Dial* received "Apostolic Beasts," the editors may have allowed as much as a month to go by before they purchased it; the records concerning "Snake," for example, indicate that it was received on February 23, 1921, and not purchased until March 21, 1921. "Apostolic Beasts" are excellent poems that far surpass "Pomegranate," and the editors may well have decided to purchase the first poem Lawrence submitted only after reading "Apostolic Beasts." Perhaps the excellence of "Apostolic Beasts" led to a reconsideration of the first poem, or perhaps the editors became aware of the design of *Birds*, *Beasts*, *and Flowers* and wanted to include representative poems from Lawrence's forthcoming volume.

Apart from their artistic excellence, the "Apostolic Beasts" doubtlessly appealed to the *Dial* because of their modern treatment of a traditional concept or image. Along with its modernity, the magazine consistently retained an interest in art and literature that exploited Christian themes and imagery. Often it reproduced modern and medieval religious painting and sculpture. In the issue for November 1926 appeared Alfeo Faggi's sculpture of Saint Francis, in November 1922 Robert Delaunay's impressionistic interior painting of the Gothic *Saint Séverin*, in January 1925 Ivan Mestrovic's sculpture *Madonna and Child*, and in April 1926 a reproduction of a twelfth-century crucifix. Among the stories the *Dial* published are modern treatments of traditional religious subjects; Victor Sharenkoff's translation of Elin Pelin's "The Mirror of Saint Christopher" in the issue for July 1924 is a representative example. In Pelin's story St. Christopher loses the image of God from his face and

begins to look like a dog. A constant do-gooder, the saint
carries people on his back across a body of water; one day he
half-knowingly carries the Devil across the lake, and as a result
the image of God returns. Saint Christopher concludes that he
purified himself because he "did good to the most malicious." [12]

In addition to stories with religious themes, the *Dial* frequently published modern poems on religious subjects. The
most famous examples are, of course, Eliot's *The Waste Land*
and Yeats's "The Second Coming," which appeared in the *Dial*
for November 1922 and July 1920 respectively. Thayer published at least two of his own poems treating religious themes:
following the reproduction of the twelfth-century crucifix in
the issue for April 1926, the *Dial* published his long poem "On
a Crucifix," and three issues later in July 1926 appeared his
short poem entitled "Jesus Again." Other poems on religious
topics were AE's "Michael" in the issue for March 1920, Marsden Hartley's "The Crucifixion of Noel" in April 1921, and
Pearl Anderson Sherry's "And the Prophets in Their Season"
in October 1926.[13]

Lawrence's treatment in "Apostolic Beasts" of the traditional images of Saint Luke as the sacrificial ox, of Saint Mark
as the winged lion and defender of heaven, and of Saint John
as the eagle whose words of intuitive truth fly to Heaven
further exemplifies the interest of the *Dial* in Christian myths
expressed in modern forms. Harry T. Moore calls the "Apostolic Beasts" poems "symbolic beasts envisioned out of Lawrence's private mythology." [14] A reading of the poems shows,
however, that Lawrence has not altered the basically traditional symbolism of the three apostolic beasts, though, to be
sure, he has to some extent reinterpreted the significance of his
symbols: ox is here Mithraic bull, eagle becomes phoenix.

All three poems are written in that vers libre then so
popular and now so period, the Lawrentian version of which
tends to disregard grammar and syntax as well as meter. But
Lawrence made his poetic line effective despite the "prosiness"
of his jagged, irregular rhythms, the rhythms of slapdash
speech: he made the image constitute the basic unit of his line

of poetry. Thus each line has an immediate intelligibility and a discernible structure, however "free" it may be. The lion of St. Mark, for example, is described as

> Ramping round, guarding the flock of mankind,
> Sharpening his teeth on the wolves,
> Ramping up through the air like a kestrel
> And lashing his tail above the world
> And enjoying the sensation of heaven and
>   righteousness and voluptuous wrath.   (*CP* 184)

Typically Lawrentian themes recur throughout the poems, endowing them with freshness by bringing to the old myths a new psychological truth. "Saint Mark" is organized as a fable relating how a lion grew wings and acquired universal freedom and power. "Saint Luke" begins with a description of the bull "since the Lamb bewitched him with that red-struck flag," and then moves to an account of his rebellion against serving God. "Saint John" describes the eagle's overwhelming knowledge of the universe, and the poet suggests that he immolate himself, as would a phoenix, so that old truth can give way to new.

Two of the most typically Lawrentian themes—sexual vitality and rebirth after symbolic destruction—occur in "Saint Luke" and "Saint John." The bull rebels because he is "constrained to pour forth all his fire down the narrow sluice of procreation" and is "overcharged" after two thousand years "by the dammed-up pressure of his own massive black blood." For "Saint John," Lawrence relies on biography for a terrible irony: because of his "proud intellect," the eagle must moult on Patmos. But Lawrence transforms the eagle into a phoenix, and avers that from the moulting will rise "a new conception of the beginning and end." With characteristic humor Lawrence adds in a little aside that at present the phoenix is only "the badge of an insurance Company" (*CP* 191).

Lawrence's next poem the *Dial* published is as representative of the 1920's as are "Apostolic Beasts," with their exploration and daring renewal of the significance of Christian icons. "Snake" is representative of its decade in a similar way, its concern with a major theme of the 1920's; in addition, it achieves a place in a quantitatively smaller category formed according to very different standards—with such work in the magazine as Eliot's *The Waste Land* and *The Hollow Men*, Yeats's "Among School Children" and "The Second Coming," and Pound's *Cantos*.[15] The basis for such a grouping is not a common theme but a degree of excellence that sets these poems apart in the literature of the twentieth century. That all were first published in the *Dial* reflects the success both of the magazine's adherence to the criterion that each work it published be aesthetically pleasing and of its effort to be cosmopolitan and eclectic. On a more complex, more significant level, these seven poems by four poets belong in the same category: they are centrally concerned with the major dilemmas of twentieth-century men and the *Weltanschauung* of the aesthetic vanguard in the 1920's, the decade that has to date determined the dominant artistic outlook of the century.

The chief technical interest of "Snake" lies in Lawrence's manipulation of the lines. Admittedly he followed the innovative vers libristes of his day and their progenitor Walt Whitman. Like the poems of "Apostolic Beasts," however, "Snake" is masterfully innovative in an aspect of the poet's conception of the function of the line that differs from the practice of both his contemporaries and Whitman. That is to say, the line in "Snake" is not so much a unit of duration or of emotion expressed in sounds as it is a unit of imagery. Each line presents an image, usually visual. The image may occur as a literal transcription of an observed act, as an abstract summation of act and meaning, or as a symbolic act or object. But for all that seeming variety, the representative and distinguishing lines in "Snake" are constituted, basically, by images. After setting down his sensory datum, the poet proceeds to set down the succeeding datum, and so on. Each line is a hard sharp gleaming tessera; the entire poem is, so to speak, the total mosaic, the completed picture composed of individual images that are the individual lines of the poem.

On the vastly more significant ideational level, for Law-

rence, "Snake" expresses the central problem of modern men
and identifies the root of all neuroses: the inability to accept
sex as the primal and natural part of the life of the senses.[16]
The meaning of the poem evolves in the dramatic interplay of
the two sharply drawn images: the educated man and the
natural snake. Both figures arrive at a neutral meeting point,
where the precedence of man over beast is destroyed; the man
must wait until the snake has drunk before he can fill his
pitcher. The narrator of the poem hears "voices in me" that tell
him to assert his dominance and destroy the snake, but on the
other hand he feels "glad" and "honored" that the snake shares
with him the water trough. Not until the snake slithers away
into a kind of sexual union with a "horrid black hole" does the
voice of "education" in the narrator force him to throw a log
after the reptile. As soon as he hurls the log, the narrator feels
regret:

> I thought how paltry, how vulgar, what a mean act!
> I despised myself and the voices of my accursed
>   human education.   (*CP* 219)

The accursed human education leads men to intellectual-
ize sex, to "think" about it; and equally unnatural is the way in
which their education leads men to rationalize their innate
moral and religious longings and wonderings. Lawrence en-
forces his point by an obvious literary allusion, which affects
both structure and meaning of "Snake" and thus orders the
poem as a whole. By his action toward the snake, the narrator
is reminded of the albatross that the Ancient Mariner killed
without reason (and perhaps of the punishment that the Mariner received). The "otherness" of the golden Sicilian snake is
as extreme as the strange beauty of the water snakes in "The
Ancient Mariner"; and in a quick change of heart reminiscent
of the Mariner's sudden intuitive empathy with the water
snakes, the narrator of Lawrence's poem wishes that the snake
would return. There is thus a further reminder of Coleridge's
poem, for besides the allusion and the common reference to
snakes, the structures of the poems are similar. After the Mari-

ner has killed the albatross, he learns repentance by seeing all
things in nature as having a place in a universal order at once
natural and divine. Even snakes are "happy living things" for
which the Mariner feels love.[17] For Lawrence the snake is not
merely a part of nature but is "like a king in exile, uncrowned
in the underworld"; the narrator asserts,

> And so, I missed my chance with one of the lords
>   of life.
> And I have something to expiate;
> A pettiness.   (*CP* 219)

Keith Sagar points out that the poem functions on more
than one level; it is not only a dramatic narrative but a psychological analogy. The snake serves as an analogue of the poet's
own manhood, the "I" of the poem as opposed to the "voices in
me," or in Freudian terms, the ego that mediates between the
id and the universe. According to Sagar, "As the snake issues
clear from the burning bowels of the earth, so the man must
meet him with a response (gladness and humility) which
issues clearly from his own bowels without the intervening of
the superego (the voices of his education)." [18]

Understanding the motives for the action that expresses
the conflict of "Snake," the throwing of the log, relies on the
interpretation of the central symbol in the poem. One interpretation is clearly sexual. The snake comes from a "fissure" in the
earth, recalling the "fissure" of "Pomegranate." In the early
poem in the *Dial* the sexual implications of the term were
merely suggested by such phrases as "The end cracks open
with the beginning" (*CP* 123). In "Figs," another poem from
Birds, Beasts, and Flowers, the word "fissure" is explicitly
identified as "the female part" (*CP* 94). In "Snake" the phallic
snake and the "fissure" unite in a sexual metaphor. When the
snake returns to a "horrid black hole," the narrator feels "a sort
of horror" and throws the log. But the union of the snake and
fissure suggests a meaning that transcends the sexual metaphor. In terms of the esoteric iconography with which Lawrence was familiar, the return of the snake to the black hole

symbolizes not only the union of life and death but the soul's emergence, through death, into immortality. Life issues forth from the dark, abiding unknown, and thence it returns. The poet thus hints at a complex religious symbolism, especially in his vision of man's world as, in reality, an underworld in which one of the lords of life roams unacknowledged and uncrowned and in danger of attack by the ignorant. The "horrid" black hole possesses horror only to the uninitiate who fail to perceive that death is the gate through which one passes to that more glorious life of the "upper" world.

Explicitly Lawrence attacks the "voices of education" that persuade the narrator to throw the log; Sagar points out that the poet is also implicitly and symbolically attacking Christianity. The civilizing influences of formal education and institutional religion unite to destroy the natural responses in men. In an essay Lawrence asserts that "the Christians, phase by phase, set out actually to *annihilate* the sensual being in man." [19] In Judaeo-Christian lore the snake belongs to the underworld and represents evil, but for Lawrence the snake represents "a deep, deep life which has been denied in us, and still is denied." [20] Unable to participate in the affective, natural life represented by the snake, the narrator attempts to destroy it. When he throws the log, the snake that earlier had "looked around like a god" becomes "convulsed in undignified haste" (*CP* 218, 219). In sum, the pettiness—ugliness, disharmony —the narrator has brought about is his own stultification and is due to his domination by the great institutions of civilized man.

In several ways "Snake" appealed to the interests of the *Dial*, apart from the aesthetic pleasure the poem gives. In depicting a struggle between primitive, natural instinct and stereotyped, civilized response, the poem accorded with the interest of the magazine in the primitive. More importantly, the psychological implications of the poem reflect the *Dial*'s concern with the theories of Freud and their applications to works of art. Further, the techniques of "Snake"—the exact words and the precise images that describe the narrator and the snake, and the intimation rather than explicit statement of the theme—reveal the influences of the Imagists and establish the poem with other Imagist poems in the *Dial*. (Although the magazine did not espouse any particular poetic theories, it nevertheless reflects the predominant Imagist influence at the beginning of the 1920's.) The striking and unmistakable sexual images, even though they do not call attention to themselves, made the poem seem avant-garde in its day and therefore attractive to the *Dial* as a voice of liberation.

Again, the suggestion in "Snake" that the "voices of education" or precepts of Christianity destroy man's affinities for natural goodness is an assertion that the *Dial* would have wished to examine. One of the consistent and basic interests of the magazine was the reform of education. Its advertising pages carried notices of "new" schools for the young; in the issue for July 1921 the *Dial* announced that its Educational Service had compiled a list of schools "which are applying the scientific principles of modern psychology to the development of an improved type of education." [21] The magazine observed Children's Book Week, and editorial "Comment" for several issues considered children's literature. At its own expense the *Dial* printed advertisements of recommended children's books. Articles on child psychology, such as Olivia Howard's "The Neglected Age" in the issue for June 1920, graced the pages of the *Dial*.[22]

The problem which Lawrence posed in "Snake" is taken up most explicitly in an editorial in the *Dial* for March 1926: "What is an education supposed to do?" Marianne Moore explored the question as she reviewed *The Religion of Undergraduates* by Cyril Harris. Miss Moore asserted that universities were just beginning "in an age of lightness" to express "a desire for the essential." The influence of the new psychology is evident in the predicaments expressed by students and quoted in "Comment": " 'Is one's conduct ethical because good ethics have been found to be good for the race and because one has the habit?' 'How good must one be to be good?' 'What am I?' 'I seem to be at war with myself. Two forces fight for possession of me. Sometimes I take sides with one, sometimes with the other. More often I merely look on.' " [23]

The questions of the students and especially the last comment reveal as well as any statements could the situation of the narrator in "Snake." Both Marianne Moore and D. H. Lawrence looked forward to a time when men acting according to their individual consciences would find answers to such questions. For Lawrence the traditional Christian answers seemed unsatisfactory because they were grafted onto society; they altered the values men naturally held and made men neurotic by insisting on a response contrary to their instincts. In "Snake" the narrator would have met the snake with a natural respect, but Christian indoctrination, according to Lawrence, insisted that he kill it. At the end of the poem the narrator, who should feel elevated by his action, instead feels guilty; the final judgment is made by his own conscience, and like the undergraduate in Marianne Moore's essay, he seems "at war" with himself.

Lawrence's statement of position in "Snake" effectively exemplifies the enlightened freedom that Thayer brought to the *Dial*. If there is a typical *Dial* story, poem, essay, or work of art, it is a work marked by a new freedom both of form and idea, by a new adventurousness of spirit. For Lawrence the purpose of all of his writing was to persuade readers to see the problem of modern men, of which the situation in "Snake" is exemplary; basically the problem reduces to one's inability to accept sex as the vital part of life, to regard sex as the deepest mystery without analyzing it as Freud was doing. The entire history of mankind is recapitulated in the modern failure to accept the sensual life without imposing intellect upon it. Man was driven from Paradise, "Not because we sinned. But because we got sex into our head" (*FU* 121).

The wide interests of Thayer that permitted him to accept both Lawrence and Freud without becoming editorially partisan to either also permitted him to publish other works like "Snake" that express so effectively the central problems of twentieth-century society. Eliot's impression that the century is a waste land and Yeats's private mythology that accounts for the decline of Christianity in our age may conflict perhaps with Lawrence's diagnosis of the twentieth-century malaise. Yet all

three views are encompassed in the embrace of the *Dial* because Thayer and the rest of his staff found in each poet's work
the rare blend of a new, significant, and tenable idea and
matchless aesthetic form.

The records of the *Dial* and the letters and diary of
Lawrence do not indicate whether any other poems from *Birds,
Beasts, and Flowers* were submitted to the magazine. Certainly
any poems submitted after "Snake" would have been artistically inferior—and perhaps would have been rejected. On the
other hand, the conjecture that "Pomegranate" was published
because of the value of the other poems in *Birds, Beasts, and
Flowers* suggests that any poems submitted after "Snake"
would have been welcomed by the *Dial*. Most probably Lawrence declined to submit poetry and sent instead his works in
other genres which the magazine published in issues subsequent to the one for July 1921, containing "Snake." Indeed
in that month Lawrence wrote presumably his first letter to
Thayer, recommending "The Gentleman from San Francisco"
and *Sea and Sardinia*. From July 1921 until October 1923,
when the collection of *Birds, Beasts, and Flowers* was published, the *Dial* printed—instead of Lawrence's poems—*Sea
and Sardinia*, "The Gentleman from San Francisco," "An Episode" from *Aaron's Rod*, *The Fox*, "Indians and an Englishman," "Taos," and "Model Americans."

After *Birds, Beasts, and Flowers* in 1923, Lawrence published no new volumes of poetry until *Pansies* appeared in
1929. Significantly, the *Dial* reflects this hiatus; in 1929 it was
the first American magazine to publish a group of poems from
the new book, in the issues for May and July. To Marianne
Moore, early that year Lawrence sent the complete manuscript
from which Miss Moore chose eleven poems.

The fact that the *Dial* was the first American magazine to
publish part of *Pansies* assumes greater significance when one
considers the publishing history of the volume. In January
1929 two copies of the manuscript which Lawrence was sending to Curtis Brown were confiscated by the British postal
authorities. The Home Secretary, Sir William Joynson-Hicks,

had begun a witchhunt for underground copies of *Lady Chat-terley's Lover*, searching even the homes of Lawrence's friends. The seizure of *Pansies* was merely an extension of Joynson-Hick's search, and the confiscation of *Pansies* produced the same effect as the ban on *Lady Chatterley's Lover:* the books enjoyed a greater commercial success than Lawrence had anticipated. Another result of the seizure was the omission of fourteen poems from the bowdlerized English and American first editions.

For the *Dial* the confiscation of *Pansies* is important in several ways. First, the publicity the volume of verses received would have increased the prestige of the *Dial* as, for at least two months, the exclusive source in America for the poems. Thus even in its last issue the magazine led the vanguard. Second, the seizure of his manuscripts forced Lawrence to retype the poems, and as he retyped, he revised. The revisions he typed out in the manuscript he sent to the *Dial* are relatively minor, if one judges them according to the variations between the texts of the poems in the *Dial* and those in the American first edition that Knopf published. The number of variations— sixteen changes in eleven poems—suggests, however, that the manuscript used by Knopf is not the one that Lawrence sent to the *Dial*.

If the *Dial* manuscript is not unique, the various changes in the poems are inexplicable. The great number of variants in the *Dial*'s versions of *Pansies* excludes the possibility of print-ers' errors, especially in light of the *Dial*'s abhorrence of errors and the careful proofreading by the staff to avoid them. Moreover, some of the changes are too strategic to allow for a printer's carelessness and, if anything, seem attributable to an editor's whims. But Miss Moore, as her letter to Lawrence attests, never allowed into print any changes, textual or me-chanical, in a contribution without first consulting the author. It is thus unlikely that Miss Moore revised the poems from Lawrence's manuscripts and that Lawrence anyway would have accepted so many of her revisions. Upon mailing page proofs of *Pansies* to Lawrence, she requested him to telegraph any changes he wanted to make; and Lawrence chose not to reply to indicate any changes. Instead he wrote Miss Moore later, approving of her selection of his poems. If Miss Moore had revised his poems, why did Lawrence not also comment on the revisions, somewhere in his correspondence, as previously he had commented on the *Dial*'s editorial changes?

The variations in the poems from *Pansies* in the *Dial* occur in vocabulary, mechanics, and structure. Least important are the mechanical changes in punctuation, capitalization, and variant spellings; while other changes, such as the arrangement of lines in stanzas, affect the meter, emphases, and meanings of certain poems. In "When I Went to the Circus—" appear two structural and two mechanical variants. The last line in the third stanza of the poem in the Knopf edition appears separately as a third one-line stanza in the *Dial*— "Then came the hush again, like a hush of fear"—and stanzas four and five in the Knopf version are combined as the fifth stanza of the poem in the *Dial*. Minor changes in the poem in the *Dial* are the period after "star" in the second line of the fifth stanza and the pluralization ("horses" instead of "horse") of the first word of stanza six. Of these four changes the most important is the appearance of the one-line stanza, which focuses on the mood of the people and thus emphasizes the central concern of the poem.

Another of the *Pansies* contains an even greater number of changes than "When I Went to the Circus—." The first poem of the group appearing in the last issue of the *Dial* bears a title change, "To Let Go or to Hold on—?" adding the second "to." In addition to the change in title, three minor and three major changes further suggest that the *Dial* used a manuscript different from that published by Knopf. Changes in spelling and capitalization, such as placing an accent on "debris" and spelling "civilization" with a "z" rather than "s" and capitalizing the first word of a line, are relatively insignificant. On the other hand, two structural changes alter the meaning of the poem and another sets in sharper focus the theme of the poem. The version in the *Dial* reads, instead of "make a new job of the human world," "make a job of the human world"—"make a job" sounding peculiarly British and more acceptably Lawrentian. Instead of "Can we let go?," the line in the *Dial*, expressed as the first line of stanza seven and repeated as the second line, reads "Can we let it go?," changing again the intention of the poem. Finally, the *Dial* sets in a separate stanza the last two lines of the next-to-last stanza in the Knopf version—"Must we hold on?/ Or can we now let go?"—and thereby calls attention to the argument of the poem.

Three other poems from *Pansies* have variants in the *Dial*. In "What Would You Fight For?" only a minor textual change, the spelling of "fellow men" as two words instead of one hyphenated word, indicates perhaps a whim in typing. But in "Work" and in "Attila" appear significant structural changes. In "Work," as in "When I Went to the Circus—" and "To Let Go or to Hold on—?," a line is presented by itself to gain attention and force: "And so it will be again, men will smash machines." Also the word "the" before "machines" is omitted in the *Dial* but included in the Knopf version. In the fourth stanza of the poem, the *Dial* more carefully establishes the pattern of verse than does the poem as published by Knopf: the last four words, "in its own foliage," appear as a sixth line and thus more obviously recall the cadence of line four, "the tissue they weave." Finally, "Attila" in the *Dial* consists of four short verse-paragraphs, the middle two beginning, in parallel fashion, "For after all" and "And after all." In the first American book edition the middle two verse-paragraphs are combined and the force of this parallel construction is obscured. Thus for every substantive change in structure and in vocabulary, the *Dial* version of the selections sharpens, emphasizes, and improves the poems.[24]

Moreover, the extent and the frequency of the changes prove a significant fact: the magazine was temporarily in possession of the first revision of the manuscript. In February 1929 Lawrence requested Marianne Moore to send the manuscript to Curtis Brown after she had chosen the poems she wanted to publish (*CL* 1129). As there is no manuscript of *Pansies* in the

Dial papers, it seems safe to conclude that Miss Moore sent Curtis Brown's representative the manuscript, that it arrived safely, and that Lawrence used the *Dial*'s manuscript when he revised further some of the poems in the volume.

The *Dial* was also the first to publish the original fore-word to *Pansies*, which Lawrence mailed with the poems. Part of it appeared as a brief preface to the ten poems in the issue for July 1929. In a letter to Lawrence on March 28, 1929 Marianne Moore requested two sentences of the preface for the *Dial*; Lawrence agreed, indicating that he had written a new introduction for the book. The *Dial*'s foreword reads:

> *Pensées*, like pansies, have their roots in the earth, and in the perfume there stirs still the first grim scent of under-earth. Certainly in pansy-scent and in violet-scent it is so: the blue of the morning mingled with the corrosive moulder of the ground.[25]

In the book version of the introduction to *Pansies* Lawrence is concerned with vindicating himself from the charge of obscenity. The passage in the revised introduction that corresponds to the preface in the *Dial* lacks the poetic structure and diction of the original version:

> The fairest thing in nature, a flower, still has its roots in earth and manure; and in the perfume there hovers still the faint strange scent of earth, the under-earth in all its heavy humidity and darkness. Certainly it is so in pansy-scent and in violet-scent; mingled with the blue of the morning and the black of the corrosive humus. (*SLC* 27)

Critics generally agree that by and large the poems in *Pansies* are inferior even to Lawrence's earliest poetry. For Harry T. Moore the poems are "not so much authentic poetry as thoughts crystallized in verse forms." Richard Aldington claims that the poems "came out of Lawrence's nerves, and not out of his real self." Auden attacks the short poems in the collection by asserting that "a poem which makes a single point and is made up of no more than one or two sentences can only be organized verbally." [26] Correctively, Keith Sagar suggests

that "Lawrence himself never took *Pansies* as seriously as his
hostile critics" and points out that Lawrence in the introduction to the volume reveals that he was fully aware of any
shortcomings the poems possess.[27] An often-quoted letter Lawrence wrote to the Huxleys, as well as the introduction to *Pansies*, reveals what Lawrence was about in the volume: "I have
been doing a book of Pensées, which I call pansies, a sort of
loose little poem form: Frieda says with joy: real doggerel.—
But meant for *Pensées*, not poetry, especially not lyrical poetry" (*CL* 1106). It is in the light of the author's express
intention that one judges the poems, and Lawrence makes no
pretensions to excellence. Yet Lawrence may have undervalued
Pansies, and critics may have been too eager to accept Lawrence's estimate. Admittedly, there are weak poems in the volume, but others, such as "Attila" and "November by the Sea—"
—two of the poems chosen by Miss Moore—more than justify
the volume as an important addition to the Lawrence canon
and to modern poetry.

The selections in the *Dial* reflect the range, both in length
and quality, of the *Pansies* collection. Miss Moore chose not
only lyrical and comparatively successful poems such as "November by the Sea—" but also "Censors," a personal diatribe
rather than a formulated poem. Yet all the *Pansies* in the *Dial*
reflect the editor's tact, and objectionable, vindictive poems,
such as "Editorial Office," are omitted. Of the eleven poems,
only one in addition to "Censors" is flat and direct and representative of Lawrence's poems of statement: "What Would
You Fight For?" The other nine are lyrical and Imagistic. The
first poem from *Pansies* in the *Dial*, "When I Went to the
Circus—" is a long catalogue of Lawrence's impressions of
circus life and his comparisons of the animals and circus people
and the audience. The idea that Lawrence presents so effectively and imagistically in "Snake" is stated rather explicitly in
"When I Went to the Circus—": the audience was "frightened
of the bare earth and the temporary canvas / and the smell of
horses and other beasts"; they "applauded with hollow, frightened applause"; they "seemed to resent the mystery that lies in

beasts." In short, "modern people are depressed" because of their alienation, and even the children "vaguely know how cheated they are of their birthright/ in the bright wild circus flesh" (*P* 32–35).

If the poems in the volume are not as successful as the earlier *Birds, Beasts, and Flowers*, they have still, as Pinto points out, a quality of freshness and directness.[28] "Whatever Man Makes–," brief though it is, exemplifies the better poems in *Pansies:*

> Whatever man makes and makes it live
> lives because of the life put into it.
> A yard of India muslin is alive with Hindu life.
> And a Navajo woman, weaving her rug in the
>   pattern of her dream
> must run the pattern out in a little break at
>   the end
> so that her soul can come out, back to her.
> But in the odd pattern, like snake-marks on the
>   sand
> it leaves its trail.   (*P* 37)

The epigrammatic and satirical qualities of the poems from *Pansies* that the *Dial* printed are among their chief aesthetic virtues. In "Lizard," for example, Lawrence describes a lizard listening "to the sounding of the spheres" and asserts that "if men were as much men as lizards are lizards/ they'd be worth looking at" (*P* 148). In "Censors" Lawrence manages in a few short successful strokes to burlesque the bane of his life. Unlike "live, sunny men" who laugh, "censors are dead men"; anything alive is dangerous and must be executed–

> And when the execution is performed
> you hear the stertorous, self-righteous
>   heavy breathing of the dead men,
> the censors, breathing with relief.   (*P* 154)

The other poems from *Pansies* in the *Dial* reflect the range of the excellence of the volume. The first poem in the group in the magazine, "To Let Go or to Hold On–?" is a rather long rhetorical discussion about whether men should die

and surrender to a new and better civilization or try to forge a
new world for themselves. The second poem, "Things Men
Have Made—," is in contrast a short nostalgic assertion that
objects are valued because of the labor that produced them.
"Sea-Weed" presents an image of seaweed moved by the winds
and tides. "Attila" describes the ancient Hunnish leader and
concludes that because "he helped to smash a lot of old Roman
lies" he is "a man of peace" (*P* 103). Lawrence here is taking a
smack at the British; during the First World War, the most
popular epithet, among the Allies, for the Germans was
"Huns," to equate their wartime atrocities in Belgium with the
Huns' devastation of the late Roman Empire. In wrecking the
prewar world of lies and illusions, the Germans, suggests
Lawrence, brought men closer to truth. The message of
"Work" is that the purpose of labor is to involve men in life:
"When a man goes out into his work / he is alive like a tree in
spring" (*P* 40). Finally, the weakest and best poems are represented respectively by "What Would You Fight For?" and
"November by the Sea—." The first asserts that lives and wives
and sometimes sons and countries are not worth fighting for—
only "inward peace" is worth the fight. The latter is a description of a sunset over a sea that mingles with the poet's own
thoughts of death.

Like "Snake," Lawrence's early masterpiece, "Sea-
Weed," "Attila," "Lizard" and "November by the Sea—" rely in
varying degrees on imagery for their structure and meaning.
In the later poems, Lawrence paints a single image, and despite his denials that he was an Imagist (à la Amy Lowell),
such a poem as "November by the Sea—" constitutes a perfect
if belated example of Lawrence's Imagist technique. In his last
poem in the *Dial*, he works out a detailed analogy of life's
ending with the sun setting on the eternal sea: the end of the
day, the end of the year, and the end of the poet's life. And
these endings of three natural cycles contrast to eternity and
the unchanging sea. The poem recalls Shakespeare's sonnet
73—"In me thou see'st the twilight of such day / As after sunset
fadeth in the West"—but unlike Shakespeare, who compares

himself in successive quatrains to a winter-stripped tree, a sunset, and a dying fire, Lawrence equates the setting of the sun over the water ("A few gold [November] rays thickening down to red") and his death ("the sun of my soul" is "setting behind the sounding sea between my ribs") and accomplishes by one startling image what Shakespeare communicates by three. "November by the Sea—" expresses the poet's mythopoetic attitude toward nature, his feeling that, truly viewed, the universe is a vast web of analogies. Yet in that vital and basic respect in which Lawrence declares his Romantic heritage, "November by the Sea—" relates not so much to Charles Baudelaire's "Correspondences" as to the lyrics of an earlier Romantic poet, the German Friedrich Hölderlin. Like Hölderlin, Lawrence invokes the classical and preclassical pasts in his nature images and thus not only universalizes his own individual tragedy but also manages, by the very fact of his utterance, to achieve and assert a sense of personal wholeness and fortitude in the face of death. The result is a lied worthy to be placed with those of Hölderlin, Heine, Mörike, and von Hofmannsthal. (In 1934 Josephine Johnson recalled the opening of Lawrence's masterful poem with the title of her prize-winning novel of a dreary farm life, *Now in November*.) Like "November by the Sea—," each of the other successful poems in *Pansies* avoids flat direct statement and becomes expressive through a basic image. The selection by Miss Moore of such poems reveals her own Imagist bias as well as her taste and acuity as editor. On the other hand, such poems as "Censors" and "What Would You Fight For?" reveal a policy of electicism that prevented anyone's labeling the magazine as Imagist.

In addition, some of the themes in the poems from *Pansies* —as well as the excellence of style—reflect the interests of the *Dial*. The burlesque of censors would appeal to editors who were always wary of suffering the fate Lawrence met at censors' hands. Lines from "To Let Go or to Hold on—?" apply perhaps to the perennial interests of the *Dial* in new aesthetic forms: "Have we got to get down and clear away the debris / of a swamped civilisation, and start a new world of man / that will blossom forth the whole of human nature?" (*P* 8–9). Finally, the assertion Lawrence makes at the opening of "Work" would apply equally to Scofield Thayer—who founded the new *Dial* of the 1920's because he wanted an aesthetic outlet and left the magazine for another artistic purpose, the writing of poetry—and to Marianne Moore, devoted as she was to the craft of poetry: "There is no point in work/ unless it absorbs you/ like an absorbing game" (*P* 40). Thus until the very end of the *Dial* Lawrence's work continued to exemplify its interests.

The first works by Lawrence in the *Dial* were autobiographical sketches; and these one may regard as an appropriate introduction to the magazine. The main body of his contributions begins with the poems he submitted from *Birds, Beasts, and Flowers*. After their publication, Lawrence left off writing poetry to produce the essays, stories, and novels for which he is famous; in these intervening years the *Dial* reflects Lawrence's worth by publishing more of his fiction and essays than any other American magazine. It is appropriate that at the end of the *Dial*'s career and near the end of Lawrence's, the magazine again published his poetry and thus brought full circle the relationship of the artist and his publisher. The last poem by Lawrence in the magazine, "November by the Sea–," anticipates the poet's death. On the birthday of the solar heroes, the winter solstice, the sun in Lawrence declines with the sun of the universe to the sea—

> downward they race in decline
> my sun, and the great gold sun.

It was also the last sun to illumine the face of the *Dial*.

8

REVIEWS AND ADVERTISEMENTS
IN *THE DIAL:* A SUMMARY

ALTHOUGH LAWRENCE'S WRITING IN the *Dial* is the most important and most interesting, indeed the essential, aspect of his relationship with the magazine, two other facets of the relationship merit detailed comment in a general survey: the reviews of Lawrence's work and the advertisements in the *Dial* for his books.

Consideration of the advertisements and reviews of Lawrence's work aids importantly in the attempt to fill in and to give perspective and depth to Lawrence's relationship with the magazine. Although ancillary to Lawrence's writing itself, the reviews and advertisements provide, so to speak, a mirrored backdrop for the stage across which Lawrence's works paraded, and reflect the work, magnifying it and enclosing it, giving for each poem and story that appeared in the *Dial* a relevance to the total effect of Lawrence's production. Take the reviews and advertisements away, and Lawrence's work stands as forcefully as ever; but it stands on a bare stage, and the absence of counterplay with the reviews and advertisements results in a sense of loss of the richness and complexity that all three, taken together, can provide.

During all the years that the *Dial* published such a variety of Lawrence's work, the magazine's editors and its commissioned reviewers were at the same time tracing his progress outside the *Dial*'s pages. The reviewers focused more often than not on work by Lawrence that did not appear in the magazine, so that Lawrence's relationship with it goes beyond the works published there to include almost everything he wrote. Before 1920, even though the fortnightly *Dial* did not publish Lawrence's work itself, his publications were the subject of five reviews; in Thayer's *Dial* eighteen reviews focused on Lawrence's writing.[1] Eleven of the reviews were signed by such leaders of the New Movement as T. S. Eliot and in length ranged from a single paragraph discussing Lawrence's writing in general to long, detailed analyses of specific works, essays focusing on a single publication. But the importance of the reviews of Lawrence's work in the new *Dial* transcends the mere frequency of their appearance, for Thayer's critical review was unique in its departure from the humanistic and impressionistic criticism dominant in the 1920's.

In his reminiscence of the decade, Malcolm Cowley suggests that reviewers for the *Dial*, at least before the 1920's, had a rather lackadaisical approach to their work. According to Cowley, reviewing for the *Dial* was a way of "earning a few dollars" so that "you didn't exactly starve." At the *Dial* office Cowley and his writer-friends were given "half a dozen bad novels to review in fifty or a hundred words apiece." Unfortunately, the reviewers were not paid until their reviews were published, which might be weeks or months. So the young reviewers hastily leafed through the books, took a few notes, and then carried the review copies to a secondhand bookstore. "The proprietor paid a flat rate of thirty-five cents for each review copy. You thought it was more than the novels were worth." The next day they wrote the reviews.[2]

For the old *Dial* and for a few fledgling writers like Cowley, this romanticized reminiscence is fair enough. But for the long reviews of Lawrence's work in Martyn Johnson's *Dial*, such an offhand approach to criticism is negated by the high quality of the reviews. Certainly such a reviewer as Edward Garnett, who helped Lawrence get his work into print, is different in kind from the reviewers whom Cowley described.

Moreover, like Garnett's review, Conrad Aiken's assessment of Lawrence's poetry and Henry B. Fuller's remarks about *Twilight in Italy* and *The Prussian Officer* reveal not only comprehension but also a close attention to style and techniques in Lawrence's work. The only review that might support Cowley's contention is Homer E. Woodbridge's discussion of *The Widowing of Mrs. Holroyd;* but because Lawrence's play is incidental in the reviewer's consideration of many plays, Woodbridge could not be expected to analyze it in any detail.[3] Finally, one takes Malcolm Cowley's comment on his generation of *Dial* reviewers as the backward glance of a mature writer toward his youth, with all the idealized half-truths of any such recollection. An examination of Cowley's own reviews in the *Dial* does not suggest that his review assignments were executed in a few minutes on a park bench on a sunny New York afternoon.[4]

For Thayer's *Dial* there can be little question that high aesthetic standards were applied rather carefully to each work reviewed in the magazine. In his *Dial* there is, to be sure, a variety of approaches to criticism, each review reflecting the taste, style, and ideology of its author. For most of the reviews, however, the approach is objective and analytic rather than subjective and impressionistic. The authors of *The Little Magazine* hail the *Dial* of the 1920's as the magazine that "introduced a new criticism to America—a criticism of learning and insight, and a criticism that kept a close eye on the organization of the work under discussion." Reviews in the new *Dial* were in sharp contrast to those in Johnson's magazine; the criticism in the *Dial* before the 1920's "was not criticism of literature from an aesthetic or technical approach at all, but simply an estimate of American thought as revealed in literature."[5]

The reason the *Dial* succeeded in establishing a new critical approach lies in the very principles that governed its editorial selection of fiction, poetry, and essays. The sole criterion of excellence was applied to critical essays and permitted a wide range of reviews. The *Dial* welcomed the new criticism of

Ezra Pound, T. S. Eliot, Kenneth Burke, and Yvor Winters, and thereby it became the chief outlet for one group of the New Critics. On the other hand, it welcomed the appraisals of such writers as Babette Deutsch, an early critic of Lawrence's work in the new *Dial*, whose approach was completely different from the intellectual, objective, highly organized analyses of Kenneth Burke. Unlike Burke, Babette Deutsch does not impose order or devise categories, but instead weaves in and out among the works she is examining, interjecting her responses —however introvert—to each. The qualities and features common to the *Dial*'s reviews are their intensity, urbanity, and acceptance of aesthetic criteria as ultimates. It is not surprising that the fiction and poetry that appeared toward the front of the *Dial* were contributed by the very writers whose reviews were published toward the back.[6]

In Thayer's refurbished *Dial*, the first review to consider Lawrence's writing was a portion of Gilbert Seldes' column "The Theatre" in the issue for August 1920, one month before Lawrence's first work in the *Dial*, "Adolf," was published. The reviewer discussed a new series of *Plays for a People's Theatre*, which Thomas Seltzer, Lawrence's American publisher, was bringing out. For this series Lawrence had written *Touch and Go*, which was to be the first play in the volume, and a preface that was designed to announce the "People's Theatre." Douglas Goldring, editor of the series, also had written a play, *The Fight for Freedom*, and an introduction to the volume and had placed his introduction and play first, thus making Lawrence's preface superfluous and inappropriate.[7] In his review Seldes praised Lawrence's preface but expressed his doubts that either play would long remain in a repertory of a people's theater. He concluded that "Mr. Lawrence, of course, cannot escape his genius. The secondary qualities of *Touch and Go* are superior to big things in the work of many other dramatists."[8]

The next reference to Lawrence's work appeared two issues later in October 1920. In a review of *Georgian Poetry, 1918–1919*, entitled "Weary Verse," Amy Lowell singled out

Lawrence's poem "Seven Seals," his only contribution to the anthology. Miss Lowell, a leader of the Imagist group, had managed earlier to persuade Lawrence to contribute to her anthologies, although Lawrence never thought of himself as an Imagist any more than he imagined himself a Georgian. Naturally the Imagist reviewer attacked the Georgian poets represented in the volume: "Here are nineteen poets, in the heyday of their creating years, and scarcely one of them seems to have energy enough to see personally or forge a manner out of his own natural speech." On the other hand, Amy Lowell praised Lawrence enthusiastically: "As a poet, Mr. Lawrence is rising in stature year by year; his last volume, *Bay*, is the best book of poetry, pure poetry, that he has written, although it does not reach the startlingly human poignance of *Look! We Have Come Through*. It is unfair to Mr. Lawrence to be represented by one poem, the editor should take heed and give us more of him in the future." [9]

Lawrence's poetry was also the subject of the next *Dial* review of his work, which appeared in the issue for January 1921. Lawrence's *New Poems* was included along with F. S. Flint's *Otherworld*, Louis Untermeyer's *The New Adam*, and Arthur Symons' *Lesbia and Other Poems* in an article by Babette Deutsch entitled "Poets and Prefaces." The reviewer was concerned that notable poets, like "a certain Irish playwright . . . feel the necessity for preface-writing." She observed that all four prefaces were concerned with distinguishing poetry from prose. Quoting from Lawrence's preface, she said that, "Instead of emotion recollected in tranquility, the contemporary poet seeks 'mutation, swifter than iridescence, haste, not rest, come-and-go, not fixity, inconclusiveness, immediacy, the quality of life itself, without denouement or close.' " Miss Deutsch commented that "this is what the prose writers also are seeking. Hence, perhaps, in part at least, the need for explanation and examination."

The subsequent critical examination was more successful in pointing out the similarities of prose and poetry than their dissimilarities. Miss Deutsch stated that both poets and prose writers affirm a *Weltanschauung*, as they free themselves from "a Scylla in the image of a Queen Victoria and a Charybdis in the guise of a long, lank Lilith." Contemporary poetry—that is, that of the early 1920's—was like contemporary prose; it was, wrote Miss Deutsch, "at once a reaction and a revelation." As the prose writers were using the stream-of-consciousness technique, so the poets used images or dreams rooted in "primitive impulse and barbarous taboo." Miss Deutsch concluded that the poets' "need for self-explanation" came from a "subconscious fear of their own iconoclasm—of substance even more than technique." [10]

The first review in the new *Dial* to discuss more than one of Lawrence's works appeared three issues later. In an essay of three and a half pages Evelyn Scott, an avant-garde novelist and a rather frequent contributor to the *Dial*, reviewed *Women in Love* and *The Lost Girl*. Echoing Lawrence's pronouncement at the end of 1912 that he would "always be a priest of love" (*CL* 173), Miss Scott characterized Lawrence in the title of her review for April 1921 as "A Philosopher of the Erotic." Unfortunately the essay rambles discursively; the reviewer seems more concerned about the origin of art and its definition than with the novels. First she categorizes Lawrence with Michelangelo, El Greco, and Cézanne, men who substitute "an individual affirmative" for "the interrogation of existence." The purest art, she says, expresses "the most individual experience" but "there is something negative, deathly in this pure art." This discussion brings her somehow to *Women in Love*, which "is not pure as an art form . . . because it is too limited for Lawrence's conviction of reality."

The review becomes more perceptive as Miss Scott spends three sentences describing *Women in Love*. Then she returns to her discussion of the pure art form, to which this novel cannot belong for another reason: it "lacks the quality of the arrested ephemeral." In the surrounding abstruse discussion, occasional phrases break through to indicate that the reviewer's reading of the novel is correct: Miss Scott observes that "the polarized relations of Ursula Brangwen and Rupert Birkin . . . are obviously tendered as a solution of the erotic problem."

The Lost Girl is compared to *Women in Love:* both novels employ the framework of "a search for temporal solutions," but *The Lost Girl* has "an objective sequence" that *Women in Love* does not. Evelyn Scott accurately observes that "Lawrence, the Englishman, accomplishes a sort of mystical identity with the sense-enwrapped Italian, Francesco Marasco [of *The Lost Girl*]" and that both books are remarkably parallel in theme and structure. Except for these rather obvious conclusions, the review does little to advance an understanding of Lawrence's work. Instead, the reader is presented with Miss Scott's own assessment of the artist's dilemma—"the intoxication of self-annihilation balanced against the intoxication of self-assertion"—and with her personal interpretation rather than a straightforward delineation of Lawrence's ideas.[11]

In February 1922 Padraic Colum reviewed *Sea and Sardinia*, parts of which had been published in the *Dial* in the issues for October and November 1921. The reviewer compared Lawrence's travel book to John Millington Synge's *The Aran Islands* and George Borrow's *The Bible in Spain*. Although Lawrence's work is not equal to Synge's and Borrow's, it belongs with them as a "journey into the writer's self . . . the quest that is rarely spoken of—the secret quest."[12] In Lawrence's travel the quest is for a male civilization unlike that of the female European countries. Because his quest is not satisfied, the book remains only a memorable one. Although *Sea and Sardinia* does not have the comprehension of the great travel books, it has "apprehension." Quoting from the book, Colum points out that the descriptions unfold in a way that recalls the art of "the most revealing paintings," suggesting that Lawrence's imagistic technique was not confined to his best poems, such as "Snake," but operated also in his most successful prose. Concluding the discussion, the reviewer uses the word "remarkable" to characterize both Lawrence and Jan Juta, Lawrence's artist friend, whose paintings were reproduced in color in *Sea and Sardinia* and whose portrait of Lawrence the *Dial* reproduced a year later in its issue for February 1923.

The next reference to a work by Lawrence appeared in T. S. Eliot's "London Letter" in the *Dial* for September 1922. In this particular "Letter" Eliot discusses the capacious topic of "The Novel" and includes Lawrence in his consideration of the genre. He characterizes Lawrence's progress as being accomplished by "fits and starts" and asserts that "he has perhaps done nothing as good as a whole as *Sons and Lovers.*" Lawrence's greatest weakness, for Eliot, is a failure to get beyond theory, as evidenced by the fact that Lawrence requires, at the end of *Aaron's Rod*, "the mouthpiece for an harangue." Eliot nevertheless adds that "there is one scene in this book—a dialogue between an Italian and several Englishmen, in which one feels that the whole is governed by a creator who is purely creator, with the terrifying disinterestedness of the true creator." [13]

After the reference to *Aaron's Rod* in Eliot's "London Letter" in the issue for September 1922, Lawrence was not reviewed until April 1923. In that issue appeared an anonymous review of *The Gentleman from San Francisco* in the department of "Briefer Mention"; it was to be the only review of Lawrence's work during that year. The reviewer does not point out that Lawrence was the translator of the title story— he does point out that the book had "evidently been lucky in its translation." For satire, the title story "makes one seek English comparisons, all the way back to Swift," and the reviewer concludes that "the work is new, individual, authentic." [14]

The next year, 1924, Lawrence's work was the subject of three signed reviews; two of them were lengthy and were prominently featured in their issues. The first of the long reviews was written by Alyse Gregory, who became managing editor of the *Dial* in January 1924, the same month that her review of Lawrence's work appeared in the magazine. Running seven and one-half pages, her assessment of four works by Lawrence was to be the *Dial*'s longest review of his work.

The title of Miss Gregory's review shows the influence of the earlier long piece about *Women in Love* and *The Lost*

Girl. In her review of those novels Evelyn Scott had called Lawrence "by accident a novelist, actually . . . the priest of an age almost intolerably self-aware." Alyse Gregory took her cue from the Scott review and entitled this second discussion "Artist Turned Prophet." The bibliographical headnote for the review indicates that Miss Gregory's province includes four works formally listed as being under review. The early novels, *Sons and Lovers* and *The Rainbow*, fare well in Alyse Gregory's survey. "No one," says Miss Gregory, "could read [*Sons and Lovers*] without feeling in its pages something wholly new and vital in the literature of our day." *The Rainbow*, although "less integrated as a work of art," is praised for its descriptions of the English landscape and its characterization.

Fortune turns with *Women in Love.* Its appearance, says the reviewer, was "a very pitiful and unexpected spectacle." She denounces it as dogmatic and autobiographical, making one wonder why *Sons and Lovers* escaped her wrath. *The Lost Girl* only affirms her belief that Lawrence's powers have been lost in "the hermetic cell of dogma," drawn there by "the very tiger that he had loosed so magically with his own hands, the tiger of sex." *Aaron's Rod*, "The Ladybird," "The Captain's Doll," and *The Fox*, Miss Gregory correctly observes, are all obsessed with "seeking out some male purpose greater than sex."

When Lawrence turns to metaphysics in *Psychoanalysis and the Unconscious* and *Fantasia of the Unconscious*, according to Miss Gregory, he fails completely. "And really what a comic picture he presents in his new role of spiritual leader to mankind: this bearded, fox-eyed, irascible prophet with a thundering Jehovah-complex." In *Studies in Classic American Literature* Lawrence becomes a "Babe Ruth of literature," throwing only one theme—that America "bolted from the domination of Europe, only to find herself unable to establish a separate life of her own." Regarding Lawrence's only book-length criticism, Miss Gregory is also one of the earliest critics to observe correctly that Lawrence's essays reveal more about himself than about American literature.

Turning finally to *Kangaroo*, the reviewer speculates

whether it is possible that the novel has come from "one of the best established [authors] in the Anglo-Saxon world of letters." The construction she finds bad, the characters unbelievable, and "the dialogue and reflections vulgar and wearying beyond belief." The novel is redeemed by a few phrases that recall an older and better writer. Nevertheless, says Miss Gregory, "even if he should never write a sentence again penetrated with that quality of mobile response to the savage and destructive beauty of life . . . we shall continue to revere and respect him." [15] The complimentary close of Miss Gregory's review hardly compensates for the ceremonial burial of Lawrence's talent in the rest of the essay, and may well account, in part, for Lawrence's absence from the *Dial* while she was managing editor.

During Miss Gregory's editorship two other reviews of Lawrence's work appeared in the *Dial*. The issue for February 1924 contained Herbert J. Seligman's "D. H. Lawrence, Translator," a review of Lawrence's translation of Giovanni Verga's *Mastro-Don Gesualdo*. As the author of an early critical study, *D. H. Lawrence: An American Interpretation*, which Thomas Seltzer published in 1924, Seligman was an obvious choice for reviewer. In contrast to Alyse Gregory's opinion of Lawrence, Seligman had only praise for his skill at translation, attributing the success of Verga's book to the compatibility of Lawrence's style for the Sicilian master's vibrant moods. Lawrence's words are "heavy with earth awareness," he feels "with the expanse of the body, with skin pores and limbs," and his speech has a "kind of atomic weight so that it radiates the sense, odour, colour, and massiveness, as well as trembling movement of animate and inanimate beings." In sum, according to Seligman, "Lawrence has been able to give out this work again, in his own idiom." [16]

For the issue of June 1924 Conrad Aiken, altogether a more formidable critic than Seligman, reviewed *Birds, Beasts, and Flowers* in a five-page article entitled "Disintegration in Modern Poetry." An important poet of the New Movement, Aiken was a frequent contributor of reviews and critiques to

the *Dial* and also had been on the staff during the years
1917–20, when Martyn Johnson was publisher. Like Babette
Deutsch, Aiken discusses the difference between poetry and
prose, but unlike Miss Deutsch he focuses on Lawrence's
work: phrases from the poems are "excellent bits of descriptive
prose, sharp and exact . . . but their excellence, it must be
insisted, is a prose excellence, level, cumulative, explanatory."
According to Aiken, poetry must contain "sharp, brief suggestions" and a "total elimination of the personal presence," and it
is only rarely that both conditions exist. This was doctrine
acceptable to the Pound-Eliot axis, but hardly to Lawrence and
his supporters. Aiken attacks Lawrence's view of the world as
"infantile" and "obsessed." "Figs, tortoises, goats, dogs, flowers
—all, to Mr Lawrence, write in sex-martyrdom." His conclusion is that "Mr Lawrence has carried disintegration a long
way back" and that "his structure is casual, slipshod, and
rhythmless . . . a prose structure." [17]

Conrad Aiken's review of Lawrence's poetry is much like
Lawrence's analysis of American writers in *Studies in Classic
American Literature:* both reviewers tend to reveal as much
about their own theories of art as they do about the work under
consideration. In an earlier review of Lawrence's poetry in the
Dial for August 9, 1919, Aiken had established his criterion for
successful poetry; it consisted of "that sort of brief movement
when, for whatever psychological reason, there is suddenly a
fusion of all the many qualities, which may by themselves
constitute charm, into one indivisible magic." Aiken admired
most the poems of the Imagists, especially those of John Gould
Fletcher, for their metrical quality that fused dissonant elements into a unified whole.[18] In the early poems by Lawrence,
such as "Look! We Have Come Through," Aiken glimpsed the
possibility that Lawrence might allow emotion to dominate
intellect and produce metrical verse. Instead, Lawrence proceeded to use the image as the unit that constitutes a poetic line
and discarded rhythm and meter as controlling forces for the
line; as Aiken's review shows, he was out of sympathy with
that development. Moreover, Lawrence's development as a poet

was away from the Georgians and the Imagists toward a personal style that assimilated and built on those two early influences and in which the poet's voice could always be heard. For Aiken, Lawrence's *Birds, Beasts, and Flowers* was a falling away—a "disintegration"—of his poetic ideal.

The next five reviews in the *Dial* of Lawrence's work were all anonymous and were printed in the "Briefer Mention" section of the magazine; fortunately the *Dial's* records reveal the identities of the reviewers of most of these books. In the issue for June 1925 Henry McBride, the columnist for the magazine's short-lived "Modern Forms" and throughout the 1920's the sole contributor-editor of its monthly chronicle "Modern Art," reviewed Lawrence's coauthorship with Mollie Skinner of *The Boy in the Bush.* For McBride, the work "acquires no polish from the Lawrence touch," and he concluded that "occasional lucky phrases do not offset the vast reaches of careless writing." [19] By contrast, Lisle Bell in the next issue of the *Dial* for July recalled Seligman's earlier estimate of Lawrence as a translator and found his efforts for Verga's *Little Novels of Sicily* to be "good fortune for the reader no less than for the [original] author." [20]

Two other brief, unsigned reviews by Alyse Gregory appeared in the issues for November 1925 and June 1926, the first of *Saint Mawr* and the second of *The Plumed Serpent,* respectively a novella and novel that grew out of Lawrence's Southwestern and Mexican experience. In the review of *Saint Mawr,* Miss Gregory expressed again her preference for Lawrence's early works such as *The Fox* and *The Lost Girl.* Of *The Plumed Serpent* she concluded that "if one is interested in the revival of ancient religious cults, in bullfights, and in revolutions, there is much that is instructive and entertaining in this volume, but if one's chief interest is Mr Lawrence there is nothing new to learn." [21] Bullfights were one of Miss Gregory's aversions, and it may be that the emphasis on blood and violence in *The Plumed Serpent* assured her antipathy to the novel.

In an intervening issue between November 1925 and June

1926, when Alyse Gregory's reviews appeared, an anonymous reviewer—whom the *Dial* papers do not identify—assessed *Reflections on the Death of a Porcupine and Other Essays.* Writing in the issue for April 1926 the reviewer praised "The Crown," an essay Lawrence had written in 1915 for John Middleton Murry's little wartime magazine, *Signature* (*RDP*, p. i). The other essays in the volume reflect a later Lawrence and exhibit "a vulgarity unprecedented and phenomenal," but " 'The Crown' restores one's faith in Lawrence's singular and eccentric genius." It contains "passages of a deep and penetrating beauty, burning with intensity, rich in imagery, and fecund in philosophic suggestion." This early assessment of "The Crown" reveals the remarkable insight of the *Dial*'s critics, for this essay, written about the same time as *The Rainbow*, is generally recognized to be a basic source for explanations by Lawrence of the symbolic meanings of his novels, poems, and stories.[22]

In the issue for October 1927 appeared a third and final signed review by Conrad Aiken of Lawrence's work. The reviewer's growing disaffection for Lawrence is evident in his characterization of Lawrence's *Mornings in Mexico* as merely "one more of his attempts to rifle the soul of a landscape and its people." The failure of the work, says Aiken, lies primarily in Lawrence's passion for exposure. "His desire to see things naked has itself become increasingly naked, not to say brutal; his passion for understanding, for exposing, has become almost synonymous with a passion for destroying." The reviewer compares a passage from the book to a passage from *Sons and Lovers*, calling attention to the assertion that Lawrence's prose had become "slipshod and journalistic." Aiken does not compare *Mornings in Mexico* to *Sea and Sardinia*, a more appropriate volume in the same genre, but apparently he has the Sardinian travel book in mind when he avers that in the past Lawrence "selected the one or two details which might magically imply a whole scene, drenched with scent and sound." By comparison *Mornings in Mexico* is "tiresomely explicit."[23]

Toward the end of the 1920's—and of the *Dial*—its reviews of Lawrence's work appeared less frequently in the magazine, presumably not from any editorial lack of interest but because most of Lawrence's work had already been reviewed there. In the years after 1926 until the last issue of the *Dial* in July 1929, Lawrence produced four major works: *Mornings in Mexico*, published in June 1927, *The Woman Who Rode Away and Other Stories* in 1928, *Lady Chatterley's Lover*, published in various editions in May, July, and November 1928, and the *Collected Poems*, published in September 1928.[24] That only the last of these major works was not treated in the *Dial* hardly constitutes an omission, since the magazine had already considered in its reviews every volume of Lawrence's poetry which comprised the *Collected Poems. New Poems, Love Poems, Bay, Amores, Look! We Have Come Through,* and *Birds, Beasts, and Flowers* all received some notice—from an incidental comment in a summary review by Amy Lowell to a five and one-half page essay by Conrad Aiken devoted exclusively to Lawrence.

The last collection of Lawrence's short stories to appear before his death, *The Woman Who Rode Away and Other Stories*, was reviewed by Henry McBride in the issue for August 1928. It is perhaps the most representative of the briefer, unsigned reviews of Lawrence's later work, echoing as it does the sentiments of Alyse Gregory's three reviews and Conrad Aiken's last review of Lawrence's work. Certainly McBride's remarks show him at his most urbane and wittiest.

> Mr Lawrence reduces all humanity to Adam and Eve and studies them in the nude. Not a hint of fig-leaf, though the stories date distinctly from "after the fall!" Lords and ladies, boot-blacks and kitchen-maids are at bottom, just Adams and Eves. . . . In the end too much nudity, like too much of anything else, surfeits. Readers, even sympathetic ones, now begin to smile when Mr Lawrence's characters undress.[25]

Finally, in the "London Letter" for the issue of February 1929, the London correspondent, Raymond Mortimer (who in 1923 succeeded T. S. Eliot in this post) considered his country's censorship of *Lady Chatterley's Lover* and Radclyffe

Hall's *The Well of Loneliness*, the decade's notorious depiction of lesbians. Mortimer has little praise for Lawrence's novel or for the view of existence it presents. Comparing *Lady Chatterley's Lover* to Aldous Huxley's *Point Counter Point*, in which a character speaks as a mouthpiece for Lawrence, Mortimer asserts that the novelists "have both got it into their heads that the development of the brain entails atrophy of the capacity for love." He concludes hopefully that such ideas are merely "growing pains," a part of the twentieth century's "crisis in the growth of consciousness." [26]

Certain conclusions are suggested by a retrospect of all the reviews of Lawrence's work. The most significant is that during the 1920's there is observable in the *Dial* a definite trend, a movement away from complimentary reviews of Lawrence's early work to qualified or noncommittal praise and finally to a complete disenchantment. Many reviewers—among them T. S. Eliot, Alyse Gregory, Conrad Aiken, and Henry McBride—suggest that the early promise of Lawrence, although it was not lost, at least changed its direction. The reviews of Eliot, Aiken, and Miss Gregory express a preference for the early novels, especially *Sons and Lovers* and *The Rainbow*, and deplore the failures of Lawrence's later novels, *Aaron's Rod*, *Kangaroo*, and *The Plumed Serpent*. In his "London Letter" in the issue for September 1922, Eliot still saw Lawrence as a "true creator," and in her long review in January 1924 Miss Gregory continued to "revere and respect him." On the other hand, by June 1926 Miss Gregory suggested that Lawrence had nothing new to say, and Aiken's review in the issue for October 1927 described Lawrence's work as "tiresomely explicit."

A second conclusion is that the reviews in the *Dial* adumbrate, to a remarkable degree, today's major critical opinions of Lawrence's work. Critics after 1920, and writing outside the *Dial*, have held that Lawrence's early novels are his best, that his poetry is an uneven achievement aesthetically, that he excelled in descriptive travel essays, and that his translations reflect his genius for entering another writer's world and faithfully reproducing it in English. Finally, then, the assessments of Lawrence's work by the *Dial*'s reviewers suggest the success of Thayer's policy of representing eclectically as many different critical points of view as possible. This guiding principle of the *Dial* resulted not only in its taking the lead in publishing the best writing of the 1920's but also in its earning recognition as a reliable authority for critical judgments.

For Lawrence, who wisely tended to discount reviewers' and critics' opinions (however much they wounded his self-esteem), such essays were probably more important as advertisements for his work. In effect, these reviews were influential in conjunction with the advertisements from his publishers that appeared in the *Dial*. The number of advertisements for Lawrence's work is twice that of his contributions and more than triple the number of reviews of his writing. In all, seventy-one advertisements referred specifically to one or more of his current publications: thirty-eight were placed by his major American publisher, Thomas Seltzer, in issues from July 1920 until July 1924; one by Mitchell Kennerly for *Sons and Lovers* in October 1921; one by B. W. Huebsch for *Amores, Look! We Have Come Through*, and *New Poems* in April 1921; one by New York's Holliday Bookshop, which advertised in the issue for November 1921 that it sold all of Lawrence's works; two by the Dial Press in the issues for September and October 1924 for *Stories from The Dial*, which included "The Gentleman from San Francisco"; and twenty-eight by the *Dial* itself among its house advertisements.[27] In addition, advertisements appeared for *Georgian Poetry*, to which Lawrence contributed, and for magazines other than the *Dial* in which Lawrence's work appeared—the *Athenaeum, English Review, Nation*, and *Bookman*. Frequently some of these magazines were offered as a joint subscription with the *Dial*.[28]

The most prominently featured advertisements were those of the Thomas Seltzer firm. In the issue for April 1922 Lawrence's American publisher bought the entire fourth cover and devoted two-thirds of the space to Lawrence's work, incorrectly announcing *Aaron's Rod* as the third novel in a trilogy with

The Rainbow and *Women in Love*. In every issue from August 1923 through May 1924 Seltzer bought the entire third cover and devoted at least part, frequently one-third or more, of the advertisement to Lawrence's work. In nine other issues Seltzer purchased full-page advertisements; in the issues for February 1921 and June 1923 he used the entire space to announce that he was publishing new works by Lawrence—*The Lost Girl* in 1921 and *The Captain's Doll* and *The Gentleman from San Francisco and Other Stories* in 1923. In some other issues, especially in 1920, 1921, and 1922, Seltzer's advertisements occupied no more than one-eighth of a single column (one-half the width of the magazine's page). Over the years every work by Lawrence that Seltzer published was advertised in the *Dial*.

The quality of Seltzer's advertisements varies. In some advertisements, such as the full-page advertisement at the back of the *Dial* for March 1923, the contents are arranged attractively, the various sizes of type have a pleasing range, and a pen-sketch of Lawrence appears in the upper left corner. Complimentary quotations from reviews in various journals are well-chosen. Sometimes the advertisements refer to the *Dial* if the work advertised or a part of it had appeared earlier in the magazine; for example, the advertisement in the issue for November 1921 in which the second installment of *Sea and Sardinia* appeared, describes the work as "The Travel Book of the Season" and asserts, "You have sampled portions of this book in the pages of the *Dial*. The whole is just as delicious." Comments in other reviews describe the books in terms then avant-garde but now "period" and amusing. The advertisement for *Aaron's Rod* in the issue for July 1922 summarizes the novel as an account of "love and marriage in our day." At other times Seltzer used advertisements to emphasize Lawrence's progress artistically, as in the issue for April 1922, where he reported that Lawrence had just received the James Black Tait Award for Fiction for *The Lost Girl*.

The *Dial* for July 1924 printed what was to be Seltzer's last advertisement in the magazine; it is the only one of his,

after June 1920, that does not refer to a specific title by Lawrence. Lawrence's correspondence reveals that at least by
March 1924, when Mr. and Mrs. Seltzer called on the writer at
Kiowa Ranch, the publisher was having financial difficulties.
Lawrence wrote to Koteliansky that "Seltzer and Mrs. Seltzer
are not so nice. She is the bad influence. He says he lost $7000
last year. And simply no money in the bank, for me. I don't like
the look of their business at all" (*CL* 785). Perhaps Seltzer's
advertising in the *Dial* was not sufficiently helpful. Other writers Seltzer published—notably Ford Madox Ford and Hemingway—found themselves in the same predicament as
Lawrence.[29]

Lawrence's correspondence with friends and with his
agent Curtis Brown reveals a growing disaffection for Seltzer
(*CL* 775, 707, 814, 822). By February 1925 Lawrence had
decided to send his work to the more reliable firm of Alfred
Knopf (*CL* 826, 831). As late as August 1929 Lawrence was
still embroiled with Seltzer and was trying to persuade Curtis
Brown to secure the rights of publication that Seltzer had
transferred to Boni and Liveright (*CL* 1183). After 1924
Boni and Liveright were the only publishers to advertise Lawrence's work in the *Dial*. In the 1920's when he published
Lawrence's work, Knopf did not buy space in the *Dial*, not
only because it was a rival of his own *American Mercury* but
also because H. L. Mencken, then editing the *Mercury*, could
not abide Lawrence's views and literary style.

The other important advertiser for Lawrence, in addition
to Thomas Seltzer, was the *Dial* itself. After 1924 it was almost
his sole advertiser; of thirteen advertisements for Lawrence's
work, twelve were house advertisements; the other was Boni
and Liveright's advertisement for two of Lawrence's books
reprinted in their Modern Library, *Sons and Lovers* and *The
Rainbow*. As early as April 1921, however, the *Dial* had included Lawrence in its advertisements. In that issue the editors
announced their first award from Edward O'Brien, who in his
annual anthologies of short stories rated leading American
reviews by the quality of their fiction. In 1920, and for every

year thereafter, the *Dial* was the only magazine in America to receive a "100%" award rating, which meant that all the fiction in the magazine belonged in qualitatively the highest category of all the fiction published in leading American magazines. In addition, O'Brien further categorized the best stories into four groups, and in 1921 "Adolf" by Lawrence was one of the eleven stories from the *Dial* selected for the first group—a fact to which the *Dial* called the attention of its readers in April 1921.

Other house advertisements in the *Dial* featured Lawrence for various reasons. In some issues these house advertisements served to announce the writers whose work would appear in forthcoming issues; Lawrence's *Sea and Sardinia* was so announced in the issue for October 1921, *The Fox* in June 1922, "The Woman Who Rode Away" in April, May, and June 1925, "Glad Ghosts" in June 1926, "Two Blue Birds" in January, February, and March 1927, "The Man Who Loved Islands" in June 1927, "In Love?" in October 1927, and "a group of poems" from *Pansies* in June 1929. Usually the announcements of forthcoming publications were part of a double-page house advertisement at the rear of the magazine. One such advertisement, first published in July 1923 and reprinted in the issues for October 1924 and February 1925, described the work in the *Dial* as "The Classics of Today and Tomorrow" and included Lawrence along with Joyce, Yeats, Sherwood Anderson, Van Wyck Brooks, Thomas Hardy, William Carlos Williams, Edwin Arlington Robinson, and E. E. Cummings—contributors to the *Dial* who virtually made up a roll of some of the foremost writers of the late nineteenth and early twentieth centuries.

In still other ways the *Dial* could be called Lawrence's most faithful advertiser. The magazine featured a column entitled "Among Dial Advertisers," which focused on new works coming from the presses of its advertisers. In the issue for November 1921 the anonymous columnist announced Seltzer's forthcoming publication of Lawrence's book of poems, *Tortoises*, and *Sea and Sardinia*. Along with a subscription to the *Dial* the editors frequently offered a book from a specified list;

twice works by Lawrence were included in such a list. In its Christmas advertisement in December 1922 the magazine offered a copy of *Sea and Sardinia* and a year's subscription for ten dollars (hardly a bargain, since a year's subscription to the *Dial* and a copy of *Sea and Sardinia* each sold for five dollars anyway). A year later, in the issues for November and December 1922 the magazine offered *Aaron's Rod* and a year's subscription for five dollars.

Lawrence was also included in the most lavish advertising venture ever engaged in by the magazine. Between November 20 and December 10, 1921, the *Dial* mailed to selected lists of names thirty thousand copies of a handsome brochure, assembled by Gilbert Seldes and dubbed the Peacock Folder because on its front cover was reproduced Gaston Lachaise's stone sculpture of a peacock, published in the *Dial* for April 1921. The other three pages of the Peacock Folder included eight other works of art reproduced in the magazine, reprints of commendatory passages about the *Dial* from newspapers and other periodicals, editorial assertions about the aims and achievement of the *Dial*, and an impressive list of contributors. Lawrence was one of the forty-three contributors named.[30]

Additionally, the *Dial* advertised Lawrence's work in the clipsheets that it distributed to publicize its forthcoming issues. Each clipsheet consisted of short selections from articles, stories, and poems in the issue and a leading short summary paragraph that revealed what the *Dial* considered to be the most important contributions to that issue. For at least eleven issues of the clipsheets the *Dial* announced a forthcoming poem, or story, or essay by Lawrence in its summary paragraph; on three occasions it quoted from one of his works or reprinted it entirely; once the magazine reproduced part of a review of a work by Lawrence.

The occasions on which Lawrence is referred to in the clipsheets virtually span the 1920's: the clipsheet released on September 22, 1921 announced the forthcoming issue for October that contained the first installment of *Sea and Sardinia;* the clipsheet of June 30, 1929, for the last issue of the *Dial*, saluted

Lawrence's ten poems in that issue and reprinted one of the poems. The first clipsheet to mention Lawrence also quotes a paragraph from *Sea and Sardinia;* under the heading, "Volcanoes and Sentiment," the *Dial* reprinted the passage in which Lawrence suggests that the proximity of Mount Etna makes the Sicilians "so terribly physical all over one another" (*SeSa* 7) – surely one of his more amusing conjectures.

At least four of Lawrence's short stories and his novella, *The Fox*, were announced in the summary paragraphs of seven clipsheets. In the clipsheet released on June 24, 1922, the *Dial* referred merely incidentally to *The Fox*, noting only that it was fiction "from England (D. H. Lawrence)." In the clipsheet for the July 1925 issue, which the magazine released on June 25, 1925, Lawrence's story, "The Woman Who Rode Away," received top billing, appearing first in the summary paragraph that led the release. As if to welcome him after his absence from the magazine, the staff writer, presumably Marianne Moore, elaborated by summarizing the story in a long sentence, an unusual if not unique accord under the limitation of the available space. In the clipsheet for the following issue the reader was reminded of the second installment of Lawrence's story about "a woman's adventures among Indians in contemporary Mexico." In the clipsheets for June 29 and July 26, 1926 "Glad Ghosts" received the same treatment as "The Woman Who Rode Away"–top billing and a short summary in the June clipsheet and a reminder of the concluding installment in the other clipsheet. "Two Blue Birds" and "In Love?" received less emphatic notice in the clipsheets for March 25, 1927 and October 27, 1927, although the October clipsheet described the second story as "one of Mr Lawrence's characteristic satires."

In the clipsheet for September 27, 1927, the summary paragraph announced the forthcoming review by Conrad Aiken of *Mornings in Mexico*, omitting there to furnish the reviewer's name. On the second page, however, appeared the reprint of a long paragraph from Aiken's review, entitled in the clipsheet "D. H. Lawrence," in which Aiken attacks Lawrence for his ravaging descriptions and his "desire to get under, and into, the souls of the supposedly soulless" and concludes that "for Mr Lawrence the *act* of dissection is everything, the idea behind it almost nil." For the years 1925–29 when Marianne Moore edited the *Dial*, Aiken's review was the only long, signed discussion of Lawrence's work; the inclusion of this review one need not regard as editorial statement so much as another of Miss Moore's attempts to parade Lawrence as one of the most frequent and most highly regarded contributors to the *Dial*.

By 1929 Lawrence was indeed one of the more durable glories of the magazine, and the clipsheets for the last issues not only referred to Lawrence's contributions but also reprinted them. In the summary paragraph of the clipsheet for April 26, 1929, Lawrence's name gleamed among those of other poet-contributors—Witter Bynner, Lola Ridge, and Julian Drachman. In the center column of the three-column page appeared Lawrence's contribution to the May issue, "When I Went to the Circus–." In the final clipsheet Lawrence led the list of contributors at the top of the first column, and at the top of the third column appeared the poem, "What Would You Fight For?"

The importance of the clipsheets as advertisements for Lawrence's work, as much as for the *Dial*, can hardly be overstated. Publication of the two poems and "Volcanoes and Sentiment" constitutes a hitherto unnoted set of printings of Lawrence's writing in two genres; publication of these three pieces in three issues of the *Dial* is actually accompanied by these printings. More generally, examination of the *Dial* clipsheets reveals even further the value the magazine attached to Lawrence; not only was his writing given first place in the issues of the *Dial* and touted in house advertisements, but several of his works were reprinted as "samples" for distribution to many who never read the *Dial*. In the clipsheets the frequent references to Lawrence and the terse descriptions of his works not only publicized the *Dial* but publicized Lawrence too.

Obviously to speak of Lawrence's relationship with the *Dial* and to discuss only his works published there, excluding the reviews and advertisements of his work, is to fail to grasp the entirety and complexity of the relationship. The fact that Lawrence's major American publisher advertised lavishly in nearly every issue of the magazine may reflect poor business management, but it also suggests Seltzer's awareness of the particular audience in America to whom Lawrence's work appealed. A second fact, that the *Dial* steadily reviewed Lawrence's work, suggests on one hand the appeal of the writer to the staff and, on the other, the realization of the staff that Lawrence's work in its entirety was important to the magazine's readers and thus to the vitality of the New Movement. House advertisements for his work affirm the realization at the *Dial* of his importance to the magazine's readers, while the clipsheets reveal that the *Dial* depended on Lawrence to attract new readers. The perspective on Lawrence's relationship with the *Dial* widens then to include his agents, his publishers, and, most importantly, the readership of the *Dial*—all in all, a majority of the American intellectual, literary, and artistic vanguard in the century's most brilliant decade for letters and the arts.

To a surprising extent, the *Dial*'s subscribers and Lawrence's readers were the same. The magazine's aim was to publish the works of the avant-garde as well as the established writers regardless of their ideologies and contingent only upon their excellence as literary craftsmen. Who in England was more avant-garde than Lawrence, and whose work was being followed with a more intense critical interest? Neither Lawrence nor the *Dial* was ever a financial success; each belonged not to the masses but to the microcosm of the American creative vanguard of the 1920's.

At the center of this microcosm were the *Dial*'s staff, agents, advertisers, reviewers, and contributors. It was by and large a very cohesive microcosm. Scofield Thayer agreed with Lawrence in temperament, ideology, and critical judgment. And although Lawrence did not appeal to such an antipathetic personality as Ezra Pound, agent in Europe for the *Dial*, about Lawrence's genius Pound was enthusiastic. Alyse

Gregory found Lawrence both amusing and irascible, and if she did not always agree with his views on sex and psychology, she was acutely aware that his contributions to the magazine grew infrequent. Marianne Moore and Lawrence shared few interests beyond poetry, but as editor of the *Dial*, she welcomed his work. The staff so respected Lawrence's writing that they did not change even a mark of punctuation without requesting his consent. The reviewers–except toward the end of the 1920's when both Lawrence's themes and the *Dial*'s verve were hardening–never ended a discussion, however brief, however qualified, without expressing admiration for the artist. The men who sold Lawrence's books in America looked by and large to the readership of the *Dial* for a market, just as the *Dial* depended on Lawrence's contributions to endow its pages with the glamor of his genius–and to help sell its issues.

Ten years is a long time for any relationship to endure in the literary world, and it would be indeed unusual if there were not fluctuations, turns, and unconsummated beginnings. Lawrence was ruffled when *Sea and Sardinia* was so extensively edited by the *Dial*, and yet no other magazine printed parts of the book. Lawrence brought to the *Dial* new writers and translators who caused problems for the editors but also who widened the scope of its cosmopolitanism. At one time the magazine obviously intended to publish a series of essays by Lawrence about his impressions of America; yet only two such essays appeared. Information the *Dial*'s staff received about his novels proved to be erroneous, and for some reason only tenuously explainable Lawrence did not want the magazine to publish *Kangaroo*. There are gaps of as much as two years when no work by Lawrence appeared in the magazine, either because it rejected his writing or because Lawrence or his agents submitted no manuscripts. The threat of censorship doubtless forced the magazine to decline some of Lawrence's fiction, perhaps his short story, "Sun." [31] At least one poem, "Pomegranate," was at first rejected, obviously because the *Dial* found it to be artistically inferior. Finally, there were friends of Lawrence, like Richard Aldington, who tried to lure him to the treasure chest of magazines with larger circulations than the *Dial*'s.

Yet something holds together such a literary relationship: the consonant tastes and judgments of editors and contributors, the greater willingness of editors to publish more of an author's work than do other magazines, the gracious hospitality and respect of the staff for a writer's work, the more frequent appearance of a contributor's name in "Notes on Contributors" and the house advertisements, the rate of payment that permits the contributor to buy more groceries, books, and travel tickets, even perhaps the comfortable feeling of a familiar signature on checks. All of these, the essentials of payment and the small comfortable touches of friendly editors, held Lawrence to the *Dial*. Largely as a result of his relationship with the *Dial*, Lawrence found an audience in America for his work—and helped foment a revolution in attitudes and manners. The offspring of the fertile union—the small *Dial* with a circulation that never exceeded twenty-two thousand, and Lawrence, a writer in a strange, new country—were articles in the New York *Times*, poems and stories in *Vanity Fair* and the *Atlantic Monthly*, and a ranch in New Mexico, the only home Lawrence and Frieda ever owned.

So a literary relationship begins and lasts, grows beyond the initial partners, comes to fruition, scatters seeds to places still unseen.[32] How does it end? The best literary relationships, like the best marriages, last till death. Even the avant-garde who proclaim freedom in sex and love exhibit a remarkable personal constancy. Until its final issue of July 1929, a dying gasp for many of its critics, the *Dial* paraded Lawrence first; *Pansies* blossomed on these first—and final—pages. Lawrence, in this case the more reticent of the married couple, curtly wrote to a friend about the death of the *Dial*: "Don't bother to send on the *Dials*. By the way, those are the last numbers, it is now dead." But a more public and significant appreciation of the relationship was expressed—an appreciation that sums up the mutual importance to each other of D. H. Lawrence and the *Dial*. The New York *Times*, in taking note of the passing of the *Dial*, applied to the defunct magazine a line from Lawrence's poem, "When I Went to the Circus—," which had appeared in the *Dial* for May 1929:

"THERE WAS NO GUSHING RESPONSE, AS THERE IS AT THE FILM." [33]

APPENDICES
NOTES
INDEX

Contributions, Reviews, Advertisements

Lawrence's Contributions to *The Dial*

"Adolf," LXVIX (September 1920), *269–76*.

"Rex," LXX (February 1921), *169–76*.

"Pomegranate," LXX (March 1921), *317–18*.

"Apostolic Beasts," LXX (April 1921), *410–16*.

"Snake," LXXI (July 1921), *19–21*.

"*Sea and Sardinia:* As Far as Palermo, The Sea," LXXI (October 1921), *441–51*.

"*Sea and Sardinia:* Cagliari, Mandas, Sorgono: The Inn, To Nuoro," LXXI (November 1921), *583–92*.

"The Gentleman from San Francisco," LXXII (January 1922), *47–68*.

"An Episode," LXXII (February 1922), *143–46*.

The Fox, LXII (May–June 1922), *471–92, 569–87;* LXIII (July–August 1922), *75–87, 184–98*.

"Indians and an Englishman," LXXIV (February 1923), *144–52*.

"Taos," LXXIV (March 1923), *251–54*.

"Model Americans," LXXIV (May 1923), *503–10*.

"The Woman Who Rode Away," LXXIX (July–August 1925), *1–20, 221–36*.

"Glad Ghosts," LXXI (July–August 1926), *1–21, 123–41*.

"Two Blue Birds," LXXXII (April 1927), *287–301*.

"The Man Who Loved Islands," LXXXIII (July 1927), *1–25*.

"In Love?" LXXXIII (November 1927), *391–404*.

"When I Went to the Circus," LXXXVI (May 1929), *383–84*.

"*Pansies:* To Let Go or to Hold On, Things Men Have Made, Whatever Man Makes, Work, What Would You Fight For? Attila, Sea-Weed, Lizards, Censors, November by the Sea," LXXXVI (July 1929), *543–48*.

Reviews in *The Dial* of Lawrence's Work

H. E. Woodbridge, "Plays of Today and Yesterday" (rev. *The Widowing of Mrs. Holroyd*), LVIII (January 16, 1915), *46–50.*

Edward Garnett, "Art and the Moralists: Mr. D. H. Lawrence's Work" (rev. *The White Peacock, The Trespasser, Sons and Lovers, The Widowing of Mrs. Holroyd, The Prussian Officer*), LXI (November 16, 1916), *377–81.*

Henry Blake Fuller, "Embracing the Realities" (rev. *The Prussian Officer, Twilight in Italy*), LXII (March 22, 1917), *237–38.*

William Aspenwall Bradley, "Some Modern Singers" (rev. *Amores*), LXII (April 19, 1917), *352–54.*

Conrad Aiken, "The Melodic Line" (rev. *Look! We Have Come Through*), LXVII (August 9, 1919), *97–100.*

Gilbert Seldes, "The Theatre" (rev. *Touch and Go*), LXVIX (August 1920), *215.*

Amy Lowell, "Weary Verse" (rev. *Georgian Poetry, 1918–19, Bay, Look! We Have Come Through*), LXVIX (October 1920), *424–31.*

Babette Deutsch, "Poets and Prefaces" (rev. *New Poems*), LXX (January 1921), *89–94.*

Evelyn Scott, "A Philosopher of the Erotic" (rev. *Women in Love, The Lost Girl*), LXX (April 1921), *458–61.*

Padraci Colum, "Sea and Sardinia" (rev. *Sea and Sardinia*), LXXII (February 1922), *193–96.*

T. S. Eliot, "London Letter" (mention of *Aaron's Rod*), LXXIII (September 1922), *329–31.*

Anonymous, "Briefer Mention" (rev. *The Gentleman from San Francisco and Other Stories*), LXXIV (April 1923), *413.*

Alyse Gregory, "Artist Turned Prophet" (rev. *Psychoanalysis and the Unconscious, Fantasia of the Unconscious, Studies in Classic American Literature, Kangaroo*), LXXVI (January 1924), *66–72.*

Herbert J. Seligman, "D. H. Lawrence, Translator" (rev. *Mastro-Don Gesualdo*), LXXVI (February 1924), *191–93.*

Conrad Aiken, "Disintegration in Modern Poetry" (rev. *Birds, Beasts, and Flowers*), LXXVI (June 1924), *535–40.*

Henry McBride, "Briefer Mention" (rev. *The Boy in the Bush*), LXXVIII (June 1925), *519.*

Lisle Bell, "Briefer Mention" (rev. *Little Novels of Sicily*), LXXVIX (July 1925), *76.*

Alyse Gregory, "Briefer Mention" (rev. *Saint Mawr*), LXXVIX
(November 1925), *431.*

Anonymous, "Briefer Mention" (rev. *Reflections on the Death of
a Porcupine*), LXXX (April 1926), *341.*

Alyse Gregory, "Briefer Mention" (rev. *The Plumed Serpent*),
LXXX (June 1926), *520.*

Conrad Aiken, "Mr Lawrence's Prose" (rev. *Mornings in Mexico*),
LXXXIII (October 1927), *343–36.*

Henry McBride, "Briefer Mention" (rev. *The Woman Who Rode
Away and Other Stories*), LXXXV (August 1928), *172.*

Raymond Mortimer, "London Letter" (mention of *Lady Chatterley's Lover*), LXXXVI (February 1929), *136–41.*

Advertisements in *The Dial* for Lawrence's Work

The first entry identifies the firm placing the advertisement.

Seltzer, LXVIX (July 1920), *iv.*

Putnam, LXVIX (October
1920), *ii.*

Seltzer, LXVIX (October
1920), *viii.*

Dial, LXX (February 1921),
xii-xiii.

Seltzer, LXX (February 1921),
v.

Seltzer, LXX (March 1921), *v.*

Seltzer, LXX (April 1921), *v.*

Huebsch, LXX (April 1921),
viii.

Seltzer, LXX (June 1921), *v.*

Seltzer, LXXI (September
1921), *vii.*

Kennerly, LXXI (October
1921), *iii.*

Dial, LXXI (October 1921),
xviii.

Seltzer, LXXI (October 1921), *v.*

Seltzer, LXXI (November
1921), *ix.*

Holliday Bookshop, New York,
LXXI (November 1921), *xx.*

Dial, LXXI (November 1921),
xxiii.

Dial, LXXI (December 1921),
xxxii.

Seltzer, LXXII (February
1922), *v.*

Seltzer, LXXII (March 1922), *v.*

Seltzer, LXXII (April 1922),
4th cover.

Seltzer, LXXII (May 1922), *xx.*

Seltzer, LXXII (June 1922),
xiii.

Dial, LXXII (June 1922), *xix.*

Seltzer, LXXIII (July 1922), *ix.*

Seltzer, LXXIII (August 1922),
4th cover.

Seltzer, LXXIII (September
1922), *xxiv.*

Seltzer, LXXIII (October 1922),
vi.

Dial, LXXIII (November 1922),
xxx–xxxi.

Seltzer, LXXIII (November
1922), *3rd cover.*

Seltzer, LXXIII (December
1922), *ix.*

Dial, LXXIII (December 1922),
xxxvi–xxxvii.

Seltzer, LXXIV (January 1923),
vii.

Seltzer, LXXIV (February
1923), *xiii*.

Dial, LXXIV (February 1923),
xxx–xxxi.

Seltzer, LXXIV (March 1923),
vii.

Seltzer, LXXIV (April 1923),
ix.

Putnam, LXXIV (April 1923),
xi.

Seltzer, LXXIV (May 1923),
xxviii.

Seltzer, LXXIV (June 1923),
vii.

Seltzer, LXXV (July 1923), *v*.

Dial, LXXV (July 1923), *xx*.

Dial, LXXV (July 1923), *xix*.

Seltzer, LXXV (August 1923),
3rd cover.

Seltzer, LXXV (September
1923), *3rd cover*.

Nation, LXXV (September
1923), *xxviii*.

Seltzer, LXXV (October 1923),
3rd cover.

Seltzer, LXXV (November
1923), *3rd cover*.

Seltzer, LXXV (December
1923), *3rd cover*.

Seltzer, LXXVI (January 1924),
3rd cover.

Seltzer, LXXVI (February
1924), *3rd cover*.

Seltzer, LXXVI (March 1924),
3rd cover.

Seltzer, LXXVI (April 1924),
3rd cover.

Dial, LXXVI (May 1924), *xv*.

Seltzer, LXXVI (May 1924),
3rd cover.

Seltzer, LXXVI (June 1924),
3rd cover.

Dial, LXXVII (July 1924),
xiv–xv.

Dial Press, LXXVII (October
1924), *ii–iii*.

Dial Press, LXXVII (October
1924), *iv*.

Dial, LXXVII (October 1924),
xv.

Dial, LXXVIII (February 1925),
vii.

Dial, LXXVIII (March 1925),
vii.

Dial, LXXVIII (April 1925),
xi.

Dial, LXXVIII (May 1925), *x*.

Dial, LXXVIII (June 1925), *vii*.

Dial, LXXX (June 1926), *vii*.

Dial, LXXXII (January 1927),
vii.

Dial, LXXXII (February 1927),
vii.

Dial, LXXXII (March 1927),
vii.

Modern Library, LXXXII (May
1927), *v*.

Dial, LXXXII (June 1927), *vii*.

Dial, LXXXIII (October 1927),
vii.

Dial, LXXXVI (June 1929), *iii*.

APPENDIX B

SEA AND SARDINIA in the *Dial*

Based on the Compass Books edition (New York, Viking Press, 1963).

"As Far as Palermo"

> Two paragraphs, beginning "Where does one go?" and ending "Let it be Sardinia," *p. 3*.
>
> One paragraph, beginning "There is a fortnightly boat," *p. 3*.
>
> Four paragraphs, beginning "Under the lid" and ending "I have got so far," *pp. 4–5*.
>
> Eight paragraphs, beginning "Humanity is, externally" and ending "can never be physically near enough," *pp. 6–8*.

"The Sea"

> Four paragraphs, beginning "The fat old porter knocks" and ending "on the undarkening sky," *pp. 20–21*.
>
> Twenty-eight paragraphs, beginning "I felt very dim" and ending "Beppina, as most babies are," *pp. 33–38*.
>
> Three paragraphs, beginning "We strolled for ten minutes" and ending "turns us down with a bang," *pp. 39–40*.
>
> Four paragraphs, beginning "Slowly, slowly we creep" and ending "and we get off that ship," *pp. 52–53*.

"Cagliari"

> One paragraph, beginning "Strange the feeling round the harbor," *p. 53*.
>
> Two paragraphs, beginning, "On the great parapet" and ending "the seated carabinieri into the hall," *pp. 55–56*.
>
> One paragraph, beginning "Followed another white-satin marquise," *p. 57*.
>
> Three paragraphs, beginning with the third sentence of the paragraph that begins, "The crowd is across the road" and ending, "without the awe this time," *pp. 61–62*.

Two paragraphs, beginning "They are amusing" and ending "mess of modern adoration," *pp. 66–67.*

"Mandas" Entitled in the *Dial:* "To Mandas"

Two paragraphs, beginning "The coach was fairly full" and ending with the first sentence of the third paragraph, "They were very happy," *pp. 69–70.*

Eight paragraphs, beginning "After a long pull" and ending with the middle sentence of the eighth paragraph, "Yes, we chimed, it was a shame," *pp. 72–74.*

"To Sorgono" Entitled in the *Dial:* "Sorgono: The Inn"

Eleven paragraphs, beginning "In the bar a wretched candle" and ending "a high, dark, naked prison-dungeon," *pp. 99–100.* The *Dial* combined the tenth and eleventh paragraphs.

Seven paragraphs, beginning "In dithers a candle" and ending "I sat holding the candle," *pp. 101–2.*

Three paragraphs, beginning "The bus starts at half past nine" and ending with the next to last sentence of the third paragraph, "They are ready for us when we are ready," *pp. 111–19.* The *Dial* included this section as the first part of the next chapter, "To Nuoro."

"To Nuoro"

Four paragraphs, beginning "The automobile took us" and ending "have perfected oneself in the great past first," *pp. 121–23.*

Corrections and Additions to
Warren Roberts, *A Bibliography of*
D. H. Lawrence;
The Soho Bibliographies (*London, 1963*).

THE CORRECTIONS AND ADDITIONS to Roberts's *Bibliography* are offered in no sense pejoratively. We are grateful for the thorough and generally accurate descriptions made in Roberts's work. In the light of Lawrence's peripatetic habits while preparing and handling manuscripts and because of the profusion of his publications, this latest *Bibliography* is admirably accurate. Just as Roberts in the preface to his work invites anyone to "remedy the deficiencies," so we shall be receptive to any corrections to Lawrence's bibliography as regards the *Dial.* Items below are keyed to numbers of Roberts's bibliographical entries.

Corrections

For corrections to Roberts's bibliographical notation of *Sea and Sardinia*, A20, see Appendix B.

For corrections to Roberts's bibliographical notation of *Aaron's Rod*, A21, see chapter 5, n. 7.

Babette Deutsch's review of *New Poems*, A11, "Poets and Prefaces," appeared in the *Dial*, LXX (January 1921), 89–94 (not January 1920).

Reviews of Lawrence's Work in *The Dial*

Edward Garnett, "Art and the Moralists" (rev. *The White Peacock, The Trespasser, Sons and Lovers, The Widowing of Mrs. Holroyd, The Prussian Officer*), LXI (November 16, 1916), 377–81.

Henry Blake Fuller, "Embracing the Realities" (rev. *Twilight in Italy, The Prussian Officer*), LXII (March 22, 1917), 237–38.

William Aspenwall Bradley, "Some Modern Singers" (rev. *Amores*), LXII (April 19, 1917), 352–54.

Amy Lowell, "Weary Verse" (rev. *Look! We Have Come Through, Bay*), LXVIX (October 1920), 424–31. No reviews of *Bay* are cited in Roberts.

T. S. Eliot, "London Letter" (mention of *Aaron's Rod*), LXXIII (September 1922), 329–31.

Raymond Mortimer, "London Letter" (mention of *Lady Chatterley's Lover*), LXXXVI (February 1929), 136–41.

The Dial Clipsheets Reprinting Work by Lawrence

"Volcanoes and Sentiment" (retitled passage from *Sea and Sardinia*), clipsheet of September 22, 1921.

"When I Went to the Circus—," clipsheet of April 26, 1929.

"What Would You Fight For?" clipsheet of June 30, 1929.

Work by Lawrence in Other Periodicals

"Poems from a Pointed Pen," *Vanity Fair*, XXIV (March 1930), 38 and 108: "All I Ask," "Energetic Women," "Censors," "I Wish I Knew a Woman," "Talk," "Old People," "Choice," "Tolerance," "Compari," "Wellsian Futures," "To Women, As Far as I'm Concerned," "The Ignoble Procession," "Let Us Be Men," "I Am in a Novel," "No! Mr. Lawrence," "The Oxford Voice," "Natural Complexion," and "How Beastly the Bourgeois Is," all from *Pansies*, A47.

1 In the Beginning, 1913–1920

1   John Middleton Murry was long associated with various little
magazines. Murry edited the *Athenaeum* for the issues from April 1919
until February 1921, when the magazine merged with the *Nation:* see
F. A. Lea's *The Life of John Middleton Murry* (London, 1956), pp.
65–82, for an account of Murry's position with the *Athenaeum.*

Signature was a short-lived wartime effort of Murry, Lawrence,
and Katherine Mansfield. Only three issues of the magazine appeared
from October 4 to November 1, 1915 (according to *The Union List of
Serials in Libraries of the United States and Canada*, ed. Edna Titus
Brown, 3d ed. [New York, 1965], V, 3871). This little magazine is
notable for its having published the first three parts of "The Crown,"
an essay Lawrence wrote expressly for *Signature* and one that explains
the symbolic conflicts in his novels. For Lawrence's comments on
Signature, see H 251, 253–57, 293; *CL* 364, 369, 370; and "Note to
'The Crown,' " in *RDP*, n.p.

The *Adelphi*, like *Signature*, was established primarily as an outlet for Lawrence's work, but because Lawrence was displeased with
Murry's editorial supervision and quarreled with him about the magazine, Lawrence became only an occasional contributor (*CL* xlviii, 747,
749, 753, 792, 821, 877, 881–84). The magazine was a rather sporadic
effort and persisted—according to Lawrence—only because Murry refused to "dry up" (*CL* 977). Murry edited the magazine at three intervals of its publication: for the issues from June 1923 until July–August
1930, from July 1931 until September 1938, and from July 1941 until
June 1948. See *The Union List of Serials*, 3d ed., I, 65; and Frederick
J. Hoffman, Charles Allen, and Carolyn Ulrich, *The Little Magazine:
A History and a Bibliography* (Princeton, 1946), p. 386. The terminal
date of Murry's editorship is supplied by Lea, p. 320.

Rhythm was begun by Murry when he was an undergraduate at
Oxford University in June 1911. From its beginning, this ambitious,
cosmopolitan review betrayed its undergraduate origins, and when Edward Marsh contributed financially, *Rhythm* became the leading
Georgian review. Lawrence first met Murry and Katherine Mansfield
when, after submitting a story, he was invited to the office of *Rhythm*
in London. As the magazine waned in popularity, the editors tried to

revive it by changing its title in May 1913 to the *Blue Review* before abandoning the enterprise in July 1913. See Lea, pp. 27–35; and John Middleton Murry, *Reminiscences of D. H. Lawrence* (New York, 1933) pp. 27–29.

2   Warren Roberts, *A Bibliography of D. H. Lawrence*, Soho Bibliographies Series (London, 1963), pp. 245–59. Roberts does not indicate whether magazines in which Lawrence's work was published are American or English. To establish nationality we have relied on *The British Union Catalogue of Periodicals*, ed. James D. Stewart, Muriel E. Hammond, and Erwin Saenger, 4 vols. and supplement to 1960 (New York, 1957), and upon the *Union List of Serials*.

3   A suggestion of at least one biographer, Richard Aldington, in *Life for Life's Sake* (New York, 1941), p. 233.

4   Harry T. Moore, *The Intelligent Heart: The Story of D. H. Lawrence*, rev. ed. (New York: Grove Press, 1962), p. 206.

5   Roberts, *A Bibliography*, p. 278; and see *CL* 1057.

6   An estimate of Carl R. Dolmetsch, The Smart Set: *A History and an Anthology* (New York, 1966), p. 15.

7   Nicholas Joost, *Scofield Thayer and* The Dial (Carbondale, 1964), pp. 42, 91.

8   Roberts, *A Bibliography*, pp. 20, 250, 252, 268.

9   "Saving the World," *Smart Set*, LXVIII (July 1922), 144, as quoted in William H. Nolte, *H. L. Mencken, Literary Critic* (Middletown, Conn., 1966), p. 247. Nolte adds, p. 246, that Mencken "read the Lawrence canon assiduously and published some of his early short stories in the *Smart Set*." The only such stories published after Mencken came to the *Smart Set* were Lawrence's "The Shadow in the Rose Garden" and "The White Stocking"; inasmuch as Willard Huntington Wright did not leave his editorship until February 1914, the first story, in the March 1914 *Smart Set*, was of course purchased by Wright, not Mencken. And "The White Stocking" may well have been held over from Wright's editorial regime.

10   No volumes or months are given for *Playboy;* the numbers of the issues in which Lawrence's work appeared are 4 and 5.

11   Nicholas Joost, *Years of Transition:* The Dial *1912–1920* (Barre, Mass., 1967), pp. 142–44.

12 For this count we have used Elizabeth Wright's *Index to Fifty Years of* Poetry, A Magazine of Verse (New York, 1963), p. 187. For Miss Monroe's review of the *Collected Poems* and *Pansies*, see *Poetry*, XXXV (February 1930), 273.

13 Dolmetsch, *The Smart Set*, p. 188; *CL* 222.

14 *The Letters of Ezra Pound: 1907–1941*, ed. D. D. Paige, Harvest Books (New York, 1950), p. 17.

15 *Ibid.*, p. 22.

16 *Ibid.*, p. 155; for Pound's letter to Harriet Monroe, p. 22.

17 Joost, *Scofield Thayer*, p. 167.

18 Pound, *Letters*, p. 234 (to Lincoln Kirstein).

19 Moore, *The Intelligent Heart*, pp. 217–18.

20 Aldington, *Life*, pp. 140–42, 228–35, 301–7, 321–23, 329–36. For Pound's feud over Amy Lowell's appropriation of Imagism, see his *Letters*, pp. 33–132 *passim*.

21 See, for example, his "To the Slave in Cleon," the *Dial*, LXIV (March 14, 1918), 226–27; "To Sappho," LXIV (May 9, 1918), 430–31; "New Paths," LXV (September 5, 1918), 149–50; "La Grosse Margot," LXVI (May 17, 1919), 510; "Henri de Régnier," LXI (September 21, 1916), 151–72; "The Emerald Way," LXI (November 30, 1916), 447–48.

22 Aldington, *Life*, p. 301.

23 Roberts, *A Bibliography*, pp. 15–46.

24 For complete bibliographical details of these early reviews, see Appendix A, second part.

25 Roberts does not cite this review; see the *Dial*, *LXI* (November 16, 1916), 379–81.

26 Roberts does not cite this review; see Henry Blake Fuller, "Embracing the Realities," *Dial*, LXII (March 22, 1917), 237–38.

27 Roberts does not cite this review; see William Aspenwall Bradley, "Some Modern Singers," *Dial*, LXII (April 19, 1917), 352–54.

28   Conrad Aiken, "The Melodic Line," *Dial*, LXVII (August 19, 1919), 97–100.

29   For a more complete discussion see Joost's *Scofield Thayer* and *Years of Transition*. Our account of the *Dial* essentially relies on these two volumes.

30   The surname of the agent is not identified in Lawrence's correspondence; her first name is recorded as Louise (*CL* 484).

31   See Waldo Frank, "Vicarious Fiction," *Seven Arts*, I (January 1917), 294–303; Lawrence was mentioned favorably if briefly, p. 302. The content of Waldo Frank's letter is inferred from Lawrence's reply of July 27, 1917.

32   For a convenient source of "War and the Intellectuals," see Randolph Bourne, *The History of a Literary Radical and Other Papers*, ed. Van Wyck Brooks (1920; reprint ed., New York, 1956), pp. 205–22.

33   See G. A. Janssens, "*The Seven Arts* and *The Dial*," *Papers on Language and Literature*, IV (Fall 1968), 442–58, for a more qualified view of this connection.

34   Roberts, *A Bibliography*, pp. 254–63.

2 Lorenzo Comes to *The Dial*, 1920–1922

1   See Harry T. Moore, *The Life and Works of D. H. Lawrence*, rev. ed. (New York, 1964), pp. 313–18, for the titles listed here in the text.

2   *Ibid.*, p. 14. For the brief discussion of Lawrence's life see pp. 145–47, 171–72, 182, 193–94, 196–203, 209–11, 225–26, 249–50, 268–69.

3   See Appendix A, first part, for a list of works by Lawrence in the *Dial*.

4   For details, see Nicholas Joost, *Scofield Thayer and* The Dial (Carbondale, 1964), *passim*, the source for the brief discussion here.

5   *Ibid.*, p. 255.

6   For details of Lawrence's treatment during World War I and his struggles with censors over *The Rainbow* and *Women in Love*, see

Harry T. Moore, *The Intelligent Heart: The Story of D. H. Lawrence*, rev. ed. (New York: Grove Press, 1962), pp. 254–311; for a discussion of new themes in his works after the war, see Moore's *Life and Works*, pp. 145–91. For an account of Thayer's efforts on behalf of the *Little Review*, see Nicholas Joost, *Years of Transition:* The Dial, *1912–1920* (Barre, Mass., 1967), pp. 247–52, 301, n. 3. Thayer's rejection by the draft is reported in Joost, *Scofield Thayer*, p. 6.

7   *Living Art* came about largely because many of the paintings Thayer admired were unsuitable for reproduction in the *Dial*. For details of this elaborate project, see Joost, *Scofield Thayer*, pp. 211–43.

8   Nicholas Joost, in *Ernest Hemingway and the Little Magazines: The Paris Years* (Barre, Mass., 1968), p. 9, refers to Thayer's visit to Freud. See Philip Rieff's introduction to *Psychoanalysis and the Unconscious and Fantasia of the Unconscious* (New York, 1960), pp. vii–xxiii; and Frederick J. Hoffman, "Lawrence's Quarrel with Freud," *The Achievement of D. H. Lawrence*, ed. Frederick J. Hoffman and Harry T. Moore (Norman, Okla., 1953), pp. 106–27. Mark Spilka, in *The Love Ethic of D. H. Lawrence* (Bloomington, Ind., 1955), pp. 60–61, suggests that Lawrence had to outgrow or else dismiss Freud's theories. *Sons and Lovers*, according to Spilka, "takes its strength from Lawrence's psychology and its weakness (inadvertently) from Freud's" (p. 61). For further discussion of Lawrence's reaction to Freud and Jung, see William York Tindall, *D. H. Lawrence and Susan His Cow* (New York, 1939), pp. 31, 38, 58; and David J. Gordon, *D. H. Lawrence as a Literary Critic* (New Haven, 1966), pp. 56–57, 76, n. 2, and especially p. 57, n. 9.

9   For Thayer's views about freedom of sex and expression, see his editorial "Comment" in the *Dial*, LXVIII (May 1920), 674–76; LXXI (November 1921), 624; LXXII (April 1922), 446–47; LXXII (June 1922), 664; LXXIII (August 1922), 240; LXXIII (October 1922), 460–62. His *aperçu* of Lawrence is published with the permission of his representative, Charles P. Williamson.

10   See, for examples, the issues for April, May, June 1925; June 1926; January, February, March, June, October 1927; June 1929.

11   John Middleton Murry, *Reminiscences of D. H. Lawrence* (New York, 1933), pp. 90–93; quotation, p. 92. Lawrence's letter to Murry in March 1919 corroborates Murry's account (*CL* 578).

12   Typescript in the *Dial* Collection. All of the materials quoted from the *Dial* papers are unpublished except as specified, and are printed with the permissions of Charles P. Williamson, representative of Scofield Thayer; of Louisa Dresser, Curator, Worcester Art Museum;

and of Donald Gallup, Curator of the American Literature Collection, Beinecke Library, Yale University. There is no indication that Pound sent "Adolf" and "Rex" or that Aldington directly sent them; but Mountsier did not.

13   Keith Sagar, *The Art of D. H. Lawrence* (Cambridge, Eng., 1966), p. 100.

14   Moore, *Life and Works*, p. 176.

15   In the *Dial*'s records of purchase, the sums paid to Lawrence for his work are not always commensurate with the *Dial*'s rates, as in this instance.

16   See John F. Sullivan, *The Externals of the Catholic Church*, 3d ed. (New York, 1918), p. 314. The symbols of the Evangelists are of very ancient date, originating in St. John's Apocalypse. "The human head indicates St. Matthew—for he begins his Gospel with the human ancestry of our Blessed Lord. The lion, the dweller in the desert, is emblematic of St. Mark, who opens his narrative with the mission of St. John the Baptist, 'the voice of one crying in the wilderness.' The sacrificial ox is the symbol of St. Luke—for his Gospel begins with the account of the priest Zachary. And the eagle, soaring far into the heavens, is the emblem of the inspiration of St. John, who carries us, in the opening words of his Gospel, to Heaven itself."

17   Warren Roberts, *A Bibliography of D. H. Lawrence*, Soho Bibliographies Series (London, 1963), pp. 54, 261–62, erroneously says that the *Dial* published intact the first two chapters of *Sea and Sardinia*.

18   Referred to in Joost, *Scofield Thayer*, p. 53.

19   Also in the *Dial* papers. Parts of the letter appear in Joost, *Scofield Thayer*, pp. 58–59.

20   Although this letter is not in the *Dial* papers, its contents are evident from Thayer's reply to Koteliansky.

21   Gregory Zilboorg was a Russian living in New York who translated Russian materials and contributions for the magazine. Before 1920 he had contributed political articles such as "Russia and International Economics," *Dial*, LXVII (September 6, 1919), 198–201. He also translated *He, the One Who Gets Slapped*, by Leonid Andreyev, published in the *Dial*, LXX (March 1921), 250–300.

22   As she wrote in (Mabel Dodge Luhan), *Lorenzo in Taos* (New York, 1932), p. 280.

23   See *Die Neue Rundschau*, XXXIII (April 1922), 393–402, for the German version of Bunin's story.

24   Roberts, *A Bibliography*, p. 204.

25   Typescript by Seldes in the *Dial* papers indicates that he purchased the story for the magazine. "Kasimir Stanislawowitch" appeared in the *Dial*, LXXIII (July 1922), 41–47.

26   See *Dial*, LXXX–LXXXI (June–August 1924), 481–92, 31–43, 105–20, for "Reminiscences of Leonid Andreyev." See also, *Dial*, LXXXII (February 1927), 164, for Alyse Gregory's short unsigned review of *Mitya's Love*, printed in "Briefer Mention." See also, *Dial*, LXXXIII (October 1927), 271–82, for "Reminiscences of Tolstoy."

27   See the *Forum*, L (September 1913), 343–52. Roberts, *A Bibliography*, p. 23, identifies Kennerly's printing of *Sons and Lovers* as the first American edition.

28   The erroneous belief that *Aaron's Rod* is part of a trilogy with *The Rainbow* and *Women in Love* persists still in advertising. See the back cover of the Compass Books edition of *Aaron's Rod* (New York, 1961).

3 Lawrence, *The Dial*, and Mabel Dodge Luhan, 1921–1925

1   For Mabel Dodge Luhan's autobiography, see *Intimate Memories*, 4 vols. (New York, 1933–37), respectively entitled *Background*, *European Experiences*, *Movers and Shakers*, and *Edge of Taos Desert*. Also see her account of D. H. Lawrence, *Lorenzo in Taos* (New York, 1932). For a recent popular sketch of her, see W. G. Rogers, *Ladies Bountiful* (New York, 1968), pp. 106–35. According to Rogers, Carl Van Vechten's *Peter Whiffle: His Life and Works* (New York, 1922) depicts Mabel Dodge in New York and Florence in the guise of the fashionable radical hostess Edith Dale, pp. 119–96 *passim*.

2   Edward K. Brown and Leon Edel, *Willa Cather: A Critical Biography* (New York, 1953), pp. 169, 198.

3   "The Art of the American Indian," *Dial*, LXVIII (January 1920), 57–65; "*Na-Ka-Vo-Ma*": *Hopi Snake Dance, The Legend of the Deer, The Corn Dance*, LXVIII (March 1920), [342]; "Vaudeville," LXVIII (March 1920), 335–42.

4 "A Symposium of the Exotic" (rev. Elsie Clews Parsons, ed. *American Indian Life* [New York, 1922]), *Dial*, LXXIII (November 1922), 568–71.

5 Mary Austin, "Zuni Folk Tales" (rev. Frank Hamilton Cushing, *Zuni Folk Tales* [New York, 1921] and *Outlines of the Zuni Creation Myth* [New York, 1921]), *Dial*, LXXI (July 1921), 112–17; Mabel Dodge Luhan, "Southwest," *Dial*, LXXIX (December 1925), 477–84; Elizabeth Shepley Sergeant, "The Wood-Carver," *Dial*, LXXX (May 1926), 397–402; Henry J. Glintenkamp, *Blind Woman and Boy*, *Dial*, LXXVI (April 1924), 308, and *Group of Mexican Boys*, LXXX (April 1926), 288; Lowell Houser, *Christo* [*sic*], *Dial*, LXXXVI (April 1929), 318; Katherine Gorringe, "The Ukiah Big-Time," *Dial*, LXXXVI (July 1929), 580–85; Amy Lowell, "Songs of the Pueblo Indians," *Dial*, LXVIII (September 1920), 247–51. As regards the cuts by Glintenkamp and Houser that are in the Dial Collection and have been listed in Alice Mundt, comp., "Exhibition Catalogue: Drawings and Prints," *The "Dial" and the Dial Collection* (Worcester, Mass., 1959), pp. 92, 104, we have used the titles for these pictures as they were published in the *Dial*, not the exhibition catalogue.

6 Carl Van Vechten, *Spider Boy* (New York, 1928), p. 164.

7 Luhan, *Lorenzo*, pp. 3–5.

8 The pertinent dates are those cited in Warren Roberts, *A Bibliography of D. H. Lawrence*, Soho Bibliographies Series (London, 1963), pp. 53, 54, 66. For the poems in the *New Republic*, see "Medlars and Sorb Apples," XXV (January 5, 1921), 169; "The Revolutionary," XXV (January 19, 1921), 231; "Humming-Bird," XXVI (May 11, 1921), 325. Incidentally, where in Sicily would Lawrence have seen a hummingbird, a creature exclusively of the New World?

9 Luhan, *Lorenzo*, pp. 4–5.

10 *Ibid.*, pp. 5–7.

11 Diana Trilling, ed. *Selected Letters of D. H. Lawrence* (New York, 1958), p. xxxii.

12 See "The Woman Who Rode Away" in D. H. Lawrence, *The Woman Who Rode Away and Other Stories* (New York, 1928), pp. 47–90, and p. 52 for the quotation.

13 Luhan, *Lorenzo*, pp. 40–41, 61.

14 *Ibid.*, pp. 52, 64–66, for the unfinished novel; p. 13, for his expression of belief in the Indians. See Frieda Lawrence, *"Not I, But the Wind . . ."* (New York, 1934), p. 136, for her account of the unfinished novel; and Luhan chapter, "America," pp. 135–53, for her account of the Lawrences' American experience.

15   See Stuart Sherman, New York *Herald Tribune Books*, June 14, 1925, pp. 1–2, for the review of *St. Mawr* (New York, 1925). The text of Lawrence's "Model Americans," *Dial*, LXXIV (May 1923), 503–10, was first reprinted in *Phoenix: The Posthumous Papers of D. H. Lawrence*, ed. Edward D. McDonald (New York, 1936), pp. 314–21, and later in Lawrence's *Selected Literary Criticism*, ed. Anthony Beal (London, 1955), pp. 414–21.

16   See "The Dance of the Sprouting Corn" and "The Hopi Snake Dance," *Theatre Arts Monthly*, VIII (July 1924), 447–57, and VIII (December 1924), 836–60; "Just Back from the Snake Dance—Tired Out," *Crazy Horse*, No. 11 (September 1924), 26–29; and "Indians and an Entertainment," New York *Times Magazine* (October 26, 1924), p. 3.

17   Roberts, *A Bibliography*, pp. 76, 270. See also Luhan, *Lorenzo*, pp. 209–10 (for the description of the cave), 222, 237–38, 253.

18   Luhan, "Southwest," pp. 479, 483, 484.

19   Luhan, *Edge of Taos Desert*, p. 333.

20   Luhan, *Lorenzo*, pp. 52–58 reprints most of "Indians and an Englishman"; for the remark about history, see pp. 252–53. See chap. 3, n. 15 for the relevant publication data; titles in the text are those Mabel Luhan cited inaccurately. All of the manuscript she quotes in these pages is identical with the essay in the *Dial* except for two sentences added to the ends of paragraphs 12 and 13 of "Indians and an Englishman" and paragraphs 8 through 12 of her manuscript. These paragraphs, omitted from the *Dial's* version, constitute paragraphs 1 through 6 of "Certain Americans and an Englishman," New York *Times Magazine* (December 24, 1922), pp. 3, 9.

21   William York Tindall, "D. H. Lawrence and the Primitive," *Sewanee Review*, XLV (April–June 1937), 198–211, especially 211.

22   As quoted in Stephen Potter, *D. H. Lawrence: A First Study* (London, 1930), pp. 119–20; our interpretation of Lawrence's affinity for the "primitive" differs from Potter's.

4 Lawrence and *The Dial* of Marianne Moore

1   Harry T. Moore, *The Intelligent Heart: The Story of D. H. Lawrence*, rev. ed. (New York: Grove Press, 1962), p. 220.

2   *Ibid.*

3   Compton Mackenzie, *My Life and Times*, IV (*Octave Four, 1907–1915*) (London, 1964), 224–25.

4   *Ibid.*, pp. 167–78.

5   Mackenzie, *My Life and Times*, VI (*Octave Six, 1923–1930*) (London, 1967), 131. See also *CL*1208; and Roberts, pp. 88–91, especially p. 90.

6   Mackenzie, VI, pp. 131–32.

7   *Ibid.*, pp. 84–85; Faith Mackenzie's remarks as quoted by her husband.

8   Kyle Crichton, untitled, original memoir, in Edward Nehls, *D. H. Lawrence: A Composite Biography* (Madison, Wis., 1958), II, 413, 525.

9   Faith Compton Mackenzie, *As Much As I Dare* (London, 1938), p. 221.

10   Nehls, *D. H. Lawrence*, II, 455.

11   Warren Roberts, *A Bibliography of D. H. Lawrence*, Soho Bibliographies Series (London, 1963), pp. 88, 91–101 *passim*.

12   *Ibid.*, pp. 113–19.

13   In Marianne Moore, *Predilections* (New York, 1955), pp. 103–14; quotation, p. 107. The two letters by Lawrence that Marianne Moore prints are on pp. 107–8 of the essay; the latter of the two has been reprinted in *CL* 1142.

14   As quoted in Nicholas Joost, *Scofield Thayer and* The Dial (Carbondale, 1964), p. 258.

15   *Ibid.*, pp. 258–59.

16   Roberts, *A Bibliography*, p. 119; *CL* 1163–1246 *passim*.

5 Lawrence's Fiction in *The Dial*

1   The magazines that published some work by Lawrence for the first time during this period are: *Atlantic Monthly, Bookman, Laugh-*

ing Horse, Creative Art, Golden Book, Literary Digest International Book Review, Metropolitan, Nation, New Republic, New York *Evening Post Literary Review,* New York *Herald Tribune Books,* New York *Times Magazine, Southwest Review, Theatre Arts Monthly, Travel,* and *Vanity Fair.* Three others had published Lawrence's work before 1920 and published his work again in issues during the period from September 1920 until July 1929: *Forum, Poetry,* and *Smart Set.* See Warren Roberts, *A Bibliography of D. H. Lawrence,* Soho Bibliographies Series (London, 1963), pp. 245–81, for this count, although he does not always include all periodical contributions in the "Contributions to Periodicals" of his bibliography.

2 Roberts, *A Bibliography,* pp. 88–91. "The Man Who Loved Islands" was not included in the English printing; for the reason, see pp. 100–103.

3 Dates assigned by Keith Sagar, *The Art of D. H. Lawrence* (Cambridge, Eng., 1966), pp. 169–70, primarily based on *CL* 810, 870–73, 918, and H 658. See also Mabel Dodge Luhan, *Lorenzo in Taos* (New York, 1932), pp. 237–38.

4 For the complete letter, see pp. 42–43.

5 Ivan Bunin, *The Gentleman from San Francisco,* trans. Bernard Guilbert Guerney (New York, 1933), p. 313.

6 *Dial,* LXXVI (March–May 1924), 213–35, 311–33, 423–44.

7 The excerpt in the *Dial* begins with the paragraph that opens, "As he lay thinking of nothing": *Aaron's Rod,* Compass Books (New York, 1961), p. 179. Several words in the *Dial's* excerpt are different from those of the Compass Books edition. In the first line of the last paragraph (p. 182), the *Dial's* passage substitutes "dispersed" for "disappeared," and in this case, the *Dial's* word seems more appropriate, suggesting an error in the Compass Books edition. In the same paragraph, after the phrase "Let themselves foolishly be taken" (p. 183), the *Dial* has a colon, and after the word "prisoners" it has a semicolon. Moreover, this paragraph is not separated from the one that follows, as it is in the Compass Books edition. For the phrase "in cautious dejection" at the end of the first paragraph on p. 183, the *Dial* reads "in humiliation." In the first sentence of the second paragraph on p. 183, the *Dial* substitutes "surrounded" for "seized." And in the magazine the last sentences of the second paragraph on p. 183 have been altered and combined to read, "And away they marched, the dejected youth between them." The next two paragraphs are not reprinted in the *Dial* except for the last sentence of paragraph four on p. 183, which is also the last sentence of the excerpt, "The scene was ended."

8   Quoted by Harry T. Moore in *"The Plumed Serpent:* Language and Vision" in *D. H. Lawrence: A Collection of Critical Essays*, ed. Mark Spilka, Spectrum Books (Englewood Cliffs, N. J., 1963), p. 70.

9   See Harry T. Moore, *The Life and Works of D. H. Lawrence*, rev. ed. (New York, 1964), pp. 210–11; and Moore, *"The Plumed Serpent,"* in Spilka, p. 63; and Sagar, *The Art of D. H. Lawrence*, p. 160.

10   See the letter of Gilbert Seldes to Scofield Thayer, p. 60.

11   *The Utopian Vision of D. H. Lawrence* (Chicago, 1963), p. 53.

12   See Moore, *Life and Works*, pp. 179–80, 235; Julian Moynahan, *The Deed of Life: The Novels and Tales of D. H. Lawrence* (Princeton, 1963), pp. 196–98; and William York Tindall, *D. H. Lawrence and Susan His Cow* (New York, 1939), pp. 72–73.

13   Cf. "Saint Loup: A Portrait," *Dial*, LXVII (October 1920), 347–50, to *Remembrance of Things Past*, trans. C. K. Scott-Moncrief (New York, 1924), I, 764 ff.

14   Nicholas Joost, *Scofield Thayer and* The Dial (Carbondale, 1964), p. 195.

15   *Dial*, LXXIII (July–November 1922), 1–22, 162–80, 246–70, 411–24, 509–24.

16   "The New Song," *Dial*, LXXVIX (November 1925), 355–69. "Lt. Gustl," *Dial*, LXXVIX (August 1925), 89–117.

17   "German Letter," *Dial*, LXXIII (December 1922), 645–54; LXXIV (June 1923), 609–14; LXXV (October 1923), 369–75; LXXVI (January 1924), 58–65; LXXVII (November 1924), 414–19; LXXIX (October 1925), 333–38; LXXXIII (July 1927), 53–59; LXXXV (July 1928), 56–58. "Death in Venice," *Dial*, LXXVI (March–May 1924), 213–35, 311–33, 434–44. "Disorder and Early Sorrow," *Dial*, LXXXI (October–November 1926), 269–84, 402–22. "Loulou," *Dial*, LXX (April 1921), 428–42. "Tristran," *Dial*, LXXIII–LXXIV (December 1922–January 1923), 593–610, 57–76.

18   "Comment," *Dial*, LXX (March 1921), 368.

19   Joost, *Scofield Thayer*, p. 199.

20   Eliseo Vivas, *D. H. Lawrence: The Failure and Triumph of Art*, Midland Books (Bloomington, Ind., 1964), p. 208.

21   "The Man Who Loved Islands," in *A D. H. Lawrence Miscellany*, ed. Harry T. Moore (Carbondale, 1959), pp. 265–79.

22   *Dial*, LXXVIII (January 1925), 90.

23   *Dial*, LXXVIX (July 1925), 88.

24   Moore, *Life and Works*, p. 219; and see *CL* 614–15.

25   Harry T. Moore, *The Intelligent Heart: The Story of D. H. Lawrence*, rev. ed. (New York: Grove Press, 1962), p. 433.

26   Moore, *Life and Works*, p. 219.

27   Moore, *Intelligent Heart*, p. 435.

28   Moore, *Life and Works*, p. 220.

29   *Dial*, LXXVIII (January–April 1925), 89–90, 174–80, 265–68, 354–56.

30   "Compton Mackenzie," *Dial*, LXV (November 30, 1918), 473–79; quoted in Nicholas Joost, *Years of Transition: The Dial 1912–1920* (Barre, Mass., 1967), p. 168.

31   "Mr. Mackenzie's Jest," *Dial*, LXVIII (May 1920), 611–13; quoted in Joost, *Years of Transition*, p. 169.

32   "Briefer Mention," *Dial*, LXX (Jan. 1921), 107; quoted in Joost, *Years of Transition*, p. 169.

33   *Many Marriages*, *Dial*, LXXI–LXXII (October 1922–March 1923), 361–82, 533–48, 623–43, 31–49, 165–82, 256, 272. "Miss Ormerod," *Dial*, LXXVII (December 1924), 466–74. "Love at 42 Altgeld Avenue," *Dial*, LXXVIX (September 1925), 221–30.

34   *Sherwood Anderson*, American Men of Letters Series (London, 1951), p. 189.

35   "Virginia Woolf," *Dial*, LXVII (December 1924), 461.

36   For a description of the manuscripts in the Frieda Lawrence collection, see Ted 61–63. Concerning "In Love?" Tedlock notes that the text is extensively revised and that the revisions "seem too extensive to have been done in a typescript" (Ted 63). It is interesting that another bibliographer of Lawrence's manuscripts, Lawrence Clark Powell, in *The Manuscripts of D. H. Lawrence: A Descriptive Catalogue* (Los

Angeles, 1937), does not record the variants for "Two Blue Birds" and "In Love?" (pp. 25–26) but describes "More Modern Love" as "an early version of the story published as 'In Love?' in *The Woman Who Rode Away*" (p. 25).

37   *Dial*, LXXI (July 1921), 28–32.

38   See Joost, *Scofield Thayer*, pp. 112–13.

6 Lawrence's Nonfiction Prose and *The Dial*

1   Critics generally agree that the best works by Lawrence are the novels written before 1920, especially *Son and Lovers*, *The Rainbow*, and *Women in Love;* see especially the studies by F. R. Leavis, Eliseo Vivas, Julian Moynahan, and Eugene Goodheart. For the *Dial* reviews, see Chapter 8 of this study.

2   William York Tindall, "D. H. Lawrence and the Primitive," *Sewanee Review*, XLV (April–June 1937), p. 211. Tindall later qualified his judgment; see his introduction to *The Plumed Serpent*, Vintage Books (New York, 1954), pp. v–xv.

3   Warren Roberts, *A Bibliography of D. H. Lawrence*, Soho Bibliographies Series (London, 1963), pp. 264–76.

4   See "Autobiographical Sketch," *Assorted Articles* (London, 1930), pp. 172–82; *Phoenix: The Posthumous Papers of D. H. Lawrence*, ed. Edward D. McDonald (New York, 1936), and *Phoenix II: More Uncollected Writings of D. H. Lawrence*, ed. Harry T. Moore and Warren Roberts (New York, 1968); Edward Nehls's *D. H. Lawrence: A Composite Biography*, 3 vols. (Madison, Wis., 1957–59); Mark Schorer's *D. H. Lawrence*, Laurel ed. (New York, 1968).

5   Harry T. Moore, *The Intelligent Heart: The Story of D. H. Lawrence*, rev. ed. (New York: Grove Press, 1962), p. 40.

6   See Appendix B for a comparison of the *Dial*'s excerpts and the entire work.

7   *Dial*, LXXII (February 1922), 193–96.

8   Mabel Dodge Luhan, *Lorenzo in Taos* (New York, 1932), p. 253.

9   Tindall, "D. H. Lawrence and the Primitive," p. 198.

10   For the magazines in which Stuart P. Sherman's work had earlier appeared we are indebted to his preface to *Americans* (Port Washing-

ton, N. Y., 1964), pp. xii–xiii; for the magazines in which *Studies in Classic American Literature* appeared we have followed Roberts, *A Bibliography*, p. 63. For information about Sherman's review of *Studies in Classic American Literature*, see Armin Arnold's *D. H. Lawrence and America* (London, 1958), pp. 71, 72, 135–36.

11   For Lawrence's view of professors, see *CL* 9, 27; for his feelings about the suppression of *Women in Love* and *The Rainbow*, see Moore's *The Intelligent Heart*, 253–62.

12   Lawrence's review of Sherman's *Americans* is cited as one example of a review in which Lawrence ridicules a pompous style: see David J. Gordon, *D. H. Lawrence as a Literary Critic* (New Haven, 1966), p. 39.

13   Sherman, *Americans*, pp. 19–21 *passim*.

14   *Ibid.*, p. 11.

15   For this estimate of the *Dial*, see Frederick J. Hoffman, Charles Allen, and Carolyn Ulrich, *The Little Magazine: A History and a Bibliography* (Princeton, 1946), pp. 196–98.

16   Roberts, *A Bibliography*, p. 63.

17   *Ibid.*, p. 129, specifies the newspapers and magazines in which *Assorted Articles* appeared.

7 Lawrence's Poetry in *The Dial*

1   Most critics generally agree that Lawrence is the most important English novelist of the twentieth century. Few assert that he is the best poet, and most of them attack at least some of his poems. See Harry T. Moore, *Life and Works of D. H. Lawrence*, rev. ed. (New York, 1964), pp. 259–63; Keith Sagar, *The Art of D. H. Lawrence* (Cambridge, Eng., 1966), pp. 119–20; A. Alvarez, "D. H. Lawrence: The Single State of Man," *The Shaping Spirit* (London, 1961), pp. 140–61; R. P. Blackmur, "D. H. Lawrence and Expressive Form," *Language as Gesture: Essays in Poetry*, (London, 1952), pp. 286–300; W. H. Auden, "D. H. Lawrence," *The Dyer's Hand and Other Essays*, Vintage Books (New York, 1968), pp. 277–95; Horace Gregory, "The Poetry of D. H. Lawrence," *The Achievement of D. H. Lawrence*, eds. Frederick J. Hoffman and Harry T. Moore (Norman, Okla., 1953), pp. 235–52; and in the same volume, Richard Ellman's "Barbed Wire and Coming Through," pp. 253–67. V. de Sola Pinto argues the value of all of Lawrence's poetry in "Poet without a Mask," *D. H. Lawrence: A Col-*

lection of Critical Essays, ed. Mark Spilka, Spectrum Books (Engle-wood Cliffs, N. J., 1963), pp. 127–41.

2   See Blackmur, *Language as Gesture*, pp. 277–78, and Pinto, "Poet without a Mask," in Spilka, *D. H. Lawrence*, p. 128.

3   See chapters 1 and 8 *passim* for the reviews in the *Dial* of Lawrence's work.

4   Sagar, *The Art of D. H. Lawrence*, p. 119.

5   See Warren Roberts, *A Bibliography of D. H. Lawrence*, Soho Bibliographies Series (London, 1963), pp. 113–19, 127–28, 141–45.

6   See Appendix A, first part, for complete bibliographical details.

7   Roberts, *A Bibliography*, pp. 267, 259–81 *passim*. He fails to point out that poems from *Pansies* also appeared in *Vanity Fair:* see Roberts, pp. 116–18, and Ted 103–11. See [D. H. Lawrence] "A Brit-isher Has a Word with an Editor," *Palms*, I (Christmas 1923), 153–54; and Harriet Monroe, "Comment: D. H. Lawrence," *Poetry*, XXXVI (May 1930), 90 ff. For the poems cited in the text, see *Laughing Horse*, No. 13, pp. 1–15 *passim;* "Poems from a Pointed Pen" in *Vanity Fair*, XXXIV (March 1930), 38 and 108, included: "All I Ask," "Energetic Women," "Censors"—very different from the *Dial*'s version—"I Wish I Knew A Woman," "Talk," "Old People," "Choice," "Tolerance," "Compari," "Wellsian Futures," "To Women, As Far As I'm Con-cerned," "The Ignoble Procession," "Let Us Be Men," "I Am in a Novel," "No! Mr. Lawrence!," "The Oxford Voice," "Natural Com-plexion," "How Beastly the Bourgeois Is."

8   Roberts, *A Bibliography*, pp. 199–203.

9   Pinto, "Poet without a Mask," pp. 132–35, cites these two poems as examples of Lawrence's best early work.

10   Auden, *The Dyer's Hand*, pp. 285, 292.

11   "Introduction to *New Poems*" and "Whitman" in *SLC*, 86–87, 400.

12   Alfeo Faggi, *Saint Francis*, Dial, LXXXI (November 1926) [390]; Robert Delaunay, *Saint Severin*, Dial, LXXIII (November 1922) [frontispiece]; Ivan Mestrovic, *Madonna and Child*, Dial, LXXVIII (January 1925) [42]; *A Twelfth Century Crucifix*, Dial, LXXX (April 1926) [frontispiece]; Elin Pelin, "The Mirror of Saint Christopher," *Dial*, LXXVII (July 1924), 55–58.

13   T. S. Eliot, *The Waste Land*, *Dial*, LXXIII (November 1922), 473–85; W. B. Yeats, "The Second Coming," *Dial*, LXVIX (July 1920), 466; Scofield Thayer, "On a Crucifix," *Dial*, LXXX (April 1926), 267–72, "Jesus Again," LXXXI (July 1926), 59–60; AE, "Michael," *Dial*, LXVIII (March 1920), 326–34; Marsden Hartley, "The Crucifixion of Noel," *Dial*, LXX (April 1921), 378–80; Pearl Anderson Sherry, "And the Prophets in Their Season," *Dial*, LXXXIII (October 1926), 336.

14   Moore, *Life and Works*, p. 172.

15   T. S. Eliot, "The Hollow Men I, II, IV," *Dial*, LXXVIII (March 1925), 193–94; W. B. Yeats, "Among School Children," *Dial* LXXXIII (August 1927), 91–93; Ezra Pound, "Hugh Selwyn Mauberly," *Dial* LXIX (September 1920), 283–87, "The Fourth Canto," LXVIII (June 1920), 689–92, "Three Cantos" (V, VI, VII), LXXI (August 1921), 198–208, "Eighth Canto," LXXII (May 1922), 505–9, "Part of Canto XXVII," LXXXIV (January 1928), 1–3, "Canto XXII," LXXXIV (February 1928), 113–17.

16   An assertion made by Sagar, *The Art of D. H. Lawrence*, p. 125.

17   Samuel Taylor Coleridge, "The Rime of the Ancient Mariner" as quoted in Sagar, *The Art of D. H. Lawrence*, p. 125.

18   Sagar, *The Art of D. H. Lawrence*, p. 124.

19   "Whitman" in *The Symbolic Meaning*, ed. Armin Arnold (Philadelphia, 1962); quoted in Sagar, *The Art of D. H. Lawrence*, p. 125.

20   Earl Brewster and Achsah Brewster, *D. H. Lawrence: Reminiscences and Correspondence* (London, 1934), p. 118.

21   *Dial*, LXXI (July–September 1921), v (July), viii (August), viii (September).

22   See the editorial "Comment," *Dial*, LXXI (November 1921), 624; LXXIII (November 1922), 582; LXXXI (August 1926), 177–78. See advertisements in the *Dial*, LXXI (November and December 1921), vi–viii (November), vi–viii (December); "The Neglected Age," *Dial*, LXVIII (June 1920), 697–708.

23   *Dial*, LXXX (March 1926), 266.

24   See *Pansies* (New York, 1929), pp. 7–9, 32–35, 40–41, 103, 104, for variant lines.

25   *Dial*, LXXXVI (July 1929), 543.

26   Moore, *Life and Works*, p. 259; Richard Aldington, quoted in Pinto, "Poet without a Mask," p. 138; Auden, *The Dyer's Hand*, p. 293.

27   Sagar, *The Art of D. H. Lawrence*, p. 231.

28   *Pinto*, "Poet without a Mask," p. 138.

8 Reviews and Advertisements in *The Dial:* A Summary

1   See Appendix A, second part, for bibliographical details of these reviews. See Appendix C for notices of Lawrence's writing for the *Dial* that Roberts does not cite.

2   *Exile's Return: A Literary Odyssey of the 1920's*, Compass Books (New York, 1956), pp. 50–52.

3   For a discussion of the reviews in the *Dial* before 1920, see Chapter 1.

4   See, for example, his important review of Conrad Aiken's *Priapus and the Pool* and Carl Sandburg's *Shades of The Sunburnt West* in "Two American Poets," *Dial*, LXXIII (November 1922), 563–67. There is a discussion of the review itself and Cowley's correspondence with Scofield Thayer about it, in Nicholas Joost, *Scofield Thayer and The Dial* (Carbondale, 1964), pp. 200–201.

5   Frederick J. Hoffman, Charles Allen, and Carolyn Ulrich, *The Little Magazine: A History and a Bibliography* (Princeton, 1946), pp. 196–97.

6   These reviewers included not only the editor-contributors Gilbert Seldes, Alyse Gregory, Scofield Thayer, and Marianne Moore, whose creative work appeared in the *Dial*, but also such poets and essayists as Amy Lowell, Babette Deutsch, Lisle Bell, Conrad Aiken, and Padraic Colum, all of whom reviewed Lawrence's work.

7   Warren Roberts, *A Bibliography of D. H. Lawrence*, Soho Bibliographies Series (London, 1963), pp. 42–43.

8   *Dial*, LXVIX (August 1920), 215.

9   *Dial*, LXVIX (October 1920), 424, 430.

10   *Dial*, LXX (January 1921), 90, 93.

11   *Dial* LXX (April 1921), 459–60.

12   *Dial*, LXXII (February 1922), 193.

13   *Dial*, LXXIII (September 1922), 331.

14   "Briefer Mention," *Dial*, LXXIV (April 1923), 413. The *Dial*'s records do not identify the reviewer.

15   *Dial*, LXXVI (January 1921), 67–72.

16   *Dial*, LXXVI (February 1924), 192.

17   *Dial*, LXXVI (June 1924), 536, 539–40.

18   See Frederick J. Hoffman, *Conrad Aiken*, Twayne United States Author Series (New York, 1962), pp. 23–30.

19   *Dial*, LXVIII (June 1925), 519.

20   *Dial*, LXXIX (July 1925), 76.

21   *Dial*, LXXX (June 1926), 520.

22   *Dial*, LXXX (April 1926), 341. For the significance of "The Crown," see Harry T. Moore, *Life and Works of D. H. Lawrence*, rev. ed. (New York, 1964), pp. 124–25, 138, 151, 152.

23   "Mr Lawrence's Prose," *Dial*, LXXXIII (October 1927), 343, 345.

24   Roberts, *A Bibliography*, pp. 83–109. Other works by Lawrence that appeared during these years were *Selected Poems*, a translation of *Cavelleria Rusticana*, *Rawdon's Roof* (all in 1928), and *Sex Locked Out* (1929). See Roberts, pp. 83–109, for complete bibliographical details.

25   "Briefer Mention," *Dial*, LXXXV (August 1928), 172.

26   "London Letter," LXXXVI (February 1929), 137–39.

27   For bibliographical details, see Appendix A, third part.

28   Among the magazines in which Lawrence's work appeared that were offered in a joint subscription with the *Dial* were the *Forum*, *Century*, *Nation and Athenaeum*, *Bookman*, and *New Republic*. For example, see *Dial*, LXXXIII (September 1926), vii.

29   See Nicholas Joost, *Ernest Hemingway and the Little Magazines: The Paris Years*, (Barre, Mass., 1968), pp. 93, 94, 122.

30   For further information about the Peacock Folder, see Joost, *Scofield Thayer*, pp. 40–41, 43–58, which is the source for our brief discussion here.

31   Lawrence complained in letters to friends that no review was sophisticated enough to publish this startlingly explicit story (*CL* 870–73). Since the *Dial* was the most prominent outlet in America for his work and since the magazine was known for publishing avant-garde fiction, it is difficult to believe that "Sun" was not submitted to it.

32   Seeds not only of Lawrence's genius, but of Thayer's journal as well. For an account of ways in which other magazines imitated the *Dial*, see Joost, *Scofield Thayer*, pp. 257–58. Also see G. A. M. Janssens' *The American Literary Review* (The Hague, 1968), a book devoted to tracing the tradition of the *Dial*.

33   The New York *Times*' review is discussed in greater detail in Joost's *Scofield Thayer*, pp. 259–61.